THE SAPIENCE CURRICULUM

THE SAPIENCE CURRICULUM

Teacher's Guide for an Age of Turmoil

FRANK FORENCICH

EXUBERANT
ANIMAL

Copyright © 2021 Frank Forencich

All rights reserved.

No part of this book may be reproduced, or stored in a retrieval system, or transmitted in any form or by any means, electronic, mechanical, photocopying, recording, or otherwise, without express written permission of the publisher.

Published by Exuberant Animal, Bend, Oregon
www.exuberantanimal.com

Edited and designed by Girl Friday Productions
www.girlfridayproductions.com

Cover design: Kathleen Lynch and Paul Barrett
Project management: Alexander Rigby and Dave Valencia
Image credits: cover Shutterstock/Juliann

ISBN (paperback): 978-0-9851263-4-6
ISBN (e-book): 978-0-9851263-5-3

*Mirror mirror,
Green and blue.
Are we one
Or are we two?*

CONTENTS

Foreword xi
Preface xxiii

Chapter 1: Welcome to Now 1
Chapter 2: Meet Your Mismatch 19
Chapter 3: Eye Exam 27
Chapter 4: Focus on the Park 33
Chapter 5: The Myth of Progress 36
Chapter 6: The Myth of Human Supremacy 40
Chapter 7: Teach Normal 46
Chapter 8: The Breaking of the World 54
Chapter 9: New Old Way 58
Chapter 10: We Are WEIRD 63
Chapter 11: Paleo Family Values 67
Chapter 12: Meet LUCA 71
Chapter 13: Teaching in Circles 76
Chapter 14: Tensegrity 80
Chapter 15: Rock–Scissors–Paper 85
Chapter 16: Geometry Lesson 90
Chapter 17: Corporate Crime Wave 97
Chapter 18: Money Changes Everything 103
Chapter 19: Full Circle 107
Chapter 20: The Land Is Me 115
Chapter 21: Know Habitat 119
Chapter 22: Meet Your Bioregion 125

Chapter 23: Wild Body, Wild Spirit 130
Chapter 24: Keep Your Eye on the Awe 136
Chapter 25: Radical Remembering 140
Chapter 26: Job Qualifications 145
Chapter 27: Cogito Ergo Dumb 148
Chapter 28: The Physical Life. 153
Chapter 29: The Kindergarten Model 160
Chapter 30: Nightlife 167
Chapter 31: Foodstuff 176
Chapter 32: Pause 184
Chapter 33: Let It Be. 187
Chapter 34: Hardening of the Self 194
Chapter 35: Animal Magnetism 198
Chapter 36: It's All Contagious 204
Chapter 37: Ubuntu 213
Chapter 38: The Dark Side of Us 218
Chapter 39: First, Do No Medicine 222
Chapter 40: World of Wounds 227
Chapter 41: Therapy Session 233
Chapter 42: The Art Is Long 236
Chapter 43: The Creative Imperative 241
Chapter 44: Wicked Ways 245
Chapter 45: Escape from the Drama Triangle 251
Chapter 46: Alpine Style 257
Chapter 47: Tell Me a Story. 263
Chapter 48: Believe It or Not 270
Chapter 49: The Art of the Reframe 274
Chapter 50: Stress Me Out 277
Chapter 51: Reality Is Never Wrong 287
Chapter 52: Is the Universe Friendly? 290
Chapter 53: A Why to Live 295
Chapter 54: Teach The Frog To Fight 299
Chapter 55: It's the Culture, Stupid 303
Chapter 56: Activism Is Medicine 306

Chapter 57: Life Has Standing 310
Chapter 58: What Moves People 314
Chapter 59: Breadth Before Depth 318
Chapter 60: One More Grain 322
Chapter 61: The Unknown Decathlon 325
Chapter 62: The Power of Subtraction 329
Chapter 63: Experiential Design 332
Chapter 64: Dojo Rules 336
Chapter 65: No Stick, No Carrot 341
Chapter 66: Adventure-Deficit Disorder 345
Chapter 67: Are You Coachable? 350
Chapter 68: Freedom, Discipline, Repeat 357
Chapter 69: The HEAL Curriculum 361
Chapter 70: Planet of Ambiguity 366
Chapter 71: Keep Your Eye on the Work 370
Chapter 72: Tribal Eldership 374

About the Author 381

FOREWORD

BY LAMYA ESSEMLALI

I would have liked this book to have been placed in my hands when I was younger and bored on the school benches. I would have understood my confusion better.

Apart from a "rebellious" period in high school, I have always been a good student, and I have always tried to "succeed" at school, in order to "succeed in life."

I come from a single-parent family, and my mother had a limited education that barely allowed her to learn to read and write. She raised me with a sense of the real sacredness of school, which she always presented to me as an indispensable tool for moral and financial autonomy. "If you do well in school, you will do what you want in life; you will be a free woman."

And yet, as a child and teenager, what kept me going in school was my friends, whom I considered to be my fellow sufferers. I still remember that, as a kid, I used to count the years I had left to "pull" before graduation, like a convict counting the years left to serve his sentence.

In the end, the only time I didn't feel like I was being held hostage by school was when, on rare occasions, a teacher managed to teach me something that made sense to me, something that I immediately recognized as useful and by which my curiosity was eagerly piqued because the topic spoke to my intellect and my instincts. That something always had to do with our collective history, with the way we interact with the world around us. That something always allowed me to better understand who we are, the self-proclaimed sapiens, the "wise ones." That something was always deeply rooted in the real, in short. And by real, I mean the natural world. These too-rare moments of excitement were enough to reassure me about my capacity to be passionate and to be amazed because, by dint of reacting only with boredom and indifference to everything that is proposed to you, you come to wonder if you are capable of anything else.

So fortunately, I realized that I was not intrinsically incapable of being interested in everything that was offered to me at school. I was simply resistant to anything that was not related to the understanding of everything that we did not create and on which we depend, that we damage, that we destroy. This is what I have always been passionate about. In this field, I finally found my way out of the box, and I was able to deploy a capacity for work and a personal investment that school had led me to believe I lacked.

We are probably unequal in our ability to endure this deep cognitive dissonance that undermines us from our early years of "passive life" on the school benches and still haunts us once in "active life." Is it a good thing to be resistant to that which destroys us?

Our species acquired the ability to destroy the world before we understood how it works. And therein lies the tragedy.

It has become easy for us to destroy Life and so much harder and more deserving not to save it, but simply to spare it. On the necessity and urgency of sparing the Living depend our chances of sparing ourselves. This is the great lesson of life from which all the others should follow. It is finally of an implacable logic: besides the moral and ethical considerations on the intrinsic value of the rest of the Living, if we do not apply this fundamental rule that the physical and biological world imposes on us, none of the human rules that we are taught at school will have any sense.

We have been breaking this basic rule for too long, and the consequences are just beginning to hit us. The COVID-19 pandemic is just one example. How many have realized this?

We live under the collective illusion that we are in control because we have computers and cell phones, 5G is coming, and we are sending our fellow humans into space. And yet, there are three warning signs of the extinction of a species: the population explosion, the overexploitation of resources, the occupation of all ecological niches. To see an endangered species, you just have to look in the mirror. This fact should be the basis of all our teachings, and all should take it into account, whatever the field taught. We are far from that.

I did a master's degree in environmental sciences with a specialization in biodiversity conservation at Pierre and Marie Curie University. This master's program is supposed to be one of the best in Europe. I learned a lot of interesting things there that are very useful to me today, especially about the functioning of ecosystems. But out of the dozens of professors I had during this five-year program, I can count on the fingers of one hand those who questioned us as students about our place in this world, about the role we play in this great reality show that is life. Yet many of my professors during my studies reproached me for my "militancy," my "subjective" vision of things. As if a good scientist could not be a militant and as if the anthropocentrism that places "Nature" at the service of humans was an objective vision of the real world. Is it not, rather, a world dreamed by Man, locked up in the illusion of a supremacy that bears the mourning of its "objectivity"? The idea of militant scientists is almost heresy in France. I have the feeling that this is less true in Anglo-Saxon countries. In Descartes's country, science that claims to be objective is, in reality, often a supporter of the dogma of "Man as master and possessor of Nature." In this respect, it often reveals itself as an ardent militant, with an unabashed and yet blatant subjectivity.

I learned a lot on the benches of the university, and I do not regret having spent time there. It is very useful today in my life as a scientist, activist, and militant, if only because it allowed me to recognize the essential. What is essential, beyond degrees, is knowledge, understanding of the world, experience, and a deep sense of belonging.

If I had followed the "recruitment channels" at student fairs, I would be lost in the limbo of a life that is not mine. How many people are lost in this way? Lost to themselves and lost to the world. The world needs people who are awake, educated, and aware of reality. Dreamers and utopians are not those who think that humanity must radically change; dreamers are those who are convinced that we are winning the evolutionary game. The school should be a great collective awakening; instead, it continues to manufacture zombies . . .

I am now president of Sea Shepherd France and codirector of Sea Shepherd Global, an extraordinary nongovernmental organization (NGO) dedicated to the defense and protection of the ocean and marine life.

After meeting Captain Paul Watson (founder of Sea Shepherd) in 2005, defending the ocean quickly became both an ecological emergency and a spiritual necessity. To save the ocean is to save our bodies and our souls. The ocean is the primary regulator of the climate, the primary producer of oxygen, and the primary carbon sink. It also undoubtedly contributes to the enchantment of the world. Life appeared in the ocean;

it is our cradle. But it will disappear with it; if the ocean dies, we will die. And it is dying; it will be our tomb. Today, the greatest threat to the ocean is overfishing, the insatiable appetite of billions of humans for fish, and an ocean that did not foresee this . . . And yet, only 2 percent of the world's fishing meets a subsistence need. Overfishing starves humans who really need fish as a source of protein; it also starves marine predators that can't compete with our millions of fishing vessels, and it destroys the ocean by taking thousands of marine mammals and protected species each year. And at the same time, humanity remains largely disconnected, unaware, even indifferent to the carnage perpetrated at sea. All of these reasons led me to dedicate my life to the defense of the ocean and marine animals.

With Sea Shepherd, I have led and participated in more than twenty missions at sea, hosted dozens of conferences, written books, and participated in documentaries (I particularly recommend *Seaspiracy*), all without ever having the impression that I was working or studying. Regardless, with Sea Shepherd, I have learned more than anywhere else. Sea Shepherd is a school of Life that teaches commitment, self-improvement, humility, cohesion, and team spirit. It is also a school that cultivates courage, passion, and imagination. In short, it is a school adapted to the world in which we live. There are others, in many other fields, but so few in the classic educational curriculum.

Yet the school has a fundamental role to play, the parents, the teachers, the coaches, all those who are in a role of transmission . . . The transmission of truth and the teaching of the real world are neither more nor less than the conditions of our survival as a species. For now, our legacy as *Homo sapiens* is the most massive and rapid destruction the planet has ever known. The sixth-extinction crisis unleashed by humanity has no equal in violence and scale. Just as we have a duty of historical memory for the atrocities committed against our own species, we have a duty of memory for the atrocities committed against the rest of the Living World. We have exterminated 60 percent of the wild animals in the last forty years. No human being should ignore this fact. No human being should ignore the consequences. With the power to destroy the world, we have lost the right to ignorance and inherited the duty of conscience.

In the end, this book proposes nothing more than that: to help men and women emerge in tune with the real world, a species with collective intelligence and memory, aware of the consequences of its actions: "He who plucks a flower disturbs a star," said Théodore Monod, paraphrasing Paul Dirac.

Everything is linked in the continuum of Life, both in space and in time. This essential lesson risks becoming our epitaph. I cherish the hope that, instead, we will be able to reconnect with the world around us, with the Living of which we are a part, with the past from which we come, and with the future whose possibility or annihilation we are deciding today.

May 25, 2021

ABOUT LAMYA ESSEMLALI

Lamya Essemlali is a French environmental activist and chairperson of Sea Shepherd France and second to Sea Shepherd Global. She has led several campaigns for Sea Shepherd Global in the Mediterranean Sea, the Faroe Islands, and the Indian Ocean to defend bluefin tuna, dolphins and pilot whales, and sharks.

BY DR. LOUIS FOUCHE

What a chance, what a freshness! A book on paleo-sapience. It's been a long time since anyone was interested in wisdom. Wisdom, prudence, slowness, courage, the past, the roots . . . So many old concepts, abandoned in the well-locked dungeons of the triumphant algorithmic techno-consumerism, right?

What need is there for all this nonsense when you have a smartphone? The model of personal achievement has become that of the masturbation of the narcissistic entrepreneurial performer, that of the start-up super of oneself in the start-up nation, in the digital start-up world. Number of views, number of likes, number of friends . . . The accomplished start-up lives his life as a teenager, finally shaking off the too-narrow and reactionary shackles of the dusty past of the old ones. No ties, no hindrances.

This is the "project" that some of our politicians shouted in their public meetings of electoral campaign until breaking their almost-still-mute voice, isn't it? To make of the human this emancipated being, megalomaniac, until the permanent self-satisfied ecstasy. The project was indeed this self-constructed, all-powerful, and alone individual monad . . .

What a joke! What a sham!

Because what is implied is that in order to subscribe to the infinite and eternal enjoyment of being alone and all-powerful, there is . . . a price to pay . . . You need the right subscription. Alone, sad, but rich and eternal, if you have the right package. The devil promises you so much . . . if you bow down.

But of what, by the way, would you be rich in this project? Of things, of objects, of plastic, of concrete, and of oil; but poor, to the point of crying, of depth and of true links. So much for the poor, so much for the old, so much for beauty, so much for the living and the ecology; so much the better for the salespeople of nonsense. The transhumanist hero is the dupe of a commercial system that has stolen his own life to sell him a sad face piece by piece, and as expensive as possible. This anti-hero is decorrelated from the original matrix and from the other living beings around. He is enclosed, enshrined, entangled in the imposture of his simulated happiness.

So our solitary hero thinks he is all-powerful behind his computer, but he is more helpless than Job when faced with the hazards of real life. Refugee in a digital life where everything would be perfect, he is nowhere. He no longer lives in reality. His life is a dark and algorithmic dream, endlessly reiterated. This is where the problem lies.

But fortunately, globalized techno-industrial neoliberalism has finally come to an end. Its never-satiated predation is finally coming up against a larder of resources that is beginning to be empty. Biodiversity melting, mass extinction, ecosystem destruction . . . The only thing left for the capitalist ogre to eat is the human being himself. So the digital tool has been erected as the war hammer of post-capitalism, to hypnotize and to distract . . . to death.

But the promise no longer holds. It is stale. The fake dream is only a dream. Wind and silicon dust. The real has imposed itself anyway. It is there. Like a fresh wind that sweeps away the dust. And from now on, it is well there, this reality. And only those who refuse to suffer still refuse to see. The system is dying and screaming, hideous, deformed, and monstrous like Munch's cry. The beast is dying.

The crisis we are going through has come about precisely for this reason. To avoid the worst, to make us turn around. COVID-19, in its sad and absurd narrative garb, is the herald of liberation from hypnosis. It is here to perform the obscene pantomime of the final agony, and to make the masks fall. It is here to reveal without modesty the decay of our societies. It assaults all those who continue to want to anesthetize themselves with an unprecedented shock. A huge wake-up call, a bucket of water in the face. Wake up!

This is what the world is shouting at us. This is what the living, in all the interstices left by our mortifying culture, is shouting at us. And it is high time. "It's high time," say the English speakers. It is "high time." We are in this high time. There is no other time to live in. It is the high time for heroes—for real heroes. It is the great time of courage. It is the great time of an imaginary that takes shape with the real and the living. It is high time to resume the dance with the world and with the living, a dance that we should never have interrupted. And which living being? The one that sleeps inside us, ensheathed in comfort, and the one that is dying all around us, suffocated by concrete, plastic, and oil.

This is the question for me: How to tell the story of humans who would inhabit the world in joy, beauty, love, peace? How to live together with each one—life, the world, society—in subtle diplomacy with other living beings?

The book you are holding in your hands proposes a kind of practical wisdom, a contextual wisdom. And what a joy it is to rediscover that old Aristotelian concept: phronesis. Prudence, contextual and pragmatic wisdom, the intelligence of courage. One of the key values of the ReInfo Covid collective, of which I have the honor to be one of the diplomats.

I am happy and honored to be one of the preface authors for *The Sapience Curriculum*. This book is a proposal, an opportunity. It is a guide to introduce simple words and gestures to prepare for and live in a better world.

There is no angelism in this book. There are no false pretenses. Nobody says that it will be easy. There is no deception about the difficulties of such a path. The "pfh," the fucking human factor, is exposed in an unvarnished way. But it is exposed with benevolence and empathy, with pragmatism and realism.

And in this sense, the book achieves its goal. As the Anglo-Saxons often do. It puts into simple words concepts that would take us whole books to grasp. It manages to cram each chapter into three pages to illuminate a problem and provide pragmatic answers.

You can read it by flipping through it. One chapter per day. Three pages. To meditate, to let it resonate. Yes, to let it resonate as one would let collected ancient wisdom resonate. Let it resonate like a tale told by the griot before going to sleep or an old song sung by the clan around the fire.

Put yourself in resonance with all these ancient wisdoms to shed light on the issues of a better life today. This is my proposal. Read quietly and let it resonate. Let each part of our reality be infused with these ancestral memories deposited by the first peoples as keys on the way to a certain happiness, all together and with the world.

May 16, 2021

LOUIS FOUCHÉ

Louis Fouché, born on January 23, 1979, in Saint-Maurice, is a French anesthesiologist-resuscitator at Conception Hospital in Marseille. He initially studied philosophy and ancient history, and worked as a physician at the Paoli-Calmettes Cancer Institute. He holds a master's degree in health ethics.

PREFACE

I'd really like to change the world
And save it from the mess it's in
I'm too weak, I'm so thin
I'd like to fly but I can't even swim.
—The Kinks
"(Wish I Could Fly Like) Superman"

The historian and philosopher Will Durant once observed that "education is the progressive discovery of our own ignorance." This, coming from a winner of the Pulitzer Prize and the Presidential Medal of Freedom. This, from the author of the epic eleven-volume series *The Story of Civilization*. This, from the author of dozens of serious, critically acclaimed books on philosophy, history, and the human condition.

It's a sobering thought. If a man of such prodigious achievement describes his life as the progressive realization of his own ignorance, where does that leave the rest of us? Most of us are barely treading water as it is. In fact, most of us spend our entire lives clawing and groping for any kind of knowledge we can get our hands on, and when we succeed, we're not much inclined to give it up without a fight, much less admit it in public. Ignorant? I'd rather talk about how much I know.

But of course, Durant was right. Ignorance is our ground state, the ocean that we swim in, the central fact of our existence. And if we're honest with ourselves, we find this becoming increasingly obvious with each passing year. Gradually or abruptly, we come to this realization, usually by way of some drastic act of bad judgment, sometimes by learning a new perspective that jolts us out of our complacency. We try to bluff our way through life and put up a convincing front, but deep down, we know it's all for show. Our knowledge, substantial as it once felt, is only a drop in the ocean of what's waiting to be known. As fragile, short-lived animals in a vast and unimaginably complex world, we're lucky to know much of anything at all.

To many ears, Durant's observation must sound like a Zen koan gone wrong. Of course our collective education makes us smarter and more powerful; that's the whole point of the enterprise. And now that we've been pursuing science and education for a few thousand years, we must be well on our way to knowing more than any generation that's ever lived. It's progress, after all. Every day and in every way, we just keep getting smarter and smarter. We are *Homo sapiens*, after all.

But education is far more paradoxical than most of us would like to believe. On the face of it, the process seems like a simple exercise in addition: one set of facts piled on top of another, building and growing all the way, we might suppose, to a summit of omniscience. But that's not how it really works. Adding facts on top of facts might make a mountain, but the view from the summit is unexpected and humbling. Almost every scientific discovery of the last few centuries has revealed humanity as small, temporary, and almost completely powerless in the face of a vast and mysterious universe.

Copernicus and Galileo showed us that we're not really at the center of the cosmos. Darwin exposed us as one species among millions. Edwin Hubble demonstrated the mind-boggling immensity and dynamism of the universe. Molecular biologists have shown us that the microbiome is a dominant force in the function of our bodies and even our cognition. We are, in other words, bit players on a vast and often incomprehensible stage.

But that's just the beginning. With the coronavirus pandemic of 2020, our powerlessness and ignorance have been brought into even greater relief. Suddenly, our assumptions of vast knowledge and competence have been called into question, and the ground beneath our feet feels like it's falling away. Long accustomed to thinking of ourselves as the master species, it's starting to look as if matters are no longer under our control. It's no wonder we're afraid, confused, and anxious; our assumptions of supremacy are disappearing before our eyes.

To be sure, we've got our experts. We've got a small army of virologists, epidemiologists, public health experts, and research scientists. But as this book goes to print, it's not at all clear how this pandemic will play out. The virus may simply fade away into history, or it might remain in circulation, waxing and waning as a chronic condition. Or it could gather momentum and burst into a full-blown global emergency, with millions of deaths each year. It might even bring down civilization as we know it and reduce the human population to a fraction of its former, self-declared glory.

The point is that we just don't know. And aside from following obvious public health measures and getting vaccinated, there's really not much we can do about it. And this may be the greatest consequence of all: a great humbling of human arrogance. All our delusions of grandeur, brought down by a tiny bit of nucleic code, wrapped in a protein coat. For all our expertise and advanced knowledge, we may well have to kneel before the virus.

All of which leads me to wonder about the audacity of writing a book about sapience, a subject in which my limited qualifications only seem to be getting smaller by the moment. To be sure, I've spent long years in various libraries, trained hard in the martial arts, traveled to Africa, studied with some excellent teachers, and stuck my neck out on behalf of the future. But from today's perspective, my efforts feel like drops in the ocean.

Even worse, my knowledge only seems to shrink with each passing day. I'd like to write an important book about navigating the modern world, but on most days, I'm just as confused and overwhelmed as the next guy. I'd like to brag about my qualifications, but when I get right down to it, I'm just another garden-variety primate, a bipedal chimp with a handful of ideas and opinions about what might work.

But no matter my limitations, I must step up and heed the call. The state of the world demands the effort. Our planet is on the ropes, and our society is in chaos. Everyone needs to do what they can, even in the face of radical uncertainty and diminishing qualifications.

The good news is that I've been supported in this effort by an incredible cast of fine human beings, people who've given freely of their time, knowledge, and curiosity. And while my name is on this book, their contributions are what have made it all possible. In this effort, I take heart in the words of C. S. Lewis: "The next best thing to being wise oneself is to live in a circle of those who are." These fine people include Michael Campi; Steve Laskevitch and Carla Fraga; Seby Alary; Ron Kauk; James O'Keefe, MD; Jeremy Lent; Michael Dowd; Steve Myrland; Daniel Dancer; Nick Hunt; Ken Ward; Derrick Jensen; Tim DeChristopher; Guy McPherson; Alfie Kohn; Bill McKibben; Dana Lyons; Shaun Chamberlin; Corey Jung; Susan

Fahringer; Robert Sapolsky; Pete Karabetis; Ray Sylvester; Barbara Gottlieb; Troy Corliss; Doug Peacock; Rodney King; Kari Lehr; Hana Begovic; Max Wilber; Skye Nacel; Alessandro Pelizzon; John Platt; Rita Issa; Paul Landon; Jojo Mehta; Melissa Nelson; Bruce Alexander; Clover Hogan; Kathleen Dean Moore; Giordano Nanni; Grant Wilson; Joe Gray; Mike Zwack; Travis Janeway; Elizabeth Woody; and Sam, Beth, Alex, and Travis Forencich.

CHAPTER 1

WELCOME TO NOW

> Human history becomes more and more a race between education and catastrophe.
> —H. G. Wells

Have you ever wondered why you and the people around you are suffering? Don't you find it strange that you've landed here in adulthood, in the midst of a wicked planetary crisis, with minimal preparation to meet the challenges of our day? Have you ever suspected that your education may have been an exercise in futility and a waste of precious time?

As a literate person, you've spent plenty of time in schools of various sorts. You've worked your way through the primary grades and high school and maybe even done some time in college and beyond. Maybe you were a good student, dutifully learning the material that was handed to you, all under the belief that someday, all the hard work would pay off and you'd be ready to excel, or at least make a decent go of it in the grown-up world.

But when the day finally arrived, you were shocked to discover a world in chaos. The realities of looming ecological disaster, social injustice, pandemics, and other systemic ills suddenly came into focus, and you began to feel radically unprepared, even incompetent. To be sure, you're well equipped with specialized knowledge, and you may have even performed well on standardized tests, but suddenly, none of that seems to matter. What you really need is a perspective and an orientation, a philosophy that can see you through the chaos, uncertainty, and ambiguity of our time. But no one ever seemed to teach that.

So maybe you're wondering: Why isn't there a school, a course, or a program that speaks directly to the human predicament as it is and as it will be? Why do we spend so much time learning various subjects, only to discover that in post-school life, those subjects may be entirely irrelevant to the conditions that we inhabit? Why didn't anyone teach us about activism and how to change our dysfunctional world? Why didn't anyone teach us how to recover our continuity with the planet and one another? Why doesn't our educational system teach us about the root causes of our distress?

The disconnect is striking and extremely upsetting. For many, it may well feel as if we spent our entire young lives preparing for a world that doesn't actually exist. Even worse, it sometimes seems that the education we did receive was more of a distraction than a conscious, intentional preparation for reality. And worse still, we might even come to suspect that conventional schooling, far from being a solution to our predicament, may actually be a root cause of our suffering. Maybe our standard curriculums actually *create* the culture that's proving so destructive to both people and the planet. In other words, we aren't just unprepared but actually *dis*prepared to meet the real-world challenges of our age. You might even feel duped.

PANORAMA

This book is a guide for teachers, trainers, coaches, health professionals, parents, and anyone who works with the human animal. It's designed as a remedy for our discontent and an antidote to education-as-usual. It's a set of ideas to recover our lost wholeness and prepare ourselves for the world we actually inhabit. The central theme is relevance, especially the challenge of teaching our students, clients, and patients how to adapt to the radical changes that lie in the near-term future. Think of it as the curriculum you never had.

This book is aimed at the common ground that unites today's teaching professions, especially our shared interest in promoting the health and function of the human animal. In conventional settings, many people assume that teachers, trainers, coaches, therapists, and health professionals inhabit significantly different worlds. Each field has its own curriculum, its own professional organizations, its own standards, and its own practices.

But when we look closer, the differences seem minor, even trivial. In fact, it's the overlap between these professions that really matters. We have more in common than we might think, and ultimately, our job description is identical: put the human animal back in touch with the continuities that sustain life.

No matter your specific professional niche—teacher, trainer, coach, therapist, or health professional—you can use the ideas in this book to empower your clients, students, or patients and bring them a greater sense of relevance, health, meaning, and purpose. These ideas can function as supplements, as sparks for inspiration, or as starting points for class discussions and writing assignments. Or you can simply use them to advance your own understanding of life and your preparation for the future.

WHY WE NEED THIS

In all likelihood, civilization as we know it is reaching the end of its run. The alpha issues of our day—social injustice, pandemics, and ecological emergencies—are getting more daunting with each passing hour. We are face to face with deeply embedded, systemic problems that only seem to get worse with the passage of time. Our life-support systems are in sharp decline, and humans everywhere are beginning to feel the stress. Our bodies and our spirits are suffering, and in one way or another, many of us are traumatized.

Not only is this new era unprecedented, but it's highly dynamic and fluid. Much as we might like to pretend otherwise, we're in unexplored territory now. We are, as the poet Rumi would have put it, "between stories." We don't know how to live, and we're confused about what to teach. Even worse, many of our educational institutions have failed in their basic mission and now function mostly as sorting mechanisms for moving students into academic and social pigeonholes. And most disturbing of all: we simply have no education for turmoil, resilience, crisis management, or wise action in the face of existential uncertainty.

RADICAL RELEVANCE

To get the most out of this book, it's essential to understand the deep nature of human adaptability and the power of training. In this domain, the bedrock principle comes from the world of athletic coaching. As every experienced trainer knows, the body makes extremely precise, subtle, and specific adaptations to the physical demands it encounters. And of course it would be this way; the human body is millions of years old and has survived precisely because of this nuanced ability to adapt. We have a long history of shaping our bodies to the conditions we experience in natural habitats.

In the world of athletic training and physical therapy, coaches often talk about the power of the SAID principle: Specific Adaptations to Imposed Demands. No matter what you throw at the body, it will do everything it can to remodel itself to make future encounters with that experience easier. Challenge the body with strength training, and it will immediately go to work, growing muscle fibers, tendons, and ligaments and increasing nervous-system support. Challenge the body with endurance activity, and you'll see microscopic tissue-level changes, perfectly specific to that kind of experience.

All of this makes sense at the level of athletic training and rehabilitation, but what most of us fail to realize is that this process of specific adaptation takes place continuously throughout our lives. The body—especially the nervous system—is constantly building new pathways and structures to meet whatever demands it encounters. This is why trainers everywhere are always on the lookout for ways to simulate real-world challenges. Coaches don't just give their athletes random drills; they study the detailed demands of the upcoming season, including the challenges of competition and the playoffs, then craft their training accordingly. The more precise, the better.

We see the same process in all high-performance environments. In medical school, trainers attempt to create precise simulations of surgery, emergency-room encounters, and other clinical practices, even going so far as to build detailed mock-ups of the physical surroundings. In the military, trainers prepare special-op teams by constructing actual full-scale buildings to mimic the conditions they're expected to encounter in the field. Every detail of the operation is practiced in advance; the more specific the training, the better the adaptation and ultimate performance. The closer you can get in training, the better your chances of doing the right thing in real life.

This is precisely what ought to be happening in the world of education. In fact, we can think of the entire educational enterprise as a simple, two-step process: First, determine as best you can the characteristics and qualities that your student, athlete, or client will encounter in the coming years. Second, train your people specifically for that anticipated set of conditions.

If you get the first step right, the second step will mostly take care of itself: your assessment of future conditions will tell you exactly what to do with your students and clients. But if you ignore step one or make a poor assessment of the conditions your people are likely to encounter, then the second step will inevitably be flawed, irrelevant, or even destructive.

Which, of course, is precisely what we're doing in conventional education. Even as scientists give us well-founded assessments of our climate, biodiversity, and social crises, we continue to ignore, distract, minimize, and above all, hope for the best. In this sense, modern schooling can be accurately described as a cultural case of magical thinking.

Ideally, all human education ought to follow a simple axiom: "Teach reality" or "Teach the truth." Or as many young people are now demanding: "Teach the future." In fact, one of the biggest mistakes a teacher, trainer, or coach can make is to train students in skills and perspectives that don't match up with the environment or setting they are actually going to inhabit. Obviously, reality and truth are open to interpretation, but there can be no dispute on this score: a failure to honor reality guarantees a failure of education.

Getting education right means understanding and preparing students intentionally and specifically to meet the future. But as it stands, our current educational efforts might best be described as "teaching for a future that we hope is going to happen." In most modern high schools, the one big idea that drives everything is "get good grades so you can get into college." And once you're in college, the one big idea is "get an advanced degree." But these are weak, artificial objectives that have little to do with actual challenges on the ground. By itself, a degree is no preparation for the psycho-physical challenges of rising sea levels, groundwater depletion, species extinctions, and social chaos. We need something specific, targeted, and relevant.

BIG HISTORY AND HOCKEY STICKS

To make matters worse, the modern school system is utterly failing to heed the essential lessons of Big History, especially big human history. Most history books treat our indigenous, hunter-gatherer experience as an insignificant prologue to the glories of civilization, but in fact, the story of human prehistory holds vital knowledge about who we are and what we might become. It has immense explanatory power and is highly integrative—a big idea that wraps up disparate ideas into a coherent and extremely useful whole.

When human history is taught in modern schools—if it's taught at all—it's usually presented as a set of archaic curiosities. Our ancestors are described as primitive, brutish, and unsophisticated. In our rush to celebrate the modern age of human supremacy and progress, we leapfrog over the vast majority of our time on Earth, ignoring the very paradigm that might help us find our way to a functional future. In other words, we are wasting one of the most powerful ideas in the human repertoire.

To put it bluntly, most educational programs fail to set people up for success. This stems from a failure of our imagination and our inability to appreciate the nature of social, cultural, and technological change. Most educators work under the assumption that their students will encounter a world substantially the same as the one we inhabit right now. We assume that tomorrow will be just like today, but we are tragically, spectacularly wrong about all of this.

In fact, our immediate future is best described by the hockey stick, the classic graph of radical change over time. This acceleration is most obvious in climate models and in human population growth, but today, we see a similar dynamic everywhere we look: technological change, destruction of habitat, species extinctions, and soil degradation, to name a few.

For hunting-and-gathering tribes in the Paleolithic era, change was extremely slow, and it would have been safe for elders to assume that conditions for future generations would be more or less the same as their present day. And even throughout the Middle Ages, the Renaissance, and the early days of the twentieth century, change was slow enough that education-as-usual would suffice. But today, radical change is a nonnegotiable fact of life.

Sadly, modern education makes no attempt to address this reality; it's easier to simply assume convention. We seem to believe that our systemic, planetary problems are nothing more than temporary, intermittent setbacks; if we just try harder, everything will get back to normal, and our students will succeed. But radical change is not going away. Acceleration is here to stay—at least until something breaks.

The hockey stick presents us with a monstrous psychophysical challenge, the greatest in human history. Human life is hard enough as it is, but now it's going to change in ways we can scarcely understand. We are psychologically and spiritually unprepared for what's about to come. It's no wonder we're so stressed and fearful.

ASSUMPTIONS AND PREDICTIONS

So what exactly is the specific nature of our near-term future? What kind of world will our students, athletes, clients, and patients actually inhabit? Opinions vary, but a preponderance of the evidence suggests that the following events will unfold in coming decades; these consequences are not inevitable, but highly probable:

- Human impact will continue to wreak havoc on the biosphere and life-supporting systems.
- Substantial, even catastrophic increases in sea levels will inundate coastal cities and poison freshwater aquifers around the world. Mass migrations involving millions of people will become commonplace.
- More people will compete for increasingly scarce resources, including fresh water. Continued degradation of soil, habitat, and biodiversity will lead to ecosystem crashes, with serious impacts on agriculture and food supplies.
- Energy will pose an enormous challenge. Poisonous fossil fuels will remain in widespread use, but green energy is unlikely to be an adequate replacement.
- Plastics, toxic chemicals, and endocrine disruptors will continue to be produced and will pollute soil, water, oceans, and human bodies.
- Human contact with the microbial world will increase. Viral pandemics and antibiotic resistance will become increasingly problematic across the human population.
- Social inequality and racism will continue to divide society, and the gap between rich and poor

will continue to hamper efforts toward social justice. Gated communities of various sorts will become increasingly common.
- Global supply chains will become unreliable, leading to shortages of food and products that we've come to rely on.
- Corporate power will continue to dominate government, public life, and cultural narratives.
- Lifestyle diseases such as obesity and diabetes will continue to plague a large percentage of humanity, putting continued pressure on health and medical resources.
- The right-wing embrace of authoritarian power and tyranny—backed up by violence—will continue to wield influence in America and abroad.

This assessment may sound like defeatism, but it is not. The facts are clear. Even with massive, unified, coordinated efforts across society, we are unlikely to avoid major systemic shocks and a possible failure of civilization itself. And none of this should come as a surprise. Most of this was predicted by William Catton in his 1980 book *Overshoot: The Ecological Basis of Revolutionary Change*. In short, Catton's thesis was that humanity has been living beyond the carrying capacity of the planet for quite some time, and now, we're due for a reckoning.

We hope for a quick fix in the form of green energy, but no amount of technological innovation is going to solve our crisis. On the contrary, more technology will simply do what technology has always done: provide a temporary reprieve from ecological reality, kicking the can down the road. So yes, our predicament is real. As author David Wallace-Wells has put it, "It's worse than you think ... no matter how well informed you are, you are surely not alarmed enough."

OVERLAPPING CRISES

In 2020, the coronavirus epidemic and the police killings of George Floyd and Breonna Taylor and the shooting of Jacob Blake dominated our attention, and rightly so. But the degradation of the biosphere didn't slow, and the bad news continued unabated. Headlines in the summer of that year included the following:

> "Earth Accelerating Towards Sixth Mass Extinction Event That Could See the Disintegration of Civilization"

> "Earth's Carbon Dioxide Levels Hit Record High, Despite Coronavirus-Related Emissions Drop . . . More Carbon Dioxide in the Air Now Than at Any Time in 3 Million Years"

> "Warmest May on Record, Siberia 10C Hotter"

> "Climate Worst-Case Scenarios May Not Go Far Enough, Cloud Data Shows"

> "Physicists: 90% Chance of Human Society Collapsing within Decades"

> "By 2070, More Than 3 Billion People May Live Outside the 'Human Climate Niche'"

"Canada's Last Fully Intact Arctic Ice Shelf Collapses"

"Warming Greenland Ice Sheet Passes Point of No Return"

"Record Arctic Blazes May Herald New 'Fire Regime' Decades Sooner Than Anticipated"

What's sometimes lost in the conversation is that issues of social justice, racism, viral pandemics, and the health of the biosphere are radically interdependent. All of these problems stem from a common root—our dysfunctional relationship with the natural world and with one another. If we're to make progress in any of these domains, we need to take a comprehensive, systemic, inclusive, and relational approach. Above all, it's essential that we keep our eye on the ball, which is to say, the planet. Because if the biosphere fails, nothing else matters. As Naomi Klein put it: "When your life-support system is threatened, all other problems fit inside that problem." In other words, the state of the biosphere remains and will always be the alpha issue of our day.

EDUCATION FOR THE NEAR-TERM FUTURE

No matter the details, we can say with certainty that the near-term future is going to be marked by high levels of uncertainty, ambiguity, and stress, if not outright chaos, suffering, and desperation. And so the obvious question: How do we prepare our students, clients, and patients for this unprecedented reality? Clearly, tweaks and refinements to conventional schooling aren't going to do it. Fancy new "teaching techniques" aren't going to do it. What we need is an entirely new approach to education at all levels, one aimed directly at the realities of the human predicament.

Our near-term future will demand a unique skill set, one that is certain to diverge from our conventional academic subjects and familiar professional roles. In the face of systemic breakdown and episodic chaos, we can say with confidence that practical skills will become increasingly important for survival. As global supply chains begin to falter, people will have to take on tasks that we formerly took for granted: growing and preparing our own food, fixing our own houses and machines, for example.

There's plenty of instruction available in these practical arts, and we'd do well to take advantage of what's out there. But as things grow increasingly uncertain, it will be our perspectives, philosophies, and spiritual orientations that will ultimately carry the day. In the decades to come, our students, clients, and patients will need psycho-spiritual skills such as resilience, creativity, flexibility, relational intelligence, and narrative fluency. These arts will not only make us more functional and effective, but they'll also keep depression, anxiety, and despair at bay, a challenge that is bound to become even more acute in coming years.

In particular, our students and clients are going to need a sense of wisdom or sapience to see them through. With so much ambiguity in the air, we can't simply revert to established conventions or formulas that might have worked in the past. Intelligence is all well and good, but we need something more. We need to make sense of our predicament and find our balance, even in the face of radical uncertainty. With systems crashing all around us, the question of the day becomes, "What would wisdom do?"

Even more to the point, we're coming to the astonishing realization that intelligence—the most revered of all human qualities in the modern world—doesn't seem to be delivering as promised. Challenged from every direction by a multiplicity of crises, we double and triple down on rationality and computer processing, all under the assumption that more intelligence is going to get us out of the hole. But it's not working. We have more knowledge than ever before in human history, but try as we might, we keep falling behind. This is not to say that intelligence is wrong or maladaptive or that we should abandon it in favor of irrationality and impulse. It is to say that we should put down the calipers for a while and start looking at the attitudes, perspectives, and relationships that might serve us better.

WHERE'S THE SAPIENCE?

Unfortunately, conventional education also fails in this respect. Haven't you ever wondered about the fact that we call ourselves *Homo sapiens* (the "wise animal"), yet we spend almost no time discussing or cultivating wisdom itself? When wisdom is spoken of at all in modern education, it's usually in the context of a philosophy class or religious studies. Likewise, we rarely attempt to teach these perspectives to children, assuming, perhaps, that wisdom is something only for the elderly.

To make matters worse, the conversation around wisdom seems to be declining in our culture at large. A search on Google's Ngram page shows a declining use of the words *wisdom, patience, humility,* and *modesty* over the course of the twentieth century. As a hyperactive, technological culture, we now show more interest in artificial intelligence than in organic, body-based wisdom.

But how do we educate people for sapience? We know how to train people for practical skills and knowledge, but how do we give them a sense of balance, dignity, modesty, and humility—the traits we associate with wise action in the face of radical ambiguity? No one knows for certain, but we do know this: if we don't attempt it, we are sure to fail. And as it stands, we are scarcely even trying.

THE FUTURE IS DANGEROUS

Whatever the future holds, we can be sure of one thing: it will not be safe. Big trouble is ahead. The simple, inconvenient fact is that our modern industrial-capitalistic system appears to be incompatible with a habitable planet and the creation of a functional future. To survive, many of our foundational ideas, systems, and relationships will have to change, substantially or even radically. They might change incrementally and voluntarily, but more likely, they will crash and have to be rebuilt in some new form.

And so this book is intentionally and explicitly countercultural. It points to the folly of our planet-hostile worldview and, when possible, exposes its oversights and extremity. It recommends that we throw off the myopic focus on single individuals and concentrate instead on relationships, systems, and interconnections. In the process, it will challenge convention, assumptions, and tradition.

Some of the ideas in this book might be described as "radical," but in the larger view, it's actually quite the opposite. The status quo is radical. Business-as-usual is radical. The destruction of our life-supporting systems and relationships, the stratification of society based on race—in the context of human history, especially our indigenous history, these are abnormal, extremist, even suicidal positions. In contrast, advocating for ecological preservation and social justice is primally conservative, pro-health, and pro-future.

So be forewarned: this is not a safe book. There are no promises here for a seamless transition into a functional future, no formulas for guaranteed success, no inevitable path to sapience, no slam-dunk model for personal health. If you adopt the perspectives in this book, you're going to meet resistance, and you're going to get into trouble. So be prepared; the future is not for sissies.

ORGANIZATION AND APPLICATION

As you'll see, this book consists of a series of essays, lessons, and campfire talks. Whatever you call them, the organization is nonlinear, and they can be accessed in whatever order you choose. In conventional education, administrators like to imagine that learning must come in a linear sequence, laid out in a textbook and delivered by teachers or computers. Step one, followed by step two, all the way to the PhD. Like much of what we do in the modern world, the emphasis is on order and control.

To be sure, some skills do require disciplined, sequential training, but humans are highly irrational creatures. People learn in fits and starts, making connections between ideas as they see fit. Experience—the most powerful teacher of all—comes in its own time. Like it or not, education is a messy, even chaotic business. Insights come when the brain and spirit are ready, and everyone is different.

This is particularly the case in learning to adapt to our modern predicament, a thoroughly unprecedented condition in which there are no experts, no authorities, and no best practices. Historians can tell us a lot about our trajectory, and we'd be wise to listen, but no one has ever been here before. It would be folly to assume some sort of methodical, linear progression from beginning to mastery.

In learning to live in the face of ambiguity and radical uncertainty, there can be no standardized sequence. It's a bricolage art; take whatever you have on hand and make something meaningful. Start where you are and grab what you can. Try for sequential learning if you like, but be aware that students and clients are constructing their own paths, based on their own experience and values. In this spirit, the essays in this guide can be read in any order. They all overlap and feed off one another. Start where you like and take it from there.

In any case, there are a number of ways to use this book. If you're a big reader, you can simply dive in and metabolize it from start to finish. If you're a dabbler, it's easy to drop in here and there, read an essay, and reflect on what it means for you. If you're a teacher, you can assign the whole book or particular essays as part of a class experience. One essay each week might well carry you through an entire season or semester.

Even better, you can make these readings part of a complete, whole-body experience and combine the readings with physical activity. Gather your friends, clients, or students and do some physical movement, then read together and discuss. See the appendix at the end of this book for ideas about games and movement. You can also consult *The Exuberant Animal Experience* for a complete description of team-building games and functional movement.

Many of the ideas in this book are appropriate for young people, even children, in the right circumstances. Of course, our normal impulse is to protect children from harsh reality and keep them protected from troubling ideas, at least until their bodies and minds are fully developed. This is what parents and teachers typically do.

But these are not normal circumstances. Protection and comfort are vital for the developing mind and body, but it's also true that young people deserve the truth, as well as training for the world they are about to inhabit. There is no need to terrorize them with apocalyptic images of a failing world, but they deserve to know the facts. They deserve a relevant education that prepares them for actual conditions on the ground. So use your best judgment. If you need to tone down the gravity of our situation, do it, but don't neglect the prime directive of our day: prepare to meet reality.

Your job as a teacher, trainer, or coach is to interpret, metabolize, and translate your own experience into something that others can use. Take the raw material in this book, put it in your own words, and share it with your people in a way that works for you. You are the tribal elder and the leader in this effort. This book may help you find a path, but you are the one who will do the vital work. You're about to send your students on a grand voyage into the future. Give them the best lessons you can.

CHAPTER 2

MEET YOUR MISMATCH

> Humans have dragged a body with a long hominid history into an overfed, malnourished, sedentary, sunlight-deficient, sleep-deprived, competitive, inequitable, and socially-isolating environment with dire consequences.
> —Sebastian Junger
> *Tribe: On Homecoming and Belonging*

Our bodies are ancient, and our roots go deep. Not so long ago, we were healthy, wild animals, living in intimate contact with our natural habitat and one another. But today, we're struggling to adapt—in an evolutionary blink of an eye—to some radically novel conditions.

In this big historical perspective, our collision with the modern world has been almost instantaneous. If our ancestors traveled forward in time to today, they'd be mystified, shocked, and even repelled by the magnitude of the change. In essence, we are refugees from the deep past, trying to make a go of it in a world we can scarcely understand.

This is the problem of mismatch, sometimes described as the "evolutionary discordance hypothesis." And while this may sound like just another academic curiosity, it's actually one of the most urgent and consequential problems of our age. Far from being a mere hypothesis, the effects on our bodies and our spirits are very real and sometimes catastrophic.

WIRED FOR ANOTHER WORLD

The story of the human body stretches back millions of years. Over the course of thousands of generations, every detail of our anatomy, physiology, and psychology has been sculpted for survival and reproductive success in wild, natural, outdoor environments. Our skeletal, muscular, circulatory, nervous, and hormonal systems are the way they are because they enhanced our survival prospects in natural, ancestral habitats. Every cell, organ, feedback loop, and mental inclination has been shaped by our experience as hunters, gatherers, and scavengers. We're here today because our bodies are good at surviving in ancestral conditions.

In contrast, our bodies are almost entirely unprepared for a world of cars, couches, computers, and concrete. We're just not suited for lives of sedentary work, chronic stress, technological acceleration, social injustice, and looming planetary catastrophe. Our normal, evolutionary impulses clash with modern reality, setting us up for stress, addictions, and other dysfunctions.

In essence, we are animals attempting to live outside our normal ecological range. We're round hunter-gatherer pegs trying to fit into square industrial-technological holes. If we try really hard, we can force the pegs to fit, but damage is inevitable. This is the paradox of our time: we are misfits in a world of our own creation.

PRIMAL CONFUSIONS

All of which puts us into a deep and often disturbing state of psycho-physical distress. To really appreciate the full extent of our confusion, an inventory is in order:

- *Historical confusion*: We don't really appreciate the vast scope of human evolution and the many ways the modern era is an exception to the human norm.
- *Circadian confusion*: Starved for rhythmic natural light—the primary driver and synchronizer of physiology and metabolism—our bodies are adrift and in ill health.
- *Autonomic confusion*: Under siege by random, often irrelevant stimuli, our bodies flit wildly from the fight-flight response to rest-and-digest, often independent of the facts on the ground. This is hard on our health and ability to function.
- *Physical confusion*: Our natural vagility (movement in habitat) is constrained by buildings, vehicles, and unnatural obligations. The body wants to walk, run, and explore, but it's locked down at home, in a cubicle, or in a vehicle.
- *Microbial confusion*: Our personal microbiome, inherited from Mom and the habitat of infancy, is wildly distorted by random travel and erratic contact with food and artificial substances.
- *Tribal/social confusion*: With a "tribe" of nearly eight billion people, it's almost impossible to

know who's in your circle. Alliances shift with the wind, people always breaking up and making up.
- *Bioregional confusion*: High-speed travel gives us the ability to parachute into whatever habitat we like, but the body rarely has time to adapt to or learn the local flora and fauna.
- *Cultural confusion*: With all the modern comings and goings, our cultural focus is dissolving. Our foods, rituals, languages, narratives, and beliefs have become fragmented, noisy, and incoherent.
- *Cosmological confusion*: Most problematic of all, we struggle to reconcile our animal nature with our desire to be special, exalted, and exceptional. We make up all sorts of stories to keep us apart from and above the rest of creation.

Given the breadth and depth of our confusion, it's no surprise that so many of us are suffering from ill health and a sense of psycho-physical disconnect—the truly remarkable thing is that we can function at all. Mismatch, we might well say, is a bitch.

MISMATCH AS TRAUMA

To be sure, some people adapt easily to the modern world, and with a few adjustments, many of us remain happy and healthy. But for a great many of us, the contrast is too great, the stresses of the alien environment too overwhelming to manage. Recognize it or not, our bodies feel the pull of the Paleo in every minute of every day, a frustrated longing for movement, physicality, and contact with other human beings and the living world. In this sense, mismatch must be considered a genuine form of trauma and should be treated as such.

Likewise, it's safe to assume that mismatch can also produce a form of posttraumatic stress disorder (PTSD). The trauma may not be as acute as that of combat or domestic violence, but the effects are just as real. It also shouldn't surprise us to discover that addiction in various forms is increasing around the world. When people are prevented from exercising their ancestral lifeways and are separated from the continuities that support their health, they're far more likely to turn in other directions for solace.

In fact, mismatch can also be described as a preexisting medical condition for nearly every human being on the planet, a condition that compromises our health in myriad ways. In other words, most of us are prestressed, even before we come in contact with dangerous microbes, inflammatory processes, poisonous foods, and other disease-causing agents. This is the unrecognized public health crisis of our age. Millions of people are suffering, and yet we fail to acknowledge the origins of their affliction. We pin the blame on personal behavior or flaws in physiology, but we ignore the bigger picture.

All of which adds up to a rather bleak prognosis. Human beings, even the most well adapted, have one foot deep in the Paleo, another in the modern world. But with each new round of innovation, the modern world becomes even more refined and alienated, increasingly divorced from the ancestral conditions that support our health and sanity. New technologies, new constraints on behavior, new social arrangements—each of these "developments" pulls us further away from our origins. And with one foot in each world, the stresses on the human mind and body will only increase. It's no surprise that so many of us feel like we're being torn apart.

WE'RE ALL IN THIS TOGETHER

Mismatch may well sound like a wicked, intractable problem, but the good news is that our understanding can give us fresh insight into our individual psycho-physical afflictions. In the process, our depression, anxiety, and physical unhappiness begin to feel less like a personal failing and more like the inevitable consequence of out-of-context living.

In our hyperindividualized culture, we're accustomed to blaming ourselves when our bodies and our lives go sideways: "I feel bad—there must be something wrong with me" goes the typical, unspoken refrain. But seen through the lens of mismatch, we come to view our afflictions as part of a larger whole. That is, our psycho-physical angst is simply the result of trying to live outside our normal ecological range.

In fact, aside from occasional illnesses and acute injuries, there's probably nothing wrong with you at all. And even more to the point, many of your "symptoms" can be seen as the *normal* response of a healthy, wild animal attempting to live in profoundly abnormal circumstances—all of which would be perfectly obvious to any veterinarian.

Even better, the human behavior we see around us no longer seems so arbitrary, inexplicable, and infuriating. In the conventional view, we're quick to suppose that bad behavior, anger, extremism, and narcissism are simply a consequence of poor character and ignorance or perhaps a bad upbringing. We're quick to level accusations, point fingers of blame, and even bring criminal charges against the perpetrators.

But with our new understanding of mismatch, we begin to see these behaviors as a nearly inevitable consequence of living in an alien environment. When you build an industrial civilization that's fundamentally at odds with the deep nature of the human body, you're bound to see some serious misbehavior.

Of course, this doesn't get us off the hook entirely. Character is real, and individuals must be held responsible for their actions. Personal choice does matter. It would be folly to simply abandon the concept of free will and place the totality of the blame on external conditions and the stresses of mismatch. Nevertheless, it's essential that we recognize and appreciate the power of context in shaping human life and behavior. We are not, and will never be, stand-alone organisms.

Ultimately, our struggles with mismatch should be seen as the normal response of wild animals to domestication and incarceration; anxiety, depression, physical weakness, and other afflictions are really no surprise. Everyone around us is struggling. Some of us manage to adapt, some of the time, but in general, what we're seeing is the public health consequence of civilization itself.

In turn, this understanding leads us to greater compassion, patience, and tolerance, as well as a simple life lesson: treat everyone around you like they've been traumatized. They may not show overt signs of psycho-physical dysfunction or mismatch-induced trauma, but everyone is struggling with the challenge. We're all in this together.

GIVE THE BODY ITS DUE

Make no mistake: mismatch is a serious threat to human health and our ability to create a functional future. But it's not all bad news. The suffering is real and demands our attention, but we can also see this as a chance to create something better. Anytime we experience big contrasts in life, we're moved to entertain new ideas and adopt new perspectives.

Just imagine the movie pitch: "Wild human animals loose in a modern, high-tech world." There's lots that can go wrong and plenty of room for comedy, but from the artist's point of view, this is a golden opportunity. The contrast between the old and the new creates energy, and if we can harness it, we can do some amazing things.

So it may be with mismatch. The emergency is in our face, calling on us to remake our ways of living, to craft new solutions that are consistent with the deep historical nature of the human body. Going forward, it's absolutely essential that we take the body into account in everything we do and create.

Ultimately, mismatch is far more than a medical or a health issue. It's an issue for educators, designers, planners, engineers, parents, and managers at every level. All of us need to honor our ancestry and our animal nature. Give the body what it truly needs and help it feel at home. Give the animal the room and the opportunity to move and explore, ways to connect with habitat and tribe, and the time to enjoy the experience of life.

When the body works better, everything works better.

CHAPTER 3

EYE EXAM

It's a terrible thing to see and have no vision.
—Helen Keller

Given the tumultuous state of modern society and culture, you might well come to the conclusion that humans are suffering from some kind of vision problem. That is, we can focus on things that are close at hand, but we seem to have trouble seeing big pictures at a distance. To put it another way, it appears that we've got a systemic case of myopia. Perhaps the time has come for a cultural eye exam.

Literally speaking, myopia is a condition known as *nearsightedness* or *short-sightedness*. The light that comes into the eye doesn't focus directly on the retina but in front of it, causing the image that one sees when looking at a distant object to be out of focus. The term *myopia* is from the Greek: *myein*, meaning "to shut" (from *mys*, "like a mole") and *ops*, meaning "eye, look, sight"—literally, "trying to see like a mole."

In March 2015, the journal *Nature* reported that "short-sightedness is reaching epidemic proportions." As more and more of us spend years and decades glued to electronic displays, our eyeballs actually change shape. But our literal myopia, bad as it might be, is not the real problem. The thing that really threatens our future is our inability to see the big pictures of our bodies, our lives, and our culture. We're so busy zooming in on the fine-grained details of the world that we lose sight of the vital, panoramic ideas that might really help us survive. So maybe it's time to put down the microscope and take a journey to the mountaintop instead.

The problem with our compulsive zooming is that it makes us blind to essential qualities, processes, and relationships. We come to resemble the test subjects in the classic "gorillas in our midst" experiment. In this legendary study, researchers asked their subjects to record the number of passes made by a team of basketball players during the course of a game. It's all very straightforward, except for the fact that during the game, a man dressed in a gorilla suit walks onto the court in full view, thumps his chest, and walks off. On completion of the test, researchers asked their subjects if they saw anything out of the ordinary, but a substantial number of subjects reported seeing nothing unusual. A similar experiment has even been performed by superimposing tiny gorillas on medical X-rays, with similar results.

This same kind of blindness takes place at the level of culture, compounded by our inclination toward myopic specialization. Most of us are assigned tasks at some particular level of resolution, and we're expected to stay at that level, often for an entire career. We spend our working lives "counting passes," largely oblivious to any gorillas on the court. After a few years, we get really good at our jobs, and we're rewarded for our efforts with honors, bonuses, and perks.

But along the way, we lose sight of everything that lies outside or beyond our immediate scope of interest. We become oblivious to the gorillas in our midst—the incessant destruction of habitat, the increasing fragmentation of society, and the yawning chasm between rich and poor. We're dedicated to our own level of resolution, and we can only hope that someone out there is looking at the bigger picture.

RESOLUTION IS EVERYTHING

In our quest to exercise sapience, getting the resolution right is vital. Things that appear true at one level may well appear false or trivial when we zoom out. Things that appear beautiful or healthy or sensible at one level may prove to be otherwise when we step back for a more expansive point of view. This is why it's vital that we keep moving. Getting stuck at one level of resolution is a recipe for foolishness, if not outright disaster.

Our cultural myopia is most obvious in our misunderstanding of history, specifically our single-minded focus on "short history," the story of the last few hundred or thousand years. We study the history of particular countries or even entire civilizations, then come to the conclusion that this is all there is. Depending on your short-history perspective, the world began with the ancient Greeks, or the Renaissance, or the signing of the Declaration of Independence.

But even if—particularly if—your knowledge is greatly detailed for one of these eras, you're going to wind up with some highly dubious conclusions. Just because a thing was right or true or healthy in the last few hundred years doesn't mean it has intrinsic value. To come to a truly meaningful conclusion, we need to zoom out.

THE BIG HISTORY ANTIDOTE

This is why Big History is such a vital perspective. As the name suggests, this discipline examines the entire scope of cosmic history, from the Big Bang to the present day—at last estimate, some 13.7 billion years. Professor David Christian has been credited with launching the study while teaching at Macquarie University in Sydney, Australia.

To really appreciate the power of this perspective, it's important to understand what we might call the "history of history." For most of the modern era, right up until the mid-twentieth century, historians did their work exclusively with written documents, which was all they had to go on. This meant long hours in the library, poring over books, journals, maps, and other written descriptions of how people lived in recent history.

But written documents can only take us back some five thousand years, which means that historians have been focusing on a very narrow slice of human history. This reminds us of the drunk looking for his car keys at night, under the lamppost on the street corner. The keys could be anywhere, but this is where the light is, so that's where he looks. Consequently, it's no surprise that historians have come up with some highly distorted views about the world and humanity's role in the cosmos. This would be like judging someone's entire life by their behavior over the last few minutes.

In contrast, Big History goes beyond written documents and works with all available evidence. Fossils, DNA, radiocarbon dating, as well as findings from biology, geology, and cosmology, all become part of the story. In the process, Big History takes us on a journey to the mountaintop. From this vantage point, we can generate more accurate ideas about life, biology, the body, and society. In fact, from the Big History point of view, short histories start to look fragmented, distracting, and even dangerous.

OVERVIEW EFFECT

Big History is closely related to the "overview effect," a cognitive shift in awareness reported by astronauts and cosmonauts while viewing Earth from orbit. On Christmas Eve, 1968, the *Apollo 8* spacecraft swept around the dark side of the moon, and as Earth climbed above the horizon, astronaut Bill Anders captured one of the most important photos of all time, the earthrise. The term *overview effect* was coined by science writer Frank White, who explored the theme in his 1987 book *The Overview Effect: Space Exploration and Human Evolution*.

In light of our planetary-scale predicament, this must now be considered our most vital reference perspective, the essential starting point for all our investigations into the human predicament. By taking this long view, we see entire systems at work. We see relationships, interconnections, and interdependence. We see human life in context. We see Carl Sagan's "pale-blue dot," small and beautiful, floating in space, mysterious and awesome. Fragile and precious beyond all words.

A BIG CURRICULUM

The power of Big History is foundational and should be a central theme in human education at all levels, beginning at the beginning. As it stands, most elementary schools start small with nationalistic American history. Only later, in classes on cosmology or biology, do we present our students with the expanded scope of time and space. And it's only in college that students are encouraged to really stand on the summit and survey the totality of the universe and humanity in context.

But this is simply backward. Young people are perfectly capable of understanding the vast expanse of time and space that's revealed in a Big History course, maybe even more capable than adults who've been raised on small history. And there's no reason whatsoever to restrict their vision. We may not be able to give them power, certainty, or control, but we can at least give them a full and accurate view of their world. Now more than ever, small people need Big History.

CHAPTER 4

FOCUS ON THE PARK

> The most pervasive fallacy of philosophic
> thinking is the neglect of context.
> —John Dewey (1859–1952)

In the modern Western world, we attempt to solve our problems by studying things in isolation. We put objects, animals, and people on the exam table and look for defective mechanisms and flawed components. Sometimes we get results, but when dealing with living organisms, setting is vital, a fact vividly illustrated in Bruce Alexander's legendary "rat park" studies.

As a young researcher in the 1970s, Alexander was struck by the fact that most studies of addiction were carried out on isolated rodents in cages. Cocaine and other substances were introduced, and in fact, many animals did become addicted. But Alexander objected that the rats were living in abnormal conditions, so the results could not be trusted. To test his idea, he built an enriched environment in his laboratory, complete with everything a rodent might desire: natural features, room to move, and companions to play with. When he later introduced the so-called "addictive substances," few of the animals became addicted. It seems they had better things to do with their time.

As every biologist knows, there's a big difference between results obtained by studying organisms in vitro (Latin for "within the glass") and those obtained in vivo ("within the living"). Just because an organism behaves a certain way in a cage, flask, workplace, classroom, or petri dish doesn't mean those results will be borne out in the real world. That's why biologists say *in vivo veritas* ("in the living there is truth"), a play on *in vino veritas* ("in wine there is truth").

Alexander's work is highly suggestive and consistent with our own experience. Of course our bodies behave differently in various environments. Of course there are health and behavior consequences when we're forced to live outside our normal evolutionary range. Just ask any zookeeper, or even closer to home, ask any dog owner. Force your pet to live in isolation for a few weeks, and you'll see some serious health and behavioral problems. There's nothing wrong with your dog—the problem is with the dog's world. The same principle holds true for all creatures, including us.

All of which points to our cultural failure to understand, recognize, and appreciate the power of context, setting, and environment. In a sense, we're addicted to objectification. We study things and people in isolation. We put them on the laboratory bench, run our tests, and declare our results.

As Alexander sees it, this misplaced focus goes all the way back to the earliest days of psychology. Early researchers studied individuals in the laboratory, isolated from one another, in settings we would now recognize as abnormal. Subjects were tested on all manner of tasks relating to memory and perception, and in turn, psychologists extrapolated all sorts of meanings, many of which came to influence our popular understanding of what it means to be human.

But the fact remains that people simply don't live or work in isolation. The normal, historical context for the human animal is social and, yes, outdoors. To test and evaluate people in isolation is really not much different from testing isolated rats in cages. Alexander calls this the "original sin of psychology." If early researchers had done their work on people in social groups, their findings would have been far more meaningful and relevant to human life.

For teachers, coaches, trainers, and educators, the lessons from rat park are clear, if inconvenient. In short, we need to stop looking so closely at individuals. Stop looking so closely at individual aptitudes, skills, problems, and dysfunctions. Stop with the aptitude tests, grades, assessments, and personalized programs.

In short, put your attention on the park, not the rat. Put your focus on the tribe, not the individual. Create a social culture, a setting, and a context in which your students, clients, and patients can thrive. Once you've got your park up and running, the individuals will mostly take care of themselves.

CHAPTER 5

THE MYTH OF PROGRESS

> And a step backward, after making a wrong turn, is a step in the right direction.
> —Kurt Vonnegut
> *Player Piano*

Modern people are proud of their achievements and inventions. We like to brag about our many discoveries, and we're quick to dismiss everything that came before us as primitive, unsophisticated, or just plain stupid. If it exists today, it must—by our definition—be the best possible thing. If it existed yesterday, it was nothing more than a stepping-stone to our current age of perfection and greatness.

This narrative makes us feel good, but it has a curious and highly destructive side effect. That is, our ancestors no longer inspire us. We tend to see them as infantile actors, sweaty brutes groping their way toward our current glory and greatness, out of the darkness and into the light. It's no coincidence that we describe the scientific revolution as the "Age of Enlightenment."

In the mid-twentieth century, authors C. S. Lewis and Owen Barfield described this blanket rejection of the past as "chronological snobbery," the belief that

> intellectually, humanity languished for countless generations in the most childish errors on all sorts of crucial subjects, until it was redeemed by some simple scientific dictum of the last century.

A typical example comes from the philosopher Joseph Priestley, writing in 1771: "The human species is capable of unbounded improvement ... mankind in a later age are greatly superior to mankind in a former age."

Richard Dawkins describes this glorification of modernity as "the vanity of the present, of seeing the past as aimed at our own time, as though the characters in history's play had nothing better to do with their lives than foreshadow us." Likewise, our popular language tells a similar story: insults of our day include "medieval," "primitive," "backward," "knuckle dragger," "troglodyte," and of course, "animal."

THE DELUSION OF PROGRESS

Even in the face of substantial evidence to the contrary, many of us persist in the belief that indigenous knowledge and worldviews are extinct and irrelevant. But in fact, the old ways still live, and in many ways, they're more sophisticated and sapient than our own. Our deep ancestors may have been uneducated in the modern, academic sense, but they were highly intelligent and fully capable of crafting sophisticated solutions to the challenges of life.

The myth of progress is one of the most destructive stories of our day. By devaluing our ancestry, it destroys the continuity that has long existed between generations. It leaves us stranded in the present, isolated and alone, anxious and afraid. We may well have the fanciest toys and tools in history, but we don't have the slightest idea what to do with them. In rejecting our ancestry, we also reject the sapience that accumulated across the span of thousands of generations. And so we're left with immense technological power, without the slightest idea of what any of it means.

Our ancestors may well have lived outdoors, struggling on occasion to survive, but they were not stupid. On the contrary, they knew how to survive in wild habitat and how to secure their knowledge in an oral tradition passed down from generation to generation. This is no simple matter and is well beyond the capabilities of most modern people. In fact, our ancestors passed the only intelligence test that really matters: the ability to live sustainably, in relative harmony with the biosphere. In contrast, we—the self-declared greatest people in the history of the planet—are failing the same test with flying colors.

TELL A BETTER STORY

The time has come to give up on the myth of progress. Stop telling the story of inevitable perfectibility. Just because something is here today does not make it superior. Just because something is old does not make it irrelevant. Our ancestors were not perfect, but the old ways of humanity were honed over the course of thousands of generations, by way of vast experience on the ground, in habitat. In fact, the aboriginal cultures of Australia and Africa have been the most successful on Earth.

Our arrogance is exacerbated by our misunderstanding of biological evolution. The popular assumption holds that evolution proceeds inevitably to ever-greater levels of perfection, culminating, quite naturally, in us. We see this kind of interpretation in popular advertising for a wide range of products and services. "Our widget is highly evolved" implies that it's better than whatever came before. We even speak of individual people in the same terms. If someone displays good behavior, awareness, or sensitivity, we declare that person "highly evolved." Or if someone is training hard or making an effort to become a better person, we say that they're "evolving."

But in fact, we're wrong about all of this. Evolution doesn't create better and better organisms over time. It's not the case, for example, that mammals are somehow "better" than dinosaurs. Modern humans are not "better" than Neanderthals or any of our hominid ancestors. And it's certainly not the case that humans are somehow "better" than chimps or bonobos. It always depends on context. Mutation and differential reproduction combine to produce creatures that are a better fit for a particular set of conditions, but by no means does that make those creatures superior. All it takes is a simple shift in habitat, climate, or vegetation to change everything. Yesterday's winners can easily become tomorrow's losers. "Progress" is mostly a product of the human imagination, not biology.

As teachers, trainers, coaches, and therapists, our primary duty is to tell the story of continuity and the ways that the past flows into the present. Just because something is new or modern doesn't make it better, or even good for that matter. Be skeptical of progress. Be skeptical of novelty, innovation, and even creativity itself.

The old ways worked, and we would be fools to ignore them.

CHAPTER 6

THE MYTH OF HUMAN SUPREMACY

> As far as non-humans are concerned, we have no direct duties. They are there merely as the means to an end. The end is man.
>
> —Immanuel Kant

Everyone wants to be the top dog, the alpha animal. Or so the story goes, in our culture at least. Man is always claiming to be the best, better than his peers and, in fact, better than anything else in the natural world, or the cosmos, for that matter. We feel free to label other creatures as "vermin" or "invasive species," but no one ever calls humans "invasive." On the contrary, when we colonize and dominate some new habitat, we call it "discovery," "progress," or "development." This is a story that circulates widely across our planet, so baked into modern culture that for many of us, it seems both obvious and invisible. Of course humans are the best; it would be silly to suggest otherwise.

ORIGINS

It's pretty clear how the myth got started. Our Paleolithic ancestors saw themselves as part of the great circle of life, but as soon as we domesticated the first animals and hooked oxen to a plow, our narrative began to shift, and before long, we began to imagine ourselves as the master animal. Oh sure, there were still those pesky, hungry predators to contend with, but they were eventually controlled or exterminated, which simply confirmed our narrative of superiority. No longer was the lion the king of the jungle—or the grassland, for that matter. We were.

Of course, from a biological perspective, this is mostly just a bunch of bluffing that has almost nothing to do with the facts on the ground. Humans can do some pretty fancy tricks, but so can other creatures.

Nonhuman animals have incredibly sophisticated behaviors, use tools, and engage with the world in fantastic and functional ways. And most telling of all, they are not on the verge of destroying the biosphere that supports them.

In fact, the case for human supremacy is mostly a matter of "We're the best because we say so." Our reasoning—by our estimation—is flawless: "We walk upright. We've got opposable thumbs. We've got complex societies and communal learning. We use tools. And above all, we have huge brains that dwarf anything else in the animal kingdom." We like the sound of all that. It makes us feel significant, but it's mostly just bluster and wishful thinking.

HOUSEGUESTS FROM HELL

It would be one thing if we played well with others, but supremacists make for terrible houseguests. In fact, we don't see ourselves as guests on this planet at all. We put our feet up on the furniture and even burn that furniture if it pleases us. We throw our dirty laundry wherever we like and wait around for someone else to take out the trash. We're up all night making as much noise as we want, and in the morning, we eat all the food in the refrigerator and leave our dirty dishes in the sink. And when things start to stink, we blame each other or just move into another room and continue the rave. It's our house, and we can do as we please. And as for the other inhabitants, well, they're just there to serve us. If they don't like it, they can just go somewhere else.

Examples abound: We've dammed all the great rivers of the world; we've turned almost every arable acre of land into farms and feedlots; we dominate the oceans, the skies, and even the low-Earth orbit of outer space. And not only do we lay claim to ownership of vast tracts of land and sea, but we even attempt to claim the DNA sequences of various organisms as intellectual property.

But it's all a delusion—and a dangerous one at that. Human supremacy is bad for the world, and it's bad for us. By assuming superiority, we break the world into pieces and fall out of relationship with the circle of life. From there, it's just a short step to destroying the biosphere that sustains us. This is why author Derrick Jensen believes that "human supremacy is the greatest threat to life on this planet."

BIOLOGICAL SUPREMACY

The folly of human supremacy becomes obvious as soon as we understand the grand scope of biological history, the vulnerability of all species, and in particular, the utter and complete dominance of microbial life on Earth. In fact, microbial life is the status quo on our planet. This is biology-as-usual, three billion years of diversity and power. In a very real sense, microbes are running the show.

We see hints of this power in today's viral epidemics and the growing threat of antibiotic resistance. Today, public health experts issue increasingly dire warnings of a future in which routine surgical procedures are no longer possible and people die from minor cuts and scrapes. Our relentless incursion into wild habitat puts us into closer contact with microbial life and makes us vulnerable to zoonotic diseases of all kinds.

In fact, we're only here by the consent of the microbial world. If microorganisms ever "decided" to take back that consent, our "reign" on Earth would come to an abrupt end. In other words, we aren't even close to being supreme on Earth; we're lucky to be here at all. Instead of boasting about our powers, we ought to be grateful for that fact.

WHITE AND/OR HUMAN?

At this point, we might well wonder if there's any connection between our modern attitude of human supremacy and the culture of white supremacy that's come into the spotlight in recent years. In fact, this seems to be the case. After all, the whole notion of supremacy itself is uniquely modern, Western, and yes, generally white. Native and indigenous people simply don't think in these terms. When your entire worldview is circular, supremacy of any kind doesn't really fit. When all life is interconnected and kin, it doesn't make much sense to suppose that any one animal, person, species, culture, or race would be alpha.

So yes, our belief in supremacy seems to violate the natural order of things. And from casual observation, it does seem to be the case that our most vocal human supremacists are in fact white. And yes, most white supremacists are also human supremacists. Their platform is explicitly and rigidly hierarchical; the cosmos is a pyramid with humans at the top, and white humans at the very top.

In turn, this suggests an even more radical approach to our activism. To be sure, it's essential that we dislodge and dethrone white supremacy, but that doesn't go nearly far enough. What we really need is to abandon the entire concept of supremacy itself. To make a functional society, we do need power differentials to make decisions and get things done, but at no time should people in power believe that they are better than anyone else. On the contrary, power must always be exercised with modesty and humility. Our strength and sapience lie in the circle.

SUPREMACY MAKES US WEAK

Human supremacy is foolish on its face, but even worse, it's a counterproductive way to live. It makes us feel good for a time, secure in the "knowledge" that we're in charge. But our self-declared superiority actually weakens us because it separates us from the circle of life. Standing atop our self-drawn fantasy pyramid, we can no longer access the power that flows through the biosphere. We like to think that we're in charge, but we're actually out of touch and out of the loop. It's no wonder we feel so anxious and afraid.

Human supremacy is like the rush that comes with a few stiff drinks. Drunk on our self-esteem, we celebrate our position at the apex of creation, and for a while, it all feels great. Our ego inflates and our narcissism runs wild. We pound our chests in glory, but when morning comes, our heads will be throbbing, our guts will be churning, and we'll begin to see the error of our ways.

So maybe it's time to sober up. If you really want to access the power that flows through the circle of life, clear the supremacy from your heart and mind. Join the circle and live modestly, as a participant.

In the long run, smaller is stronger.

CHAPTER 7

TEACH NORMAL

The past beats inside me like a second heart.
—John Banville
The Sea

An insane world calls the deeply sane insane.
—Marianne Williamson

Imagine a very, very large number. Now imagine a very, very small number right next to it. Unless there's some compelling reason to think otherwise, you'd probably conclude that whatever's contained within the large number is the normal state of affairs for the system or process in question. You're also likely to conclude that whatever's contained within the very small number is an abnormal exception.

This would not be unreasonable.

With this in mind, consider the fact that *Homo sapiens* has inhabited this planet for three hundred thousand years, and a lot more if we include our humanlike ancestors. In that case, human history spans something like six million years, or sixty million if you want to include our primate cousins. In contrast, agricultural civilization has been our way of life for less than ten thousand years and actually a lot less, considering the fact that animal-powered agriculture—the pivotal change in the human relationship with the world—didn't take place until some five thousand years ago. And even more to the point, the really drastic changes that mark the modern world didn't appear until a few *hundred* years ago. In other words, the modern world constitutes only a tiny fraction of human experience.

In this perspective, we begin to realize that the Paleolithic ("Old Stone Age") should be considered the norm, the reference point for all our conversations about human life, medicine, education, training, and behavior. The word *Paleo* has a couple of definitions, but for our purposes, such differences are trivial, for no matter how we define it, the Paleo encompasses a vast expanse of time, one that dwarfs the existence of the modern world.

In fact, the Paleo is such an overwhelming percentage of human experience it must be held as the gold standard for understanding the way our brains and bodies work. In 1973, the evolutionary biologist Theodosius Dobzhansky famously declared that "nothing in biology makes sense except in the light of evolution." Well said, but we might also say that "nothing in human biology and behavior makes sense except in the light of the Paleo." Or to put it yet another way, we might also say that talking about human biology, behavior, education, or training *without* referring to the Paleo is little more than taking shots in the dark. For the study of the human animal, Paleo is normal until proven otherwise.

Once we internalize the immense timescales of evolution and the nonnegotiable fact that the premodern, Paleolithic era actually constitutes the overwhelming majority of human experience, we begin to revise our entire understanding of normality itself. Suddenly, the modern world begins to look like a rather strange exception. We may even come to the conclusion that we're surrounded by abnormal creations, structures, ideas, processes, and institutions. It's no wonder our bodies and minds are so confused.

NORMAL

This calls for a review of what's truly normal for the human species:

- Nature is normal. Wild is normal. Vagility, the ability to roam freely over the land, is normal.
- Hunting, gathering, and scavenging in natural habitat are normal. Real food, derived directly from the earth and eaten with others, is normal. Robust physicality is normal.
- An integrated, participatory worldview is normal. Biophilia—the innate tendency to identify with life—is normal. Small tribal bands with personal, face-to-face contact are normal. Social equality is normal. Poetry, song, and dance are normal.
- Coherent sensory experience based in actual, on-the-ground reality is normal. Circadian and seasonal rhythm, experienced in the body, are normal. Identification with habitat and tribe is normal. Continuity between generations is normal.
- Experiential, place-based education is normal. Temporal affluence—the sense of having plenty of time to live—is normal. A gift economy is normal. And with the exception of occasional infections or injury, robust health is normal.

ABNORMAL

In contrast, today's world exposes us to an onslaught of abnormality:

- Sedentary occupations and indoor living are abnormal. Agriculture, especially its intensive, industrial form, is abnormal. Food products and edible, food-like substances are abnormal. Artificial light and noise are abnormal.
- The relentless quest for social status is abnormal. Extreme social inequality and hierarchy are abnormal. Ambition and selfishness are abnormal. Anthropocentrism and the belief in human supremacy are abnormal.
- Neck-up, cognitive education is abnormal. Literacy and measurement are abnormal. Linear, mechanical time is abnormal. Work and busyness are abnormal. Objective, nonparticipatory consciousness is abnormal.
- Money-based relationships, finance, and economics are abnormal. Wealth, affluence, and poverty are abnormal. Consumer goods, advertising, and mass media are abnormal.
- Temporal poverty and chronic stress are abnormal. Computer technology, artificial intelligence, robotics, and big data are abnormal. Movies, videos, and social media are abnormal. Cars, air travel, and chairs are abnormal.

This is not to say that all of our modern, abnormal creations are dangerous or unhealthy. To be sure, many of these things have some value, especially in moderation. Hot showers, good books, and soft beds have their place. But this historical understanding gives us pause and inspires us to return—as much as possible—to our normal conditions and lifeways. In general, abnormal just isn't working.

But who's actually teaching normal in today's world? Some native people, to be sure, some Paleo-oriented trainers, wilderness guides, progressive educators, and artists, but that's about it. And to make matters far, far worse, we have legions of people, most of them backed by institutional power, who are aggressively teaching historical and psycho-spiritual abnormality. Is it any wonder that we feel so disconnected and alienated? The abnormality is killing us.

JUST BE NORMAL

All of this suggests that the way forward is to start being normal again. But in a practical sense, there's almost no possible way that any of us can return to a historically normal, primal lifestyle. In the first place, there's not enough open land to support hunting and gathering, and even if there was, there's little chance that we could camp, wander, hunt, and gather without running into interference in the form of private property, fences, roads, and other obstacles.

And even if we could find such a place, we wouldn't have a deep oral tradition to tell us how to make a living. And even more to the point, it would be a heavy lift to get our families and friends to join us out in the bush. Most people are pretty well attached to hot showers and regular meals, so in all likelihood, we're not going to go "full Paleo" anytime soon.

But all is not lost. We can, in fact, weave some normality back into our lives, little by little, decision by decision. Step back and take a look at the way you're living. Just how abnormal is your life, your career, your dwelling? Can you move even a little toward normal? Can you add more outdoor movement?

More real food, more tribal time, more relaxation? Your body knows what's normal. Listen up and give it what it needs.

Likewise, the modern physician must take this distinction into account in diagnosis and treatment practices. How normal or abnormal is the patient's life? What are the details? If the patient is living an abnormal life, physical unhappiness and lifestyle disease should come as no surprise. And in turn, the preferred treatment strategy should be based on a return to normality. If the patient can understand and appreciate the difference between the historically normal and abnormal, he or she will take a vital first step on the road back to health.

WHO'S WHO

We can also make some adjustments in how we talk about ideas and social change in the modern world. Most of us are accustomed to the familiar divide between conservatives and liberals, but these are recent, "small-history" terms that no longer make much sense. Political conservatives, for example, typically reject the conservation of our life-supporting systems, a position that is, without question, extremely radical, if not pathological. Instead, we'd do better to substitute Big History terms, such as *normalist* and *abnormalist*.

In this model, normalists favor culture, actions, and inclinations that are historically appropriate for the human animal: human–habitat integration, circular tribal philosophy, and animism, to name a few. Abnormalists favor human supremacy and, in turn, the exploitation of habitat and people in the pursuit of corporate power and profit. Abnormalists also favor cultural practices that deviate from human and historical norms: steep hierarchy, rigid class structures, and selling off the future for the benefit of investors.

Famous normalists include indigenous people, modern Paleo enthusiasts, and deep ecologists. Famous abnormalists include most of today's right-wing talk-show hosts, techno-futurists, and corporate "visionaries." Even some well-meaning environmentalists are best described as "abnormalists." That is, the idea that people should measure, track, and control all the life processes of the biosphere is wickedly abnormal.

Abnormalists are either ignorant of human history or hostile to its implications. As human supremacists and believers in the inevitability of progress, they devalue and reject vast reaches of human experience, knowledge, and sapience. They may well have good intentions, but in their refusal to honor the depth and breadth of human history, their efforts are likely to be ineffective or counterproductive.

Using these Big History labels would go a long way in shifting our conversation toward a healthier point of view. To describe political conservatives as "abnormalist" would provoke hostility, but also curiosity and, in turn, a deeper conversation about values and what it is that really keeps us alive.

These updated Big History labels also force us to the realization that in general, modern human nation-states and corporations tend to be dominated by abnormalists. It takes a lot of aggression, ambition, and even deception to rise through the ranks to the top of the pyramid—none of which are normal human qualities. On the other hand, if you're historically normal, which is to say you value modesty, humility, and inclusion, you're unlikely to rise very high in the pyramid. In the scramble for power, abnormalists tend to prevail. Power corrupts, which is to say, power turns normalists into abnormalists.

WHY BE ABNORMAL?

In any case, the way forward is to recognize the abnormality for what it is and refuse to participate any more than is strictly necessary. Stick to the normal ways and you'll be a lot happier.

If you're a teacher, coach, therapist, trainer, or parent, teach normal whenever possible, and make sure that your people understand that this has been the default condition for the vast, overwhelming majority of human history.

By the same token, stop teaching abnormality. Or if it's strictly unavoidable, stop promoting it as if it's the only possible way to live and function in the world. Abnormal skills and perspectives might well be necessary to survive in our alien environment, but there are better ways to see and experience the world.

CHAPTER 8

THE BREAKING OF THE WORLD

> Meet the first beginnings. Look to the budding mischief before it has time to ripen to maturity.
> —Shakespeare

So where did we go wrong? We hear this question a lot these days, circulating through culture in serious conversations about the human predicament. As we reflect on the chaos of today's world and the sheer, overwhelming complexity of modern problems, we wonder about the original source of our dysfunction, the root cause. How did we come to this point, where the very habitability of the biosphere and a functional civilization are now an open question?

This theme of an original breaking is common in many world mythologies, often cast as a fall from grace or an original sin. It also shows up as a recurring motif in Robert Jordan's epic fantasy series The Wheel of Time. In this middle-earth world, the breaking was said to have taken place thousands of years before, when darkness and light, good and evil, first came into conflict. Humans, it seems, are always wondering what's gone wrong.

But history is wickedly complex, and on closer examination, we see that today's predicament has come about not as a single catastrophic break but through a series of fractures that opened into a yawning abyss between modern human life and the rest of creation.

The story begins with agriculture, of course, the original breaking of our world. The seemingly trivial act of working the land fundamentally altered the human–habitat relationship and led to the first distinction between "wild" and "tame." Land was no longer home, but something to be worked, owned, and of course, mastered.

The process intensified some five thousand years ago with the first animal-powered agriculture and domestication. Grain surpluses led to early civilizations, hierarchy, written language, numbers, and money.

Later, in the third century BCE, Euclid and Pythagoras developed geometry, and for the first time in history, humans glimpsed a realm of knowledge that promised to be universal, reliable, and certain. Plato spoke of ideal forms that exist in the superior realm of the mind, and Aristotle gave us the syllogism and the laws of rational thought. At first these discoveries were little more than interesting playthings for philosophers, but they set the stage for the next great breaking, the scientific revolution. Almost overnight, a breathtaking series of discoveries demonstrated the power of nonparticipating consciousness and psychological distance to explore, understand, and manipulate the world. Newton, Galileo, Copernicus, Francis Bacon, and Descartes pried human consciousness away from the world and destroyed what was left of human–habitat unity.

Before long, a series of inventions gave humans an increasing sense of power and control: the first pendulum clock in 1656, James Watt's steam engine in 1763, and the power loom in 1785, all of which led to yet more discoveries—germ theory, the expanding universe and the Big Bang, DNA, and all the rest. By the late twentieth century, the rift was complete, and today, humanity stands at the edge of a great chasm. Humans and nature are two.

It's an astonishing story, one that we often fail to appreciate. Growing up with modern ideas, we've become accustomed to our assumed separation. We even talk about "the environment" as if it's something outside of us. And while it may feel normal to think of nature as "other," it's not normal in the slightest. The rift creates a monstrous, gaping wound in human consciousness and experience. We long for unity, and we're starving for integration and connection, but modern culture keeps pulling us away from the original source of our lives and health. The rift lurks in the background, driving us to physicians, therapists, and one another, always in search of that primal contact and our original wholeness.

RIFT REPAIR

Today, the rift may appear and feel like a permanent, unalterable reality, an inevitable by-product of civilization itself. But it's essential to remember that the division is driven by our narrative, a story of separation, power, and control. And in this sense, it's really a kind of delusion. Human beings have always been a part of the whole and will continue to be dependent on the biosphere for survival. We really are one with the world, and now, the story of separation is starting to look like a ten-thousand-year misconception and an optical illusion of human consciousness. In short, we've been duped. As today's ecological emergency makes clear, we are not separate from life, nor could we ever be. Know it or not, acknowledge it or not, we are one.

This is something that the mystics and romantics have known for ages. The Persian poets Rumi and Hafiz encourage us to realize our preexisting wholeness and forget the distracting narratives that swarm around us. As Hafiz put it in his poem "We Might Have to Medicate You":

> *Resist your temptation to lie*
> *By speaking of separation from God,*
> *Otherwise,*
> *We might have to medicate you.*
> *In the ocean*
> *A lot goes on beneath your eyes.*
> *Listen,*
> *They have clinics there too*
> *For the insane*
> *Who persist in saying things like:*
> *"I am independent from the Sea."*

In other words, the wholeness or unity is already there; we just have to stop breaking it. Don't allow yourself to be tyrannized and traumatized by the narrative of separation. Go toward the body, toward nature, toward our life-supporting systems. If we could just tell a better story, we might feel more connected to the world. As always, the cure for bad narratives is better narratives.

CHAPTER 9

NEW OLD WAY

> Humankind has not woven the web of life.
> We are but one thread within it. Whatever we
> do to the web, we do to ourselves. All things
> are bound together. All things connect.
> —Chief Seattle

Stories are born, live for a time, then pass away into myth and legend. Other stories outlive their usefulness and disappear into the void of history, victims of their own outrageous excess.

Today's modern techno-capitalist narrative is one such story, an audacious, experimental narrative that's doomed to extinction and irrelevance. The dominant theme of human supremacy that has animated modern life for the last several hundred years is being revealed not just as an inaccurate description of life on Earth, but as destructive in the extreme.

The narrative is composed of the following elements:

- Human exceptionalism and domination of nature
- Addiction to economic growth and consumerism
- Rapacious capitalism and corporate domination of society
- Atomism (the cosmos is nothing but particles)
- Hierarchy, patriarchy, and racism

This narrative no longer serves humanity, if it ever did. In fact, this is the wickedly inconvenient paradox of our day: human supremacy is not only bad for the biosphere, but it's also bad for humans. The story has created vast wealth for some, but it also creates great suffering for humans and non-humans alike. The narrative is not healthy. It is not circular. It is not compassionate. It is not sapient.

In fact, the story is in its death throes. Most of us know that it no longer serves us, but some people and organizations are making a lot of money as a result of its continued hold on modern culture. We can expect that those who benefit will do everything possible to make certain that this narrative survives, even if human life ultimately does not.

ORIGINAL NARRATIVE

Many people have suggested that the time has come to write a new story about the cosmos and the human place in the natural world, but native people have been telling a story of interdependence, integration, and participation for a very long time. This is the Old Way narrative, a system of belief, a culture, and a vision of the world and our place in it. It's a path and a way to live. In this story, everything is alive, nothing is autonomous, and nothing stands alone.

At its core, the Old Way story is built on a unitary cosmology. When everything is interconnected and interdependent, the focus is on relations, not on static objects. Boundaries can be fuzzy and dynamic, and because everything connects, the geometry of the Old Way is circular. Everything returns. A typical passage from the indigenous elder Black Elk:

> Everything an Indian does is in a circle, and that is because the power of the world always works in circles, and everything tries to be round. In the old days when we were a strong and happy people, all our power came to us from the sacred hoop of the nation, and so long as the hoop was unbroken the people flourished.

In Old Way cultures, the world is literally alive, a view that today we call *animistic* (from *anima*, meaning "soul" or "spirit" in Latin). Every place, animal, plant, and natural phenomenon has awareness and feelings and can communicate with humans. Objects, places, and creatures possess a spiritual essence. Soul and spirit exist not only in humans but in animals, plants, rocks, mountains, rivers, and other entities in the natural environment, including thunder, wind, and shadows. Religious studies scholar Graham Harvey defined *animism* as the belief "that the world is full of persons, only some of whom are human, and that life is always lived in relationship with others."

In this kind of culture, human beings live in deep engagement with the world. Mind and spirit are always relational and interacting with the flux and flow of plants, animals, weather, and other people. There is no attempt to stand apart from nature or to be objective. In fact, precisely the opposite: the goal of life is to form an intimate, integrated relationship with the world and to penetrate deeper into its mysteries.

In this culture, people assume continuity between their bodies, habitat, tribe, and cosmos. In the Iroquois tradition, this sense of extended physicality is sometimes called the "long body." An eleventh-century official in China expressed a similar conviction this way:

> Heaven is my father and earth is my mother and even such a small creature as I finds an intimate place in its midst. That which extends throughout the universe, I regard as my body and that which directs the universe I regard as my nature.
>
> All people are my brothers and sisters and all things are my companions.

Likewise, a Zen parable:

> To your way of thinking, your skin is a thing which separates and protects you from the outside world. To my way of thinking, my skin is a thing which connects me and opens me to the outside world, which in any case is not the outside world.

With its emphasis on interdependence and continuity, it's no surprise that the Old Way embraces what we might call a "big-health" orientation. That is, health is a matter not just of individual physical welfare, but of the whole. Health is shared across communities of people and habitat.

An early Buddhist teacher put it this way: "If the people are sick, I too am sick; only when everyone is healthy will I too be healthy." Even in ancient Greece, Socrates offered a surprisingly indigenous view:

> This is the reason why the cure of many diseases is unknown to the physicians of Hellas [Greece], because they are ignorant of the whole, which ought to be studied also; for the part can never be well unless the whole is well.

Likewise, a typical indigenous maxim tells us that "The hurt of one is the hurt of all. The honor of one is the honor of all." And by extension, "The health of one is the health of all. The disease of one is the disease of all."

PRACTICE

Many of us imagine that we are powerless in the face of planetary destruction and cultural chaos, but there is something that anyone can do right now: Stop telling the story of imperialism and domination. Stop assuming that this narrative is inevitable. Stories are kept alive through repetition. If we stop honoring the dominant story, it will eventually wither away and die.

Instead, tell the Old Way story of interdependence. Our health, our happiness, even our sapience lie not in our individual brains, minds, or bodies, but in the circle. And our future—if we are to have one—will be in the circle as well.

CHAPTER 10

WE ARE WEIRD

> Western culture cuts us off from our natural roots, instead of contributing toward the cultivation of the natural beings we are. This tradition has, in this way, rendered us extraneous to our environment, extraneous to one another as living beings, even extraneous to ourselves.
> —Luce Irigaray

Locked inside Western culture, we like to think that our modern view of the world is normal, but when we take a broad historical perspective, we find that it's actually a rather strange exception to humanity-as-usual. Until quite recently, all human cultures have embraced the idea of unity and participation with the natural world. Interdependence is one of our oldest ideas, one that's common to indigenous people in Australia, Africa, and North and South America. It's been our default view for the overwhelming majority of human history.

From this historical standpoint, our obsessive focus on individuals, objects, and dominance begins to look abnormal, even deviant. This insight was famously described in 2010 by researchers from the Department of Psychology at the University of British Columbia, Vancouver. In their paper "The Weirdest People in the World?" they questioned the widespread assumption that modern research subjects are representative of our species' characteristics and behavior:

> Behavioral scientists routinely publish broad claims about human psychology and behavior in the world's top journals based on samples drawn entirely from Western, Educated, Industrialized, Rich, and Democratic (WEIRD) societies.
>
> ... [O]ur review suggests that WEIRD subjects are particularly unusual compared with the rest of the species. The domains reviewed include visual perception, fairness, cooperation, spatial reasoning, categorization and inferential induction, moral reasoning, reasoning styles, self-concepts and related motivations, and the heritability of IQ. The findings suggest that members of WEIRD societies are among the least representative populations one could find for generalizing about humans.

The WEIRD paper was perhaps written somewhat in jest, but there can be no escaping the fact that as Westerners, we see the world in a highly unusual way. We have weird ideas about the body and health, weird ideas about habitat, weird ideas about social justice, and weird ideas about the role of the individual in society. We have weird ideas about time, progress, and change. Quite clearly, we are not normal.

For example, consider the "geo-orientation" that's typical of native peoples. When giving directions or learning dance steps, indigenous people are less likely to use self-oriented terms like *left* and *right* and more likely to orient their bodies in relationship to the compass points of north, south, east, and west. Reportedly, this even extends to setting tables for meals. (The fork doesn't go on the left side of the plate, they might say, but on the north side.) This contrasts sharply with our modern, egocentric orientation, in which directions and dance steps are almost always given in reference to the self. Indeed, many modern people would be hard-pressed to refer to the points of the compass at all.

Even in matters of perception, we are strange creatures. Fascinating research on the seminomadic Himba people of Namibia shows that they are less susceptible to the famous Muller-Lyer illusion. This finding has been replicated with the Toda people of southern India and other premodern societies, including the San people of the Kalahari Desert. Researchers believe that modern Western people are the real outliers here. Our brains, conditioned by our near-constant exposure to the right angles of indoor structures, are primed to see what isn't really there.

In fact, native people are far more likely to use their entire brains and bodies in experiencing and learning habitat. This allows them to build up a holistic, integrated view of the world. This is historically normal. In contrast, WEIRD people tend to use the left side of the brain, with an emphasis on logic, language, and linear thinking. This fragmented approach to understanding the world is not just abnormal; it is also proving to be maladaptive on a planetary scale. We gain power and control, but we pay a terrible price.

MORE THAN ONE WAY TO BUILD A CULTURE

In caricature, we are the dorky kids in high school, the kids who can't dance, can't play the drums, and can't move their bodies to the beat. We're smart as hell and we can do a lot of fancy tricks with our computers, but when it comes to really knowing the Earth and our place in it, we're spectacularly ignorant. Our knowledge is fragmentary at best, catastrophic at worst.

We act like we're the foremost authority on all things under the sun, but actually, we're newcomers with an unproven set of ideas and perspectives. We have some pretty fancy tricks up our sleeves, but so does every other culture. This is why anthropology, Big History, and the humanities are so vital. When we set aside our cultural narcissism and look at the history of humanity, we begin to realize that there are many ways to see the world and many ways to live.

And so the message is clear: Stop assuming that we're the crown glory of creation. Stop with the delusions of grandeur and the outrageous mega-projects: the colonization of Mars, the expansion of artificial intelligence into every domain, geo-engineering, biotechnology, and the intensive management of every last ecosystem on Earth. We are simply one cultural variant, not the last word. Some modesty and humility would be appropriate.

CHAPTER 11

PALEO FAMILY VALUES

> One mustn't underestimate the primal appeal—to lose one's self, lose it utterly. And in losing it be born to the principle of continuous life, outside the prison of mortality and time.
> —Donna Tartt
> *The Secret History*

So how are we to live at this point in history? As modern people, we like to imagine that we've got it all pretty well wired—the myth of progress tells us so. If it exists today, it must be superior to everything that came before us, and this includes not just our tools, machines, and devices, but even our sense of morality, ethics, and judgment.

But of course, we're wrong about all of this. And now, as we come to understand more about the lives of our ancestors, we're coming to the realization that the values, ethics, and judgments of native, Paleo, and indigenous peoples might actually be a better guide to the creation of a functional future.

PALEO VALUES AND CHARACTER

Values don't fossilize, of course, but if we stopped to think about it, the ethical system of our ancestors would be completely obvious. After all, these people lived in intimate contact with sometimes-dangerous habitats and were highly dependent on one another to survive.

Under these conditions, people would have valued things like the following:

- Knowledge and understanding of habitat
- Practical skills
- Honesty and sincerity
- Modesty and humility
- A tribal orientation (*ubuntu*)

In this kind of wild, outdoor setting, the predicament is the teacher, and the lessons would have been obvious to anyone. It would have been unthinkable to lie, cheat, or steal. Boasting would have been frowned upon, and narcissism would have been an outrage. Donald Trump would have been impossible. Wealth would have been absurd. The elders knew all this, of course, and would have been quick to correct violations.

WORSHIPING THE WRONG THINGS

Paleo and native people have long had a very clear understanding of the sacred: land, tribe, food, water, ancestors, and descendants were all held in the highest regard. In fact, all of creation is considered sacred because all life is kin. But in today's world, we see what can only be described as a perversion of Paleo family values. To be sure, some of us continue to hold on to the old values of land, family, and the like, but it's becoming increasingly obvious that our problem—the problem of the modern world—is that we've been worshiping the wrong things.

In 2020, comedian John Oliver did an exposé on conditions at an Amazon warehouse. In an interview with a reporter, the manager explained her role, her priorities, and the rationale for her decisions. "Around here," she said, "speed is sacred." Likewise, an advertisement for a new email-management tool declared that "Your inbox is a sacred space."

How are we to take these statements seriously? Have we degenerated so far as a culture that we no longer list our life-supporting systems as sacred? That we rank our email inboxes at the same level as land, tribe, and ancestry? In fact, all of this smacks of idolatry. In religious circles, especially monotheism, idolatry is the worship of false gods and is forbidden. But even for the nonreligious, it just smells bad. What is there to say about a culture that worships speed and inboxes, yet fails to honor and appreciate the essentials of life itself?

Even more to the point, nothing is really held as sacred in today's profit-driven culture. In this world, we simply assume that the entire world can be dissected and broken down into bits. Nothing is off-limits. Trees, rivers, mountains, and animals can all be monetized. People are disposable objects to be hired, exploited, fired, and discarded. And in the world of Western medicine, patients are treated as medical objects, faulty mechanisms to be repaired, processed, and discharged from the system. In today's world, everything's a thing.

Anthropologist Edward Hall once made a distinction between low-context and high-context societies. The Old Way, of course, was high context; everything in life depended on everything else. Setting and conditions were always taken into account with every action and decision.

In contrast, the New Way is low context, or maybe even no context. With little respect for history, setting, or relations, we now view and treat human beings, plants, and animals as free-floating, interchangeable organisms. They don't really require anything besides chemistry to survive. They're independent and replaceable. Likewise, we treat each generation as a stand-alone cohort that's independent from whatever came before it. History is irrelevant. Native people, hippies, and ecologists have long observed that "It's all connected," but in the modern world, we might well say, "It's all disconnected."

So maybe the time has come to return to our roots. It's not necessary to live in the bush, chase animals across the grassland, or suffer all the travails of primal living; you can still enjoy a hot shower and a warm bed. What is necessary is a reevaluation of what's important and, yes, what's sacred. Assume interdependence and focus on relationship. Treat the world like everything is alive, breathing, and growing. Treat the rivers, mountains, lakes, oceans, and people with respect. It's all kin and it's all sacred.

The Paleo way isn't dead, and it's not just for hunters and gatherers. Anyone can set their values to the Old Way. It worked before and it can work again.

CHAPTER 12

MEET LUCA

> We are like islands in the sea, separate on
> the surface but connected in the deep.
> —William James

To the untrained eye, life on Earth looks like a bunch of trees, bushes, and a few animals. There's lions and tigers and bears, plants and trees, fish and reptiles and birds. As modern people, we tend to see these plants and animals as independent creatures, each with their own name, classification, and characteristics. Each animal and plant, you might say, stands alone.

This is precisely what the world must have looked like to early European explorers. When naturalists traveled to faraway lands—especially Africa—they encountered many strange and wonderful creatures, so strange and wonderful that they must have seemed completely arbitrary: giraffe, zebra, lion, rhino, and hippo, all of them unique and special in some pretty outrageous ways. And from a religious point of view, this made perfect sense. After all, the dominant narrative of the day held that these creatures were created, so of course, God could make them any way he pleased.

But then came Darwin and his famous insight that all these diverse creatures were in fact related as parts of a single immense, branching family. And not just related to their ancestors but also radically connected to the world around them. In the decades that followed, our understanding of biology coalesced, and people began to talk about the "web of life." No longer was creation "just a bunch of animals"; it was a fabric of relationship, each creature woven into its habitat in subtle and complex ways, in a marvelous dance of interdependence.

Humans, of course, are no exception. Our bodies are literally sustained by their connections to life-supporting systems and processes. The history of humanity is the story of these continuities, sustained and broken, ignored, and sometimes rediscovered. In the Paleo, people recognized and celebrated interdependence and continuity with the world. They understood the vital importance of contact, participation, and engagement. Rub your body up against the world, and it will thrive.

FALSE CONTINUITIES

But today, we're suffering from broken continuities at almost every level. Our bodies are barely connected to habitat, barely connected to one another. Our original life-giving continuities have been stretched to the breaking point, and it scares us.

As a consequence, many of us are turning to false continuities in a desperate attempt to feel connected. We attach to anything that's handy: substances, people, ideas, experiences, anything that promises to give us the primal contact that we so desperately need. In turn, these inclinations often become addictions. This is precisely the process that Bruce Alexander described in *The Globalization of Addiction: A Study in Poverty of the Spirit*. As he sees it, the prevalence of addiction is increasing around the world: "Globalization of free-market society has produced an unprecedented, worldwide collapse of psychosocial integration."

These addictions go far beyond the notorious substances that we hear so much about. Today, we've become addicted to work, ideas, sporting teams, experiences, and of course, money and power. In the absence of healthy primal connections, we reach for any point of contact we can. But these false continuities fail to satisfy our bodies and our spirits, so we continue our search, always looking for contact, connection, and continuity.

To make matters worse, modern education generally fails to honor the importance of our primal relationships. In most schools, the living world is still "a bunch of animals," and human beings are little more than fancy, stand-alone organisms. We sometimes teach the continuities in abstract ways, but almost never do students experience the feeling of being in contact with their life-sustaining communities of people and habitat.

We might suppose that physicians would step up to remind us of how the continuities support our health, but sadly, this is considered outside the job description and is left to others, who may or may not pick up the ball.

MEET LUCA

The solution to unifying this fragmented curriculum is the astonishing fact that all of us—humans and every other lifeform on Earth—have descended from a single common ancestor, known as *LUCA*, the Last Universal Common Ancestor.

In all likelihood, she was a simple microbial cell, similar to a modern bacterium. Her remains did not fossilize, but her existence has been inferred by comparing the genomes of her descendants, organisms living today. If we could play the movie of life backward, we would find LUCA at the starting point for a story that's been unfolding for almost four billion years. All living creatures on the planet are linked to this single-celled creature, the root of the tree of life.

LUCA is astonishing, but in another sense, her existence shouldn't come as a complete surprise. In 1859, Darwin proposed the idea that there was only one progenitor for all forms of life. In the *Origin of Species* he wrote:

> Therefore I should infer from analogy that probably all the organic beings which have ever lived on this earth have descended from one primordial form, into which life was first breathed.

The significance of LUCA is immense—scientifically, culturally, even spiritually. In short, LUCA unites us. She tells a story of shared origin and history. We may well behave otherwise, but we—all the plants, animals, and humans of the biosphere—are truly, literally one. We may look like singular, isolated individuals, but we are intimately related to everything that moves, breathes, and grows. The entire history of life on Earth is coursing through our veins in every minute of every day.

LUCA puts everything, even our politics, in a new light. When all life is kin, we come to a fresh understanding of who we are and what we might be doing. The prime directive is to enhance the welfare of the entire biosphere, our extended family. Whatever happens to the big family inevitably affects everything within. From this perspective, our continuing assault on the natural world begins to look very much like a case of domestic violence writ large. Habitat destruction is nothing less than violence against the family, the self, and the future. As a people, we have yet to fully appreciate the meaning and significance of LUCA, and it may be a long time before we integrate this understanding into our culture. Nevertheless, a sense of wonder is inescapable. Your body is not an arbitrary, isolated object that simply appeared on Earth. It's a leaf on an immense tree, a continuation of a process that is vast, beyond our ability to comprehend. Your body is not decades old, but hundreds of millions of years old. Every cell in your body contains a story of continuity and connection. And it's an amazing, awe-inspiring story. As Darwin himself put it, "There is grandeur in this view of life."

Believe it or not, act like it or not, we are all children of LUCA.

CHAPTER 13

TEACHING IN CIRCLES

> I live my life in widening circles that
> reach out across the world.
> —Rainer Maria Rilke

The time has come to keep things simple. As teachers, trainers, and coaches, it's easy to get wrapped up in the complexities of the body–mind and spirit and all the various dimensions of health. We get mired in the details of chemistry, brain science, physiology, psychology, and nutrition. It all seems overwhelming, but in the end, the entire enterprise comes down to four basic, life-supporting relationships: body, habitat, tribe and community, and our sense of meaning and purpose.

Sadly, modern people tend to have dysfunctional relationships at *all* these levels. Our primal continuities are broken or forgotten. Quite literally, we are out of the loop of life. To begin, many of us, possibly most of us, have dysfunctional relationships with our bodies. Driven into a frenzy of angst by relentless marketing and impossible images of physical perfection, many of us feel physically inadequate and desperate to make ourselves beautiful. Even worse, we're surrounded by mirrors, cameras, and social media, all of which drive our attention away from the world and onto ourselves. But this focus on physical perfection is historically abnormal and counterproductive. No other animal on the planet, either now or in deep history, obsesses about their appearance—or even their health, for that matter.

We also have dysfunctional relationships with habitat, the life-support system that brings us our food, our water, and our sense of wonder. The average urban dweller often has no sense of habitat whatsoever; when food is trucked or flown in from remote regions, there's not much incentive to pay attention to the land or its characteristics. It's safe to say that most humans today know more about celebrities than they do about the natural world around them. This is wildly, spectacularly abnormal.

And of course, we have dysfunctional relationships with our tribes and communities. Some of this is the simple consequence of our population explosion and the fact that there are too many people to know personally. But our tribes are always in flux now, and our alliances are always shifting. As stress circulates through the social system, polarization drives us apart and into opposing camps. And now, electronic "communication" destroys what's left of authentic conversation and easy time with one another. Untrained in this most basic of human arts, many of us have no idea how to relate to others.

Finally, many of us struggle through life without a sense of meaning and purpose. To put it another way, we often fail to connect our passion and curiosity with our work. We do what we do for money, but beyond a certain point, our day jobs often fail to give us the spiritual nourishment we need.

RECONNECT, RE-RELATE

In theory at least, the solution is simple. Turn your attention away from the noisy world of complexity and detail, and refocus your attention on the four circles of life. When things get crazy, return to these circles and get back in the loop.

If you're a teacher, trainer, coach, or therapist, use this model as a starting point for discussion and engagement. Keep reminding your students and clients about the fundamentals. Guide them through your familiar practices and content, but keep them focused. If they wander, bring them back.

If you're a physician or health professional, you can even use this model diagnostically. Ask patients about their relationships and see if you can find the weak spots.

- "What kind of relationship do you have with your body?"
- "How would you describe your relationship to habitat?"
- "What kind of relationship do you have with your community?"
- "Do you have a sense of meaning and purpose?"

These questions are almost never asked in conventional, high-speed medical practices. But this is a glaring, monstrous oversight. Knowing what we now know about how the human animal actually works, these questions are not just important, but they are probably more important than conventional measures such as height, weight, and blood pressure. Hippocrates would surely agree. If these life-supporting circles are broken, conventional treatments are likely to be ineffective, irrelevant, or even harmful. But if the circles are in place, your methods will be even more effective.

Likewise, you can teach this model to your patients as a way to simplify their own health and medical education. Help them cut through the clutter and focus on the fundamentals. Stick to the circles and you'll never go too far wrong.

CHAPTER 14

TENSEGRITY

All have their worth and each contributes
to the worth of the others.
—J. R. R. Tolkien
The Silmarillion

Integrity is the essence of everything successful.
—R. Buckminster Fuller

It might well seem obvious, but if you want to understand and work with complex systems like human bodies and ecosystems, it's essential to look at the whole thing. Fragments can be interesting and important, but it's how they relate to one another that makes the difference in what we ultimately care about: total system function.

This is precisely what we see in the world of physical training, where today's coaches and trainers are quick to emphasize whole-body integration and coordination. As they see it, strength, power, and injury resistance come from orchestration and integration of the entire system in motion, not isolation.

The body's neuromuscular system is a lot more than just a bunch of muscles, joints, and nerves. It's a tensegrity structure. That is, all the skeletal and soft tissue elements participate in carrying the loads of gravity and producing movement. As with everything in nature, it's interdependent; loads are—or should be—distributed across the body. In this paradigm, individual muscles are not considered particularly interesting. Rather, the idea is to engage "kinetic chains," combinations of muscles and neural circuits that produce movement. By learning to orchestrate these chains, our movements become more graceful, powerful, and effective. This is the path to athleticism and injury resistance. In practice, coaches often use these cues to help their athletes focus on orchestration and integration:

"Hips talk to shoulders!"
"Lift the weight with your whole body!"
"Bend your knees!"
And of course, the classic "Toenails to fingernails!"

COMPLEX SYSTEMS

We see a similar theme in all complex systems, from bodies to ecosystems. This is why the bicycle wheel is such an ideal metaphor. When the system has lots of spokes of roughly equal length, tension, and strength, all is well and the wheel rolls true. But if you lose more than a few spokes, muscles, or species, the structure becomes weak, then unstable. At this point, all it takes is a minor insult or injury for the entire system to collapse.

Which, of course, is precisely where we stand on our planet today. The loss of biodiversity and cultural diversity is the equivalent of losing spokes in our bicycle wheel. In turn, the wheel begins to wobble, which increases our stress, our fear, and our anxiety for the future. We know that something is desperately wrong with the system, the structure, the modern world, but we're not sure precisely what. Some spokes are too short, some are too long, and some are completely missing. In our fear, we keep tightening the remaining spokes, but it only makes matters worse.

WHOLE-PART-WHOLE

But how exactly does a master wheelsmith correct the imbalances in a wobbly wheel? It's an art that takes years to master, but the basics are pretty easy to understand. The first and most important lesson should be obvious but often escapes our attention. That is, *focus on the totality of the wheel.* Examine the whole wheel first and see how it behaves on the stand. Give it a spin and look for wobbles, left–right and up–down. Take your time. Watch closely and try to take in the whole thing.

Then, take your best guess as to the offending spokes. Something is broken, something is short, something is weak. Use your best judgment, pick out the offending spoke, and give the wrench a turn. But of course, this action, simple as it may seem, doesn't just adjust the spoke in question; it also affects the totality of the structure. So, you must go back to the whole and recheck the wobble. Has it gotten better or worse? Has it shifted in one direction or another? Are you adjusting in the right direction?

This process of oscillating attention is the key to success. Athletic coach Vern Gambetta has called this the "whole–part–whole" method of athletic evaluation: watch the whole athlete in motion, then focus on the offending limb or joint, apply some kind of treatment or therapy, then return your attention to the whole athlete in motion.

It's a great method, but this is about a lot more than rehabbing creaky athletes; the pattern is ideal for making adjustments to any complex system.

Our problem, of course, is that we simply aren't trained to work this way. On the contrary, we're taught to focus on the condition of individual spokes. We're trained to become spoke specialists, and we get rewarded if our particular spoke specialty works as desired.

Sometimes we get lucky and our approach actually gives a solid, whole-wheel outcome, but more often, this spoke-by-spoke approach fails to give us what we seek. An army of spoke specialists just doesn't see the big picture. In fact, we're often actively discouraged from looking at bigger pictures. The rewards go to the experts, those who keep their eyes on individual spokes.

This is particularly obvious in the domain of modern medicine, where each of the body's spokes has its own specialist practitioners, facilities, and professional organizations. Every organ, every tissue type, and every condition—every spoke gets intensive attention while the whole goes mostly ignored.

What we really need are students and professionals who are adept in whole–part–whole oscillations. We need people with fluid intelligence and the ability to zoom in and zoom out, constantly comparing their work and adjustments against the totality of the system. To put it another way, we need the training and ability to move easily from big pictures to small and back again, over and over, continuously throughout life.

TENSEGRITY IN LIFE

This is something native and indigenous people seem to understand intuitively, and in fact, it's built into their cultures and value systems. A person might specialize lightly and become a good hunter or a good warrior, but the holistic perspective is implicit and assumed by everyone. Young people are taught to ask, *How will my action or behavior affect the totality of the tribe in context?*

But such is not the case in our narcissistic modern culture. For us, it's very much the inverse. We're actively rewarded for focusing intently on ourselves, especially our personal athletic or career performance.

For the modern athlete or career professional, it's all about *my* spoke and *my* career. Who cares what effect it has on the totality of the wheel? That's not part of my job description. And besides, if I back off on my intensity, one of the other spokes might get ahead. Obviously, this is not a prescription for systemic health or sapience; it's no wonder our wheel is so wobbly.

Fortunately, a more sophisticated understanding of wheelcraft seems to come with age and experience. The master craftsperson in any discipline has an expanded view of the totality and is inherently suspicious of any single movement, action, or point of view. He or she is cautious and patient, always scanning and looking for ripple effects that cascade throughout the system. Watch and listen, then turn a spoke, just a little, then wait to see the systemic consequences. No individual action or element is good in and of itself; it's how it affects the whole that really matters.

The message is obvious. Treat your life, your community, and your culture like a wheel. Take care of all the spokes and adjust continuously. If something's short, lengthen it. If something's weak, strengthen it. If something's dormant, wake it up. If something's hyperactive, calm it down. And whatever you do, keep your eye on the whole.

CHAPTER 15

ROCK–SCISSORS–PAPER

> Action has meaning only in relationship, and without understanding relationship, action on any level will only breed conflict. The understanding of relationship is infinitely more important than the search for any plan of action.
> —Jiddu Krishnamurti

Hierarchy is dead. Or at least it should be. The grand pyramid of civilization had a good—and not-so-good—run, but it's now collapsing under the weight of its own excess. In short, hierarchy violates everything we know about the way the world—particularly the biosphere—actually works.

This disconnect is revealed in our modern competitive games and match-ups, where we're always looking to see who's alpha. But out in the real-life biosphere, the world behaves a lot more like a game of rock–scissors–paper. People call it ick-ack-ock, ching-chang-cholly, zig-zag-zog, or roshambo, but whatever we call it, the game is a perfect model for a healthy ecosystem, a healthy body, and a healthy life. Each "player" in these complex, living systems can prevail over some others at some times, but not always or everywhere. The game is internally self-regulating. This is how biospheres, ecosystems, and bodies actually work.

Our Western minds love hierarchy, and we're quick to suppose that the natural world reflects our favorite cultural paradigm. We like to lionize the lions and other so-called alpha predators, also described as "apex predators." But even these powerful megafauna can be defeated by microorganisms, insects, famine, drought, floods, or climate change. Strict hierarchy is an invention of agricultural and industrial minds; the true organization of a healthy system is circular and horizontal. There is no king of the biological hill.

The same principle holds true within the body itself. No organ, hormone, brain circuit, or neurotransmitter is alpha, not even the brain itself. All systems are regulated by some other system or informational substance. When a process moves toward extremity, another steps in to keep it in check. Extremes ultimately get regulated: blood pressure, blood sugar, heart rate, digestion, immunity, cellular growth—all are subject to control by other entities. The body is not a pyramid; it's a self-regulating circle.

Traditional Paleo cultures recognized and embraced the circular nature of the world in their daily experience. The elders knew there was always some other life process that could beat them in an encounter—predators, poisonous plants, bad weather, or disease. Indeed, the rock–scissors–paper game is still played in Indonesia as 'earwig–man–elephant.' Elephant beats man, man beats earwig, and earwig beats elephant (by crawling through its brain!).

But sadly, Western civilization is not content to accept a rock–scissors–paper reality. We find it too unpredictable and capricious; we want control. Our goal is to become, as

Descartes put it, "masters and possessors of Nature." Not satisfied with an occasional victory and reasonable security, we try to rig the game so that we are always alpha, the apex species.

Human supremacists just won't take no for an answer. Instead of being content with a modest participatory role, we try to dominate the action with powerful machines, fossil fuels, pesticides, computers, and hyperspecialization. Likewise, we try to lock down our health with "ultimate" diets, elite exercise programs, and all manner of performance enhancements. Instead of playing the game with skill, grace, and dignity, we try to rig the outcome.

But trying to gain an ultimate victory in a rock–scissors–paper world is a fool's goal. The biosphere has more ways to trump us than we could ever imagine. The diversity of microorganisms alone is beyond our comprehension. Nature is supremely creative and is constantly finding new ways to regulate errant players. As a popular Japanese saying has it, "The nail that sticks up will be hammered down." We defy the game at our peril.

To be truly healthy, we need to participate with life on equal footing and live within the circle of mutual influence and regulation. To play a sustainable game of rock–scissors–paper, we must abide by its spirit and ground rules. To play without catastrophic defeat, we must occasionally yield to other forces. This calls for modesty.

A GAMES CURRICULUM

At first glance, it might well seem that rock–scissors–paper is nothing more than a curious, trivial amusement for children and drunken college students. But there's a powerful lesson here, one that gives us an important insight into human education. That is, people often understand the world through the games we teach. As the years go by, we tend to forget the details and outcomes of the games themselves, but we remember the relationships, strategies, and psychology that come along for the ride.

It makes perfect sense to suppose that teaching different game structures will ultimately inspire people to behave in different ways. If we teach students exclusively through competitive games, we get one result; if we teach them through cooperative and circular games, we get another.

This must surely give us pause. It's obvious that modern education is structured almost exclusively around competitive games and competitive academic advancement. In fact, we might well describe modern big-box schools as factories for producing adversarial relationships. When every exam, report card, and sports game puts students in opposition with one another, we shouldn't be at all surprised to see the result: a fearful, highly stratified society in near-constant conflict. In this way, modern schools might even be described as sociopathic. If your goal was to turn people against one another, you could hardly do better than to structure students' entire educational experience around competitive games and relationships.

But as we've seen, nature is fundamentally circular. To teach exclusively via competition is to give students the wrong idea about how the world actually works, and in this respect, our exclusive focus on competitive games is really a form of educational malpractice.

In this, the cure for what ails us in education may well come down to a simple remedy: teach games that are more consistent with biological and physiological reality. If we were to do this one simple thing, our outcomes would improve immensely.

NO VICTORY

At this point in history, humility would be appropriate and sapient. Slow down, relax. Rock–scissors–paper is not the kind of game that we can "win," and trying to do so will only increase our suffering. So stop with the relentless competition in all things. Not only does it increase our stress, but it also violates the very nature of the living world.

The coronavirus pandemic has been a stark, vivid reminder of the rock–scissors–paper nature of life on Earth. Naturally, we've been quick to wish for a human victory over the virus and the promise of an ultimate fix in the form of a vaccine. But even if the vaccine works as many have hoped, it will only delay our reckoning with reality and contribute to our illusion of supremacy. The real fix here is to understand and accept the true lesson of biology: the point of the game is not to win but to keep playing.

CHAPTER 16

GEOMETRY LESSON

The object of power is power.
—George Orwell
1984

Our world is on fire. The arsonists are in charge.
—Naomi Klein

For thousands of years, human life was all about the circle. Indigenous people saw themselves as participants in the great, integrated unity of life. The circle gave them their food, their water, their health, and even, we might well suppose, their sapience. The circle sustained them.

But with the advent of agriculture, especially the animal-powered form that began some five thousand years ago, the geometry of human life began to change. Grain surpluses led to the first real affluence, population increases, and the rise of social hierarchy. The flat, egalitarian nature of human relations began to fade. As certain individuals rose in rank and took on power, the pyramid began to dominate social affairs and, in turn, the consciousness of humankind.

The pyramid became a powerful force in the human imagination, and for the first time in history, people began to think in terms of hierarchy, with kings and aristocrats at the top. This was also the origin of human supremacy, the belief that humans are, and should be, the alpha species, superior to every other life-form on the planet. In turn, this philosophy paved the way for human exploitation of the natural world.

In fact, pyramids are useful for organizing large numbers of people. When populations grow, it becomes impossible to gather everyone together and make decisions by consensus, so by consolidating power in certain individuals, the pyramid allows for a regular flow of authority and enables society to get things done.

And at first, it was pretty simple. Rulers exercised their authority by charisma, coercion, or physical force, but the distance between high and low was not extreme. Access and influence by lower-ranking individuals were still possible, and people could have a voice. But after hundreds, then thousands of years, the pyramids of social hierarchy got higher and steeper and the rulers further and further out of reach.

Which is precisely what we see in today's social order. The social and political pyramid has become so steep that the common human has no chance whatsoever of accessing or influencing those at the top; the political and economic elites are simply out of reach. The only way an ordinary person can access the top is through immense levels of wealth or fame, and even then, the chance for real influence remains a long shot.

Obviously, this structure is not democratic or humane in any meaningful sense. Those at the bottom of the pyramid have almost no real power, and even worse, those at the top are free to exercise their power in ways that are arbitrary and self-serving. In this kind of world, the circle is little more than a distant memory.

PYRAMID SCHEME

Today, almost everyone on the planet inhabits a social or political pyramid of one sort or another. And even though we rarely talk about it, the pyramid has enormous power over how we live, what we do, how we relate, and what we value.

But tragically, we almost never get an education in how the pyramid functions or how we might be able to challenge its structure. Most educators simply assume the pyramid to be a given, an unmovable social reality that cannot and must not be questioned. We teach sociology and civics classes, but most of these efforts are not really designed to tell the truth, much less confront the system itself. More likely, these courses assist in pacification and domestication and, in a sense, are actual barriers to progress.

If we were to tell the truth, we would talk about the "reverse Robin Hood" nature of pyramids in the modern world and how they enable the exploitation of those at the bottom by those at the top. Wealth and power have a positive, self-reinforcing effect—the more power you have, the more power you can get. In the process, wealth is progressively looted from those at the base of the pyramid and deposited into the accounts of those at the top. Far from being an occasional exception to business-as-usual, this is how the system is designed to function. It is fundamentally unfair and unjust. And from a Paleo, indigenous point of view, it's wickedly immoral.

THE NEUROBIOLOGY OF PYRAMIDS

The pyramid is far more than an economic and political ranking system. It has very real psycho-physical effects on everyone's bodies, a point vividly revealed by Michael Marmot in *The Status Syndrome*. By reviewing thousands of epidemiological studies from around the world, Marmot discovered that "health follows a social gradient."

To put it simply, people of high rank tend to enjoy better health. People of low social standing are far more likely to suffer the common lifestyle diseases of obesity, diabetes, heart disease, depression, and neurological disorders. This has little to do with access to doctors, clinics, and gyms but is almost certainly related to stress. After all, people of high rank have much more power and control over their lives and, in turn, tend to experience the world as a place of potential and possibility, all of which is good for the body and the spirit. But for people of low rank, power and control are fleeting; the world is more likely to feel onerous, threatening, and even hostile.

All of this adds up to a profoundly disturbing picture of pyramid dynamics: money, power, status, and opportunity flow uphill, whereas social control, stress hormones, fear, insecurity, and anxiety flow downhill. In turn, this adds up to structural, systemic health inequity. Say what you will about sugar, trans fats, and other common insults to health, if you're at the bottom of the pyramid, your health is likely to suffer.

PALEO AND REVERSE DOMINANCE

So what are we to do about the pathologies of power and the onerous nature of the pyramid? Perhaps we can take a lesson from the Paleo. In fact, native and indigenous people have long understood the problem of hierarchy, pride, and ego and the way a pyramid can overwhelm the circle. As an antidote, they devised some clever cultural practices. For example, anthropologist Christopher Boehm has studied hunter-gatherers and discovered they maintained equality through a practice he labeled "reverse dominance."

In a standard pyramidal hierarchy, a few individuals dominate the many, but in a system of reverse dominance, the many act in unison to deflate the ego of anyone who tries to dominate them. In this kind of system, people use leveling mechanisms to ensure the "domination of leaders by their own followers."

Instead of glorifying power as we do in the modern world, Paleo people sought to bring one another down to a level of shared equality. Imagine the scene when a hunting party returns to camp: A hunter has made a good kill of a large, meaty animal, but instead of bragging, he minimizes his accomplishment, a practice known as "dishonoring the meat." He understates the importance of his achievement and describes it as a "poor kill." This practice stands in marked contrast to modern cultures in which self-promotion is not only considered acceptable but is celebrated as an essential path to advancement and success.

Today, reverse dominance lives on in the world of comedy. Most comedians are quick to take aim at the top of the pyramid, using an approach of "kick up, kiss down." This ridicule of power is good entertainment, but even better, it's absolutely essential to a functional society and a working democracy. The act of kicking up and kissing down levels the hierarchy and minimizes the pathologies of power. It's healthy behavior.

CULTURE OVER PYRAMID

Some have suggested that the entire pyramidal structure must be destroyed and rebuilt from scratch, but the larger question remains: What are we to replace it with? Egalitarian power structures worked in the Paleo because conversation and consensus are possible in small groups. But what are we to do with a global population of some eight billion people and counting? And what if we were to actually succeed in tearing down the pyramids of power? Would it simply lead to chaos or yet another case of "meet the new boss, same as the old boss"?

The solution must be psycho-cultural. As it stands, many of us reflexively and unconsciously support the pyramid by showering people in power with attention and all manner of perks. This, we believe, is how the system is supposed to work. We honor famous people simply for the fact that they're famous and reward those who are already affluent. Book contracts, more powerful positions, expense accounts, and lavish honorariums tend to move upward, regardless of the recipient's character, education, or work performance. In short, a "kiss-up" behavior is built into our culture.

But it doesn't have to be this way. In fact, we can practice reverse dominance. We can stop lavishing attention and honor on the top of the pyramid. We can ignore celebrity and affluence. We can devalue power and shame the mindless accumulation of wealth. Instead, we can promote the Paleo, indigenous ethic of sharing and circularity. To be sure, some form of social ranking is probably necessary and inevitable in our hypersocial species, but let's not give it more energy than it deserves.

Finally and possibly most important, give up the belief that people at the top are smarter or more capable. These people are where they are through a combination of skin color, generational advantage, occasional merit, and luck. They are not better people.

TEACH THE CIRCLE

The trouble with the pyramid, particularly in a globalized world with billions of people, is that it's almost impossible to do anything without some sort of organizing structure. But there's no need for the pyramid to be so steep, so high, so impervious, or so destructive. So teach the old ways of the circle whenever possible, and above all, don't internalize your rank or accept what the pyramid might suggest about your capabilities. Ultimately, we will have our day. As the poet Dinos Christianopoulos put it, "They tried to bury us. They didn't know we were seeds."

CHAPTER 17

CORPORATE CRIME WAVE

> If animals could speak, we'd charge them rent.
> —Freequill

Corporate power has now become the most overwhelming social and political force on the planet, eclipsing even entire governments. In the 1970s, there were some seven thousand corporations operating internationally, but by 2008, the number had increased to about eighty-two thousand, and today there are close to a million. Corporations now account for fifty-one of the largest one hundred economic entities in the world. (The others are countries.)

This domination of society is far more than naked political and financial power. Corporations hold the most powerful megaphones on the planet—their narratives and messaging penetrate deep into our homes, our minds, and our culture, radically transforming our consciousness, values, and lifestyles.

We are constantly being sculpted, groomed, and manipulated by corporate messaging. When it comes to culture, corporate power is firmly in command. Taken together, this domination adds up to what journalist Chris Hedges calls "corporate totalitarianism."

DEATH BY A THOUSAND DISTORTIONS

This is about a lot more than money. By crafting rosy images of perfect products and services, corporate narratives drastically distort our understanding of reality and our relationships with the world. Suppose your company invents a new device. Your marketing people will design a flashy ad campaign to celebrate its many advantages: "It's shiny, fast, convenient, slick, and wonderful." It all sounds great, but at no point does this narrative mention the downsides of producing, owning, and eventually disposing of the shiny device. No one says anything about the social and environmental damage that comes from producing and using it.

In fact, the only time that negativity creeps into the process is at the beginning of the marketing pitch, when the hapless, awkward consumer, confused and overwhelmed by life, can scarcely manage his or her affairs. Life is a stressful, incoherent mess, but fortunately, salvation is close at hand with the shiny product or service. And so consumers remain duped and oblivious, lost in a world of shiny perfection.

Repeat this process billions of times across a global economy, and you'll eventually produce a state of massively distorted, fantasy consciousness in which there are no downsides to anything. Life is just one big, happy celebration of shiny devices and services; the downsides, if there are any, are far away in remote corners of the world. In other words, corporate marketing creates a very real cognitive blindness that keeps us isolated from reality, a process that might well be described as a form of anti-education.

To put it another way, the entire enterprise of corporate marketing and advertising might well be described as "distractivism," an intentional and highly conscious effort to derail human attention away from vital, life-sustaining connections. In this, we begin to realize that one of the most urgent priorities of our age is to resist the blizzard of corporate marketing stimuli that keeps us separated from authentically meaningful life and work: the intrusive ads, pop-up windows, and neuro-crafted pitches that raise our consumerist tendencies to a fever pitch. If we're going to survive as a people, we're going to have to focus.

LEGAL MACHINES

The crucial thing to remember is that a corporation is not really a human organization but a legal machine designed to internalize profit and externalize costs. And typically, those costs are borne by the public. A corporation might decide to build a fracking plant near your community. When the project is completed, the company will reap substantial rewards, but the public will be forced to pay in the form of increased noise, traffic, air pollution, and other ills. This pattern has played out all over the world with a thousand variations.

This is business-as-usual.

When the corporation succeeds, benefits go to shareholders and investors and, of course, corporate officers. And even worse, all the principals within the corporation, including the shareholders and officers, are shielded from liability, which means they can do more or less as they please. Behind the corporate veil, life is safe and easy. And most incredible of all, corporations are even considered "persons" under the law.

Trees, animals, and ecosystems have no legal standing, but the companies that destroy them do.

Ultimately, corporate behavior stems not from the decisions of individuals, but from the legal structure that drives them. In this sense, the modern corporation is fundamentally mindless. Most of the routine decisions are made by the mechanism, guided by spreadsheet. The decisions made by corporate officers are sometimes consequential, but in general, most of the "intelligence" of a corporation is structural, not human. People in a corporate setting mostly do what the structure—and the computers—tells them.

This also sheds light on the ethical nature of corporate governance. It's not exactly true that the modern corporation is immoral (although many of them are) but rather that they are *amoral*. That is, morality is simply not part of the system or the calculation. A moral perspective might come from individual officers on occasion, but morality is really a sideshow. What really matters is the legal mandate: generate profit for the investors.

This is why corporate power is so toxic to society and the planet. According to the legal structure of the corporation, there really *is* no society or planet. You can externalize costs and consequences all you like because from a legal point of view, society and the planet belong to another domain entirely. To say that corporations are immoral kind of misses the point because, in fact, morality isn't even on the radar. If an individual behaved this way—internalizing profit and externalizing costs—we'd call that person a criminal, or at least an asshole.

Given this ethical vacuum, it comes as no surprise to see corporations behaving in such a rapacious manner. Couple corporate power with a culture of imperialism, colonialism, and human supremacy, and you wind up with a mindset that attempts to profit off everything it touches. In the process, corporations turn communities into commodities. Anything can be monetized. Whether it's natural habitat or traditional human cultures, corporations are equal-opportunity destroyers.

The real solution to this nonsense would be to completely rewrite the laws governing corporations. Make them pay for externalizing costs, and make officers and investors liable for bad behavior. But this kind of reform could take generations, even with the cooperation and consent of the powerful.

In the meantime, what we really need are truth tellers to deliver a counternarrative. Teachers, political leaders, artists, and ordinary folks can pick up the microphone to remind people of the consequences of mindless consumption and devotion to corporate memes.

Likewise, we can ignore corporate messaging whenever possible and, above all, stop identifying with brands. Slick narratives are designed from scratch to manipulate our minds and distract us from the vital realities of our day. Close your ears and focus on your body, your habitat, and your people. This is where the real action is.

Second, stop worshiping corporate power and the corporate lifestyle. The top of the pyramid might seem like a fun place to inhabit, but not when you realize what it means for everyone else. Even better, do what you can to stigmatize power. Beyond the point of modest and comfortable living, wealth and power should be seen as an embarrassment. Stop lusting over private jets and race cars. If it's no longer cool to be rich and powerful, maybe people will stop with the madness.

Finally, remember that the products and services you consume come with some heavy, invisible, and highly destructive baggage. The corporation has externalized its costs onto society and the planet, which means that the price you're paying is artificially low. It may seem like you're getting a good deal on the shiny device, but if you factor in the damage to society and the Earth, the price is actually outrageous. So before you click the "Buy Now" button, imagine that the true price is a hundred times greater than what you're actually paying. This will sober you up.

CHAPTER 18

MONEY CHANGES EVERYTHING

> I am losing precious days. I am degenerating into a machine for making money. I am learning nothing in this trivial world of men. I must break away and get out into the mountains to learn the news.
> —John Muir

> Money often costs too much.
> —Ralph Waldo Emerson

We joke that it's the root of all evil, but rarely do we pause to think deeply about the ways that money has radically transformed our lives, our culture, and our consciousness. This seems like a monstrous oversight because money as we know it is a relatively new, unproven concept in human history. Our Paleolithic ancestors had virtually no possessions, no bank accounts, no credit, and no cash. Their consciousness was focused on habitat, one another, and the cosmos at large. In good years, habitat *was* their affluence. The land was their wealth.

In contrast, modern people spend much, if not most, of their time obsessing over all things financial, economic, and money related. We complain about the stress, but this is far more than a minor lifestyle annoyance. Research demonstrates that money is a profoundly disruptive, anti-tribal, even anti-human force. Kathleen Vohs at the University of Minnesota primed subjects with reminders of economics, finance, prices, and costs and discovered that

> money-primed people behave more selfishly and show a greater reluctance to be involved with others . . . Even in intimate relationships and collectivistic cultures, reminders of money weaken sociomoral responses.

Likewise, a 2015 review of money-priming experiments found two major effects:

> Compared to neutral primes, people reminded of money are less interpersonally attuned. They are not prosocial, caring, or warm. They eschew interdependence. Second, people reminded of money shift into professional, business, and work mentality.

These findings, described by Nobel Prize winner Daniel Kahneman in *Thinking, Fast and Slow*, are profoundly disturbing and inconvenient to our culture-as-usual. Obviously, people who live in the modern world are massively and continuously "money-primed." Immersed in a world of twenty-four-hour commerce, advertising, special offers, and discount pricing, we're reminded of money hundreds, even thousands, of times each day—in our cars, our workplaces, and even in our homes. If these priming events incline us even slightly away from our historically normal pro-tribal, pro-social orientation, the overall effect is destructive on a planetary scale. In effect, money is a corrosive agent, an acid that dissolves normal human communities.

Is it any wonder that so many of our modern social relations are so strained? What happens to us when most of our relationships are transactional? How does our humanity fit in? All of which leads us to another inconvenient realization. That is, capitalism—with its inherent focus on self-interest and profit—goes sharply against the grain of human history and the natural prosocial inclinations of our bodies. Our bodies crave contact and connection, but capitalism turns our priorities upside down, declaring that selfish, antisocial behavior is somehow prosocial.

To say that selfishness is the path to the common good is not only patently absurd, but it also flies in the face of our ancestry and our neurobiology. And because affiliation is essential to the functioning of our bodies, it's not a stretch to say that naked capitalism—especially its militant, extremist form—is a threat to public health and our collective future. By relentlessly driving people toward self-interest, it destroys communities and robs us of opportunities to connect. A transactional society is no society at all, merely a set of self-interested calculations.

INVERSE U

Our problem with money is rooted in our inability or unwillingness to recognize the dynamic nature of the world we live in. Out in the real world of bodies and ecosystems, everything we observe follows the classic inverse-U curve of benefit. As toxicologists so often put it, "The dose makes the tonic," and "The dose makes the poison." Small amounts can be therapeutic, but further increases eventually cross a tipping point and become toxic.

So too with money. A large body of research shows conclusively that modest increases in wealth have positive benefits to mind, body, and spirit. Up to a point, money gives us a vital sense of power and control, which eases our stress and helps us function at a higher level. But beyond the tipping point, further increases in wealth don't bring much benefit at all and eventually become irrelevant or obscene.

But as a people, we've chosen to ignore the inverse U. We act as if money and wealth have a linear, unlimited benefit and that more is always better. Not only does this assumption violate everything we know about how the world works, but it also sets us up for frustration, distraction, and ultimately, dysfunction. Humility and sapience would suggest a more modest approach. Enough, as they say, is enough.

REAL WEALTH, GIFT ECONOMY

Obviously, some degree of money consciousness is essential for survival in the modern world, and we've got to live with it as best we can. But when money comes to dominate human consciousness, society becomes automated, robotic, and in turn, dysfunctional.

And while we may not be able to escape money-priming effects entirely, we can stop making money the measure of all things. Move toward a gift economy whenever possible; monkey-wrench the economic system by giving things away. Even more importantly, stop worshiping affluence and wealth. Strive for what you need, but stop as soon as possible.

The real wealth lives in the circle.

CHAPTER 19

FULL CIRCLE

> I feel an indescribable ecstasy and delirium in melting, as it were, into the system of being, in identifying myself with the whole of nature.
> —Jean-Jacques Rousseau

Somewhere along the line, somebody took their eyes off the whole. Human intelligence, formerly a broad, inclusive aptitude that absorbed entire habitats, ecosystems, and the cosmos at large, took a turn toward fragmentation. And in the process, human consciousness became increasingly isolated and alienated.

By some accounts, this demise of holistic attention was driven by actual changes in the human brain. In *The Master and His Emissary*, Iain McGilchrist makes a powerful case that the increasing use of a symbolic alphabet led to the dominance of the left hemisphere and, in turn, our dysfunctional relationship with the world at large.

As we now know, the left and right hemispheres have distinctly different ways of attending to the world. In general, the left side specializes in linear thought, language, logic, and reason while the right side traffics in metaphor, myth, holistic imagination, and the experience of the body.

The hemispheres communicate and share many functions, but they can also inhibit one another. And when the left side begins to dominate, the result is an increasingly rigid, linear culture, a world in which hierarchy, logic, and efficiency begin to tyrannize integrated human perspectives.

It's easy to understand this leftward shift as a consequence of historical events: The invention of agriculture, our systematic extermination of predators, and an increasingly indoor lifestyle allowed for greater attention on isolated objects. In turn, the process intensified with the development of writing, the printing press, and widespread literacy, followed by the invention of industry and science, all of which combined to favor the left side of the brain. Today, we no longer scan the horizon for predators or changes in the weather. Instead we focus our attention on isolated fragments of our experience: objects, symbols, spreadsheets, sequences, and mechanical causality.

Today, we take such mental and cognitive dominance as a simple fact of modern life, and rarely do we stop to question it. But it's essential to remember that this left-dominant style is a radically abnormal way to use the human brain. In the Paleo and for the vast majority of human history, people used their entire brains and their whole bodies to learn the world. But today, we've chosen to use just a fragment of our capability. And in the process of rejecting the right side of the brain as "irrational," "impulsive," and "untrustworthy," we cut ourselves off from one of the most powerful human capabilities of all.

Naturally, some critics take issue with McGilchrist's neurological interpretation, charging that the human brain is inherently flexible and not given to such large-scale, hemispheric shifts over time. But even if the neurological explanation is flawed in some way, the metaphor certainly isn't. Dualistic explanations and interpretations are universal in our species: The Chinese gave us an entire cosmology of yin and yang. Novelist C. P. Snow famously wrote about *The Two Cultures and the Scientific Revolution*, and Robert Pirsig explored the romantic–classical divide in *Zen and the Art of Motorcycle Maintenance*. Likewise, eco-theologian Michael Dowd has made a powerful distinction between "day language" and "night language." In short, humanity is fascinated with the number 2.

In any case, our left-side dominance creates a vicious circle: intense attention to fragmented pieces of reality leads to myopia and diminished awareness of context, leading, in turn, to an abnormal state of consciousness and intense concentration on component parts, accompanied by near-total blindness of the whole. To put it another way, we might describe our condition as a "right-brain-deficit disorder."

Modern medicine is the most notorious example of fragmented consciousness and left-side dominance. The modern medical narrative—that human beings can be treated as stand-alone objects—perpetuates the myth that people are isolated, machinelike organisms. Far from being an abstract philosophy, this story has very real consequences in the ways that people relate to their bodies and the world. As long as we behave as if the human body has its own independent existence, our health is going to be compromised. In reality, human health is a unitary, indivisible phenomenon that includes mind, spirit, land, tribe, and ancestry. We might even go so far as to describe modern, context-free medicine as a kind of institutionalized, culturally driven malpractice.

But it's not just modern medicine. We see the same kind of approach in almost every modern system: education, business, government, academia. Narrower and narrower we go, until the totality of the world disappears.

USE IT OR LOSE IT

What makes this so interesting is that in all likelihood, there's a training effect at work here. Like most other tissues in the body, the hemispheres of the brain are plastic and adapt to the ways that they're used. The fibers that connect the hemispheres can stimulate or inhibit the activity of the other side, depending on how often they're fired. In turn, this allows one mode of thinking to dominate the other.

In our case, the trend is clear. As civilized culture has developed, more and more people are rewarded for left-side dominance and right-side suppression. In the process, we increasingly view the world in Newtonian terms, as a collection of measurable, trackable, and controllable objects, a view that fits perfectly with a culture of human supremacy and corporate dominance. The left side gives us the power that we seek; we can use it and profit from it.

The same principle that applies to muscle tissue applies equally to the nervous system and the brain: use it or lose it. If we habitually favor the left and inhibit the right, we'll eventually lose our ability to think holistically—to use myth, metaphor, and big-picture consciousness to understand the world. And this is precisely what we're seeing. Modern people are becoming increasingly linear in their thinking, increasingly fact-oriented and skeptical of anything that isn't nailed down with research and solid evidence. In the process, a lot of what makes us human is being left behind. In short, the left-side sciences are coming to dominate the right-side humanities.

For athletic coaches and trainers, none of this will come as a surprise. All of our physical and psycho-physical adaptations are "use dependent." We become what we do. When we practice left-side perspectives exclusively, we become left-sided athletes—adept at linear thinking and objectification but simultaneously inept at much of anything else.

All of which suggests a simple remedy. To think holistically, start using the right side of your brain. Tone down the analysis and the reductionism; let go of the linear sequences and the ceaseless quest for certainty. Open your mind and brain to poetry, myth, and the language of immediate experience. Give up the quest for control and make yourself vulnerable to feeling. Listen to the wind.

Naturally, left-side brainiacs push back on this entire line of thinking. In their opinion, cognition is a zero-sum game, a competition between hemispheres. If we open the door to the irrationality of the right hemisphere, we'll degrade the perfection and beauty of reason, and from there, it's only a short step to dysfunction, superstition, and insanity. But far from being a zero-sum game, the hemispheres work best in tandem, in conversation, in relationship. It's folly to suppose that one is, or should be, superior to the other. As in all things, a rhythmic oscillation works best.

EARTH ON THE RIGHT

This whole-brain, whole-body integration becomes even more urgent in the context of our planetary predicament and ecological emergency. The need to save habitat and species is obvious, but even more crucial is our need is to affiliate and identify with habitat and the biosphere as a whole. In other words, we desperately need an emotional connection to the living world.

But none of this is going to happen with an exclusively left-brain orientation. Research reports, data, and scientific findings have mostly failed to move the needle on ecological consciousness, much less move people to decisive action. We are besieged by numbers on climate change, sea-level rise, species extinctions, freshwater depletion, and all the rest, but most of this fails to hit the mark, something that speaking consultants understand full well. As they put it, "Numbers numb. That's why they're called numbers."

To really connect with the living planet, we need to engage and respect both hemispheres. If we simply camp out on the left side with rationality, linear thinking, and analysis, we're never going to "save the Earth." And even if we did manage to "save" her, we wouldn't really be able to appreciate what's left. We'd simply function as ecosystem managers—counting, sorting, and tracking the life around us. Life would be just another boring work project.

What we really need is authentic, whole-body physical experience. Reading about endangered habitats is all well and good, but it's even more essential that we touch the world that we're trying to save. The body craves intimacy with the planet, and no amount of left-brain analysis can substitute for genuine physical immersion. In human terms, one hour of authentic physical engagement with the living world is worth a thousand gigabytes of ecological data.

A RIGHT-SIDE CURRICULUM

It hardly needs to be said that today's modern schools are overwhelmingly left-side dominant. With the ceaseless evaluation, testing, scoring, and grading, whatever might be happening on the right side of the student's brain is dismissed as irrelevant, deviant, and even dangerous. We might even go so far as to describe the modern school system as a factory for left-brain development. In other words, the disintegration and fragmentation of human intelligence have been institutionalized. It's no wonder that so many of us feel lopsided and unbalanced.

To function properly, the right brain needs an atmosphere of safety, time, and panoramic opportunity. And most of all, it needs a nonjudgmental culture in which it's free to explore and metabolize experience. We occasionally see this kind of tone in the arts and humanities, but even here, there's a relentless drive toward measurement and evaluation. The prime directive of the modern school is to produce numbers, grades, and scores, and in this kind of culture, there's little room for subjectivity, creativity, intuition, or any other right-brain aptitudes.

Seen in the context of human history, this left-sided curriculum is spectacularly, outrageously abnormal. For the vast, overwhelming majority of our time on Earth, young people have been encouraged to use their whole brains and bodies to learn their habitat and find food. For the young hunter, discipline was important, but intuition was also vital and strongly encouraged by the elders:

> *Imagine the animals, dream of the animals. Imagine your habitat, the light, the smells, the water, and the weather. Feel this in your body as you track the animals through the bush. Feel the creatures and their movement. Identify with them, inhabit them. Become one with them.*

This is not some kind of subjective hippie nonsense; this is a practical, effective, proven way to survive in the world. Our ancestors would be perplexed by, then outraged at the way we force today's students into a rigid, left-sided worldview. Some would even call it abusive.

360 DEGREES OF INTEGRATION

In the end, it's all about balance. It would be a mistake to suppose that the left side of the brain is the "bad side," or to go all-in on everything soft, squishy, and irrational. There's nothing to be gained by rejecting rationality, linear thinking, or competence in practical matters. There is honor in reason, logic, clarity, and discipline. These tools have their place, especially in our monstrously complex, interconnected world.

However, the time has come to give the right side its due. It's time to embrace the totality of the brain and body and trust its creative powers. Learn the left-side arts, but don't allow them to tyrannize your experience. As author Jason Hickel has put it, we need to "dethingify the world." Stop with the left-side objectification of people, bodies, animals, and ecosystems. Instead, practice listening to the right side. Grok the whole thing.

CHAPTER 20

THE LAND IS ME

> There is only one core issue for all of psychology. Where is the "me"? Where does the "me" begin? Where does the "me" stop?
> —James Hillman
> "A Psyche the Size of the Earth"

So whom or what do you identify with? Where does your "me" begin and end? This is no trivial matter. How you answer this question will shape your entire life experience, your health, and your happiness.

It will also shape our ability to create a functional future.

For native and indigenous people, the answer has always been simple and straightforward. Across the planet, from North and South America to Africa and Australia, people have long identified with the land, their habitat. In every bioregion on Earth, native people express this continuity in similar ways: "I am the river, the river is me." "I am the forest, the forest is me." In Brazil, the Yanomami people say, "The environment is not separate from ourselves; we are inside it and it is inside us; we make it and it makes us."

For normal, native people, habitat is flesh. The land and the body are one thing, bound together by an ecological golden rule, a karmic principle of give and take. Aboriginal elders in Australia put it this way: "To wound the earth is to wound yourself, and if others are wounding the earth, they are wounding you." Likewise, Chief Seattle: "What we do to the earth, we do to ourselves." Also, José Ortega y Gasset: "I am I plus my surroundings, and if I do not preserve the latter, I do not preserve myself."

The Indian poet and writer Rabindranath Tagore put it this way:

> The same stream of life that runs through my veins night and day runs through the world and dances in rhythmic measures. It is the same life that shoots in joy through the dust of the earth in numberless blades of grass and breaks into tumultuous waves of leaves and flowers.

It may be tempting to dismiss these expressions of human–habitat unity as the primitive, romantic sentiments of unsophisticated native people, but white people feel it too. John Muir, Aldo Leopold, Henry David Thoreau, Rachel Carson, Gary Snyder, Arne Næss, and E. O. Wilson are just some of the voices that pull our attention back to habitat. In fact, this felt unity of body and habitat is very much a human universal, common to the vast majority of people who have ever lived. It is only us, the WEIRD (Western, Educated, Industrialized, Rich, and Democratic) modern people of the civilized world, who are blind to the connection.

The Zen philosopher Alan Watts made a particularly strong case for body–habitat continuity: "Lack of awareness of the basic unity of organism and environment is a serious and dangerous hallucination." In his book *Does It Matter*, he pointed to an explicit, palpable, almost anatomical connection between the body and the so-called outside world:

> [C]ivilized human beings are alarmingly ignorant of the fact that they are continuous with their natural surroundings.
>
> It is as necessary to have air, water, plants, insects, birds, fish and mammals as it is to have brains, hearts, lungs and stomachs. The former are our external organs in the same way the latter are our internal organs.

For some, this may sound like the ultimate in hippie talk, but this is far more than poetic language. After all, the health and function of our bodies are absolutely, completely, and utterly dependent on habitat. There can be no health in isolation. The forests, rivers, oceans, and grasslands all serve essential physiological functions that keep our bodies alive. Even the sun can be seen as an "external organ," synchronizing our metabolism via circadian rhythms.

Sadly, modern physicians often fail to see the connection. We typically view the body in isolation (in vitro), as a hairy bag of water and a handful of chemicals. It's a medical object, a mere mechanism. We examine it, probe it, measure it, all the while ignoring the larger social and natural continuities that sustain it. In the process, we congratulate ourselves on our "advanced knowledge," but from the native point of view, we are the ignorant ones. Our perspective of the body is fragmented, incomplete, and at best, only occasionally effective.

IMPLICATIONS

Once we recognize and acknowledge our continuity with habitat, we're drawn to a couple of essential but extremely inconvenient conclusions.

First, *habitat destruction is self-destructive behavior.* Cut down a rain forest, strip-mine a mountain, dam a river—these acts of violence against the land are also violence against the body and should be treated as such. There is little substantive difference between killing a person outright and destroying the habitat that keeps that individual alive. One is fast, one takes a little longer, but the end result is the same.

To put it in stronger language: habitat destruction is not only self-destructive; it's ultimately suicidal. The war on the land is a war on our bodies. Clear-cutting a forest doesn't just hurt the forest; it hurts our flesh as well. You might be able to dodge the consequences for a time and even build a temporary economy around the extractive industry, but ultimately, it's a lose-lose proposition.

The second implication is simply the inverse of the first: *habitat conservation is health care.* Or, as some have put it, "Earth care is health care." It's time to open our minds and expand our definitions to include the totality of the body–habitat. Obviously, our current health care system is unjust, unfair, and maddening in its complexity and dehumanizing effects. And just as obviously, we need health care to be universally available to everyone. But this is just a beginning. The time has come to get out of our conventional pigeonholes and start treating habitat conservation and health care as two sides of the same vital enterprise. Take care of our planet, and everyone's body is going to feel a whole lot better.

CHAPTER 21

KNOW HABITAT

> Places don't matter to people any more. Places aren't the point. People are only ever half present where they are these days. They always have at least one foot in the great digital nowhere.
>
> —Matt Haig
> *How to Stop Time*

The fundamental problem of our day is that we've forgotten our primal relationship to habitat, which is to say, we've forgotten how to be normal. Clearly, we need some remedial education on this score, but we're up against some serious cultural obstacles.

In the first place, most of us move around the modern world almost at random, chasing jobs, careers, and one another. High-speed travel gives us the ability to parachute into any bioregion with no real knowledge of the plants and animals on the ground. Most of the time, we live as aliens.

Even worse is our attitude toward the land itself. From our conventional, modern perspective, habitat is just a two-dimensional plot, a parcel, a property to be exploited. It's real estate, a place to park our stuff. It might have a few trees, maybe some water, but mostly it's just a building site. If it's level and has the proper utility hookups, you're good to go.

But genuine habitat is rich, deep, and constantly in flux. If we took the time to really learn, we'd see that even the simplest ecosystems have an extraordinary level of depth and nuance. Habitat, like the human body, is vast.

To get a sense of this depth and sophistication, try a simple thought experiment. Start by taking a quick, imaginary inventory of everything you know about the modern world:

- All the books, magazines, and stories you've ever read
- All the cities and towns you've ever visited or read about
- All the highways, streets, expressways, bike paths, and subway routes you've ever traveled
- All the buildings you've ever lived and worked in
- All the movies, TV shows, and plays you've seen
- All the scientific knowledge you've accumulated
- All the technologies, tools, and products you've ever encountered
- All the cars, trucks, boats, and aircraft you've ever seen or traveled in

Obviously, this adds up to a staggering amount of information, but now for the twist: Take all of that neurocognitive capacity and apply it to your local habitat. Imagine you could use all that "headspace" to absorb every detail of the plants, animals, light, weather, water, and soils in your bioregion.

Your knowledge would be prodigious. You'd know the intimate details of all the creatures in your world, their characteristics and their relationships. You'd see thousands of things that are invisible to the untrained modern eye: the subtle influences of climate, weather, water, and wind. You'd be able to read the spoor of animals and navigate vast reaches of terrain with the faintest clues. You'd know the natural world in a way we can scarcely imagine today.

This is precisely the realization anthropologist Jared Diamond experienced in his early travels to Papua New Guinea. Diamond considered himself a competent naturalist, but he was stunned by the knowledge of the locals, especially their encyclopedic understanding of the local bird population.

This is the normal state of knowledge for *Homo sapiens*, but today, our natural, physical knowledge of habitat is being replaced by intensive measurement, tracking, and analysis. We have reams of environmental data stored on computers, but we possess almost nothing in the way of personal, experiential, physical understanding. This turns our normal way of knowing upside down. Instead of learning habitat through our bodies, we do it through our heads, especially the left side of our brains.

These days, everyone talks about the urgent need to "save the world," but in order to save it, we have to know it. And to know it, we have to spend time in contact with it. We have to feel the rhythms, the textures, the creatures, and the forces that are the very stuff of life. So imagine the immense sophistication of your nervous system brought to bear not on the challenges we routinely experience in the modern world, but on the qualities of terrain, plants, animals, and weather that would have existed in a primal habitat.

Ideally, you'd be in a position to really learn a raw, wild habitat from birth, but for many of us, this is simply out of the question. Most of us have moved several times in our lives, and in all likelihood, your childhood habitat has been radically altered or even destroyed by what is euphemistically described as "development." So the next best thing is to find a habitat you like and immerse yourself in it. Choose some land that's accessible and walkable and go there often. Start observing the coarse-grained detail of the local plants and animals. Who lives there? How do they make a living, and how do they relate to one another?

Next, get your imagination fired up and remember your ancestry in authentic Paleo conditions. Imagine you're walking in a predator-rich environment where lions, leopards, and hyenas are common. In this world, you are not the alpha animal; you are part of the circle of life. You don't need to be terrified, but you do need to be wary. To complete the picture, imagine you haven't eaten in a couple of days, and you're starting to feel it. Forget the fact that your backpack is full of yummy snacks and that rescue is only a few clicks away. Your attention is sharp, focused, intent on any sign of animal life or edible plants. You are fully engaged.

Next, slow down. Speed is a sensation killer that obscures the world we're trying to learn. By slowing down, we see more and feel more. An indigenous farmer in Peru put it this way:

> You can run and run at five kilometers an hour, but you will see nothing. If you walk, maybe one kilometer in five hours, you will see everything.

While we're at it, we'd do well to talk less and listen more. In a normal ancestral environment, success in the hunt often hinged on the ability to keep a low profile and make as little noise as possible. Apprenticeship for young hunters would surely have included training in how to be quiet, and to this day, Native American elders in Alaska advise young people to WAIT, which stands for "Why Am I Talking?"

Naturally, this is a hard lesson for modern people to learn. To put it bluntly, most of us are loudmouths, and we use our outdoor time as one more opportunity to express our opinions about everything under the sun. Not only does this compromise our ability to learn habitat, but from an indigenous point of view, it's considered disrespectful to the land itself. Likewise, we might well ask ourselves, "Why Am I Thinking?" Let your monkey mind wind down, and start paying attention to the world of plants, animals, dirt, water, and weather.

Whenever possible, take your shoes off. The naked foot is an extremely capable sensory organ that tells important stories about the nature of habitat and the qualities of terrain, textures, heat, and cold. For modern urbanites, this practice will take some getting used to, but it's perfectly doable and enjoyable. After a few outings, the skin on your feet will start to toughen up *and* become more sensitive. Not only that, the proprioception in your ankles, knees, and hips will improve. In other words, your legs will get smarter and stronger.

As for electronics, the best practice is to leave your phone in the car. The mere presence of a smartphone is enough to hijack our attention and distract us from the goal of absorbing our surroundings. By offering the prospect of instant navigation and rescue, the phone dilutes our experience and destroys our sense of adventure. If your phone is in your pack or, even worse, in your hand, it's unlikely you'll ever enter a state of full immersion.

The same goes for headlamps and flashlights. Walking at night is one of the most powerful ways to open your senses to the subtleties of your surroundings. And if the trail is a familiar one, you can usually do pretty well without supplemental light. Just walk slower and give it time. After a few minutes, your eyes will adjust, and you'll start picking up detail. But if you turn on your headlamp, you'll destroy the ambiance and your sensitivity.

As for photography, you might want to give that a rest as well. We've all heard stories of outdoor photographers who report getting "closer to nature" through their art, and their claims may have some merit. But for the casual shooter, the camera is yet another distraction from full engagement. Remember, from a historical perspective, cameras are completely abnormal—not once did our Paleolithic ancestors look at a breathtaking sunset and wish they could get the shot.

Even more to the point, the very act of searching for ideal images distorts our understanding and appreciation of habitat. In our quest to capture the perfect image, we bypass most of what we see, including many features that would have been essential for finding food and staying alive. In a wild, natural environment, the clues that are essential to survival don't necessarily make for good pictures.

Even worse, the spectacular imagery we do capture tricks us into thinking that nature is just one fantastic light show, there solely for our entertainment. When people go into the outdoors with this expectation, many are disappointed to find that nature fails to live up to its billing. In a paradoxical way, spectacular nature photography (eco-porn) can actually turn us off to the genuine experience of enjoying the outdoor world. When tourists can buy spectacular postcards and calendars in the gift shop, there seems little point in actually going out into the park itself.

Ultimately, learning habitat is a question of attitude and relationship. To really learn the outdoor world, you'll have to abandon your cultural inclinations toward ownership, domination, and imperialism. You're not there to conquer the mountain, the land, or the river; you're a student, there to experience and learn. Forget what you know and engage your beginner's mind. Open your attention to everything you see and feel.

CHAPTER 22

MEET YOUR BIOREGION

> You cannot make the land go against itself. Not for long; the land will rebel. You must shape the vision to the land, not the land to the vision.
> —Loial the Ogier
> *The Eye of the World* by Robert Jordan

As our awareness of habitat deepens, we begin to feel more at one with the world, but we're also likely to reach some highly disruptive and inconvenient conclusions about culture-as-usual. We've noticed the lay of the land and the ways vegetation, rocks, and watersheds combine in recognizable patterns, and we're struck by a profound sense of dissonance. That is, the political and legal boundaries of our day bear almost no resemblance to the actual features of biology on the ground. The nations, states, counties, and jurisdictions that guide so much of our political and commercial behavior have almost no relationship to actual living ecosystems.

This disconnect is far more than an academic curiosity; it reveals something profoundly disturbing about our imperialistic relationship with the planet and, very often, one another. Our practice reveals not just an ignorance of habitat, but even contempt for it. When you're an alpha species, you lay down the lines wherever it pleases you. This land is our land, that land is your land, but it's all the humans' land. Earth is here to serve us, so get used to it.

Bioregionalism is the counterpoint to this flawed attitude. In the modern era, the idea dates back to the 1970s, championed by writers such as David Haenke and Kirkpatrick Sale and most famously by poet Gary Snyder. But bioregional thinking has actually been the dominant view for the vast majority of human history on Earth and is implicit in indigenous philosophy. Our current focus on arbitrary political states, regions, and districts is a recent, abnormal, and arguably insane way to subdivide the biosphere.

Any child who looks at straight lines overlaid on a map is likely to wonder what they have to do with the conditions she can see with her own eyes. She sees forests, watersheds, rivers, and oceans, but the big people say that well, no, there are actually invisible lines on the ground that must be honored. If you're standing on one side of the line, one set of rules applies, but if you're standing on the other side, it's another set entirely. To the child's way of thinking, this is just crazy.

In fact, nature doesn't care about our maps or our artificial borders. People who manage fisheries, water quality, pollution, and regional issues are coming to realize that forests, animals, oceans, atmospheres, wildfire smoke, and infectious microorganisms simply have no interest in human boundaries. Life does what it pleases.

Our modern practice of drawing arbitrary lines over living landscapes is really a kind of violence and habitat abuse, which is to say, self-abuse. The process is bad enough when it's used to chop political districts into awkward pieces to benefit political parties, but it's a thousand times worse when we use it to manipulate the biosphere for our own selfish ends. Naturally, artists have been quick to see the folly of our ways. In 1985, the Austrian artist Friedensreich Hundertwasser wrote a manifesto called "Paradise Destroyed by the Straight Line," declaring the straight line to be "godless and immoral."

Naturally, bioregionalism brings up a host of enormously inconvenient challenges. Suddenly, nationalism begins to look like a defunct, outdated concept. National boundaries forced onto the land by conquest, war, or even negotiated agreement are almost always homocentric and out of sync with nature. Even worse, as nation-states become firmly established, they give legitimacy to the idea that nature is nothing more than a two-dimensional stage for the human drama. After a few generations of nationalism, the concept begins to feel increasingly "normal."

Likewise, bioregionalism puts an entirely new frame on modern discussions of gerrymandering, the manipulation of voting districts for political advantage. What if we drew up bioregional districts instead? Instead of arguing about party affiliations and which kind of voters live in which neighborhoods, we'd draw the maps based on the lay of the land, watersheds, vegetation, and animal habitat. Forests would go with forests; grasslands would go with grasslands. In the process, every encounter with a biologically based region would remind us of our life-support system and the importance of the Earth. The beauty of bioregionalism is that it gives us a positive path forward. We can't seem to agree on much in the modern world, but we should at least be able to agree on the unity of the plants, animals, weather, and watersheds that characterize our region. In this way, bioregionalism would give us a sense of place and something real to rally around.

BIOREGIONAL ATHLETICS

In the meantime, we can practice. Whenever possible, try to draw attention to the unique ecology of the region you inhabit. Look for local foods and materials, and practice the cultivation of native plants. Likewise, give some thought to your sports and athletics. Thinking bioregionally, it suddenly seems absurd to travel long distances to do our movement practices and sports. Each bioregion has its own terrain characteristics that challenge our bodies in particular ways. If you live in the mountains, skiing, climbing, mountain biking, and hiking are the appropriate choices. If you live by the ocean, it's surfing. If you live in the plains, it's road biking and river sports.

The prime, original directive of the athletic enterprise is to move smoothly in the habitat you actually inhabit, in conditions that actually exist. Ice hockey in Las Vegas is absurd. Snowmaking is insane. If you have to get on an airplane to go play, you're missing opportunities right where you live. The time has come to stop with abstracted athletics and make our movement relevant to the places we live. In short, "Think globally, move locally."

BIOREGIONAL CULTURE

The beauty of bioregionalism is that it inspires us to create new forms of culture that honor actual conditions on the ground: cuisine, flags, narratives, songs, and stories that celebrate the unique natural history of our home bioregions. Likewise, use bioregional maps whenever possible. These maps show layers of geology, flora, and fauna and are powerful communication tools for advancing the bioregional narrative.

Bioregionalism is the way of our deep past, but it's also a path to a functional future. You may not be able to agree with your neighbor's political views, but you should at least be able to agree on the names of the plants that grow in your area, the animals that live there, and the way the weather comes and goes. It's common biological ground and a good place to start.

And as modern infrastructure collapses, we may well have to think bioregionally, whether we want to or not. One of the stark lessons of the coronavirus epidemic has been that global supply chains are probably not sustainable, economically or otherwise. In other words, each bioregion is going to have to fend for itself. When food and supplies no longer come to us from the other side of the planet, we'll have to start paying attention to the land around us.

CHAPTER 23

WILD BODY, WILD SPIRIT

> Society tames the wolf into a dog. And man is the most domesticated animal of all.
> —Friedrich Nietzsche

In a nutshell, the last ten thousand years has been a story of agriculture and domestication. First it was plants, then selected animals, and finally, people themselves. Plants were relatively easy, and the nonhuman animals took some work, but the people turned out to be a real challenge. It took thousands of years to bring wild people to heel, but today, many of us have become willing, sometimes even eager, participants in our own domestication.

If this had happened all at once, we would have noticed it immediately and rebelled. But yet again, it's the story of the frog in warming water. First we agree to wear clothing and shoes, then we agree to do the chores, attend school, and balance our checkbooks. We learn to be responsible and complete our tasks on time. We follow directions, and by the time we're finished with college, we're passive, compliant, and nonresistant, ideal subjects for life in a corporate world, where obedience is paramount. At this point, the domestication is complete, and our lives as wild animals are over.

So it's no surprise that we're suffering. We try to regain our health through all manner of substances and lifestyle tweaks, but we miss the larger point. That is, health is intimately tied to our original state of wildness. We might even say that wildness *is* health.

DEAL WITH THE DEVIL

The problem of domestication is that it systematically devitalizes the human spirit as it sucks the life out of the human animal. Domestication holds out the promise of wealth, security, power, and comfort, all at the cost of our animal vitality, our spirit and vagility.

On the face of it, it might sound like a good deal, but for most of us, it's a false promise, and for many, a lose-lose proposition.

The problem with wildness in the modern world is that it's a hugely inconvenient reality. Wildness disrupts the modern social order, reduces efficiency, and inhibits productivity. It makes us poor consumers and threatens the bottom line. It's no wonder that corporate wellness programs embrace relaxation, mindfulness, and similar practices but never encourage participants to embrace their animal nature. It's all "health and wellness," never "health and wildness."

In short, wildness is a threat to culture-as-usual. It's a revolutionary spirit. It resists incarceration of any sort, whether physical, spiritual, economic, or cognitive. It mistrusts pigeonholes, taxonomies, and human-created structures. Most of all, it distrusts social hierarchy and pyramid-shaped organizations. Wildness remembers its origins, and when threatened, it fights back.

THE DOMESTICATION CURRICULUM

Children are born wild, and if all goes well, they retain that spirit throughout their lives. But of course, we try to train it out of them. More or less intentionally, modern schools are designed to quash wildness and replace it with compliance. Learning is mostly beside the point. "Good students" sit still and do what they're told. Students with high energy and physical curiosity are accused of "acting out" and tagged with all manner of diagnostic labels, most of which have no medical basis whatsoever. If you act "wild," which is to say "normal," we'll medicate you, and if that fails, we'll kick you out of the tribe. In our modern opinion, wildness is deviant.

Naturally, this entire enterprise is doomed to fail. Wildness isn't just normal for the human animal; it's deeply embedded in every cell of every student's body. The young student has the entire history of the biosphere running through her body, the very same energy that pulses through every lion, tiger, and bear on the planet, every fish, every bird, every microbe. It's a fool's quest to try to repress this. Even if we succeed in the short term, the long-term blowback is catastrophic: epidemics of depression, anxiety, unhappiness, and suicide. This is what happens when animals are denied a chance to be who they are.

WARNING SIGNS

So how do we know if we've been duped into domestication? Warning signs include the following:

- Passive acceptance of the cultural and social status quo. Resignation: "There's nothing we can do."
- Your dreams, passions, and values aren't your own but are produced and handed to you by marketing departments.
- You reflexively go along to get along, even when your gut tells you to fight back.
- Your sense of identity and purpose is diffuse, weak, and vague. Depression nags at your soul. You'd like to follow your own path, but you don't dare rock the boat.

RECOVERY

For most of us in the modern world, our wildness is endangered. Our health is suffering and our spirits are weak. Many of us are content to accept this as our lot in life, and we visit all manner of health practitioners to set things right. But when we view it from a Big History perspective, we remember who we are and what we used to be. And now, some of us are inclined to say, "I'm in recovery from domestication."

And so the question becomes: How do we retain and regain our wildness in a world that does everything possible to make it go away? The obvious place to begin is with our physicality. When we're wild, we can feel the vitality coursing through our bodies, and we refresh that feeling with regular sessions of vigorous movement.

But sadly, the modern fitness industry misses the point. The industry promotes physical movement but labels it "exercise," something that we're supposed to do to "get in shape." At no point is there an attempt to connect the practice of movement with human or biological history. In one of the greatest ironies of the modern age, it seems that the fitness industry itself has become domesticated.

But while physicality is a necessary element of wildness, it's not enough to revive and sustain our spirit. To keep our wildness alive, we've got to act at every opportunity and at every level. Curiosity is a great starting point, and question-asking is a powerful path. Don't be content with the conventional boilerplate explanations. Don't just accept the standard methods or practices. Dig. Explore. Take charge of your education. Likewise, resistance and activism are vital. Speaking truth to power is a pure expression of our wildness. Risking for change refreshes and revives our spirits.

The problem with domestication is that it leads us toward resignation and defeatism. Beaten down by the modern world, we conclude that there's nothing that can be done. Not only is it possible to live with wildness, but we can actually use it to our advantage. Wildness doesn't just make us better animals; it can also make us better people and better citizens. Wildness doesn't turn you into a criminal or an outlaw. It turns you into an activist and a leader.

It's perfectly possible to live in the modern world and still keep one foot in the Paleo. We do this by way of memory, identity, and affiliation. Remember your deep history and your ancestry as a wild, outdoor animal. Remember your outrageous strength and adaptability. Which do you identify with? The dog or the wolf? The horse or the zebra? The common sheep or the mountain goat? The wild animals of the world are your "people," your team, your tribe, your soul mates. Think of them often.

Wildness is about health, but it's really about a lot more than that. Your wildness keeps your body strong, but it also keeps *us* strong and contributes to a functional future. As it stands, we are in grave danger of even more domestication, more robotic humanity, more passivity. And this, even beyond the rampant destruction of the biosphere, is a future that's unacceptable, a future that no self-respecting animal would want to live in.

In other words, your wildness is vital for all of us. Keep it alive.

CHAPTER 24

KEEP YOUR EYE ON THE AWE

> The smaller we come to feel ourselves compared to the mountain, the nearer we come to participating in its greatness.
>
> —Arne Næss

Something extraordinary happens when we're out in big nature, exposed to the splendor and magnificence of the natural world. It's pleasant and comforting to be in the presence of grand vistas, ancient forests, and rugged coastlines, but even more than that, the whole experience seems positively magical, even mystical. Prior to the pandemic of 2020, millions of people flocked to natural parks each year, all of us going in search of nature's grandeur. And while this kind of experience might strike many of us as spiritual, there's a lot more to it than you might think.

THE RESEARCH

Work by Professor Dacher Keltner at UC Berkeley shows that even a mild sense of awe can change attitudes and inspire prosocial behavior. People who watched a nature video that elicited awe were subsequently more ethical and generous and described themselves as being more connected to others—qualities that are commonplace in indigenous traditions. Keltner's team also found that awe makes people happier and less stressed, even weeks later. There's even a measurable health benefit. A study by Jennifer E. Stellar and Neha John-Henderson found that "positive emotions, especially awe, are associated with lower levels of proinflammatory cytokines."

Awe activates the parasympathetic nervous system, which works to calm the fight-or-flight response and dampen the production of toxic stress hormones. Awe also seems to help us break out of habitual thinking patterns and improves creativity. In other words, putting ourselves in contact with nature's magnificence is really good for us. We might even say that awe is a form of medicine.

Research by psychologists at Stanford and the University of Minnesota also shows that awe can increase well-being by giving people the sense that they have more time available, a condition known as *temporal affluence*. Keltner and Jonathan Haidt have also argued that awe is the ultimate collective emotion because it motivates people to do things that enhance the greater good. Research reported in the *Journal of Personality and Social Psychology* provides empirical support for this claim. The authors found that awe helps bind us to others, motivating us to act in collaborative ways that enable strong groups and cohesive communities. Which, of course, is an ideal quality for both ancestral and modern life.

HUMILITY AND THE AWE GAP

For those of us who've grown up in narcissistic modern cultures, the power of awe may seem counterintuitive. Most of us like feeling big and celebrating our status as the alpha species or alpha individuals, but awe in natural settings does its work in reverse. It shrinks the ego and our sense of self and, in turn, leaves more space in our consciousness for the rest of creation. Incredibly, Keltner found that when test subjects were awe-inspired, they actually signed their names smaller and drew themselves smaller. Other researchers have found that people who watched awe-inspiring videos estimated their bodies to be physically smaller than those who watched neutral videos.

All of which should give us pause. When we reflect on the radical differences between ancestral and modern environments, we're struck by what we might call an "awe gap." In a normal, outdoor Paleo world, the experience of awe would have been commonplace, even routine. Our ancestors were in daily contact with the magnificence and enormity of nature; thunderstorms, lightning displays, and animal dramas played out in real time, right before our eyes—life and blood on the grassland, fighting and fleeing just outside our camps. With no light pollution, the night sky would have blazed with an intensity that modern humans can scarcely imagine. And around a tribe's local habitat, vast reaches of unknown territory stretched to the horizon, home to anything a person might imagine. In other words, awe was a daily, health-promoting, prosocial experience.

But today, fewer and fewer of us ever go outside, and when we do, most of our parks are highly domesticated, regulated, noisy, and light polluted. Our experience of awe—such as it is—mostly derives from our contact with gee-whiz technological devices and spectacular special effects in the movies that we watch. This is massively reinforced by corporate marketing that attempts to attach our sense of awe to various products and services. In other words, our modern sense of awe is produced and managed, a plastic, manufactured, and pale imitation of the real thing.

And of course, the pandemic makes everything worse. Locked down in our homes, it's getting harder and harder to put ourselves in contact with nature's magnificence. Awe—and the health benefits that come with it—is becoming increasingly difficult to come by. We might even describe ourselves as "awe deprived." We don't hear much about this condition in the popular press, but judging from the research, it's safe to assume that this is a genuine challenge to public health and a medical condition in its own right.

The obvious solution, difficult as it may be, is to get outside—way outside. Get out of yourself and expose yourself to the outrageous power of sky, earth, wind, and water. City parks and green spaces are all well and good, but to really find the awe, you've got to expose your body and spirit to the enormity of the living Earth.

Likewise, don't allow yourself to be content with the artificial awe that's forced upon us in nearly every waking moment. Even if you can't get outside, you can still find awe in the study of human history and the depth and variety of the human experience. The great sagas of adventure, discovery, and the search for meaning can give us a sense of the enormity and magnificence of our world. Then, as soon as you're able, go to the big places, so you can feel really small.

CHAPTER 25

RADICAL REMEMBERING

> Not knowing who you are is a certain kind of hell.
> —Kelly Thompson
> *The Girl Who Would Be King*

Humanity has a memory problem. Or to put it another way, we have a crippling case of collective amnesia. We've forgotten how to be normal, which is to say we've forgotten how to be true to our bodies, our tribes, our habitat, and our evolutionary heritage. We're so consumed with the urgencies of the modern world that we're in grave danger of losing contact with the experiences, skills, and ideas that make us human, whole, and healthy.

We can see this amnesia in the decay of human vitality, resilience, and physicality that's been unfolding across the planet in recent decades. We're all familiar with lifestyle diseases such as obesity, diabetes, and all the rest, but this is something deeper, more fundamental, and more disturbing: a perplexing weakness of the human organism and erosion of the human spirit. Virus or no virus, the body is in decline, and people are in trouble. In short, modern humans are in very real danger of losing psycho-physical contact with the native biological power that sustains our bodies and our lives.

In our amnesia, we've lost contact with our native physicality and our identity as animals. We've forgotten the ancient, primal power that courses through every cell in our bodies, every minute of every day. We are sleepwalking through life, largely unaware of who we are or what we are capable of. It's no wonder we're suffering from so much disease and malaise; this deep amnesia is a kind of disease in itself.

To put it another way, we're like confused superheroes. We've got the cape and the boots and a vague expectation that maybe we ought to be doing something extraordinary, but we just can't feel our power. And so we stumble through life, only half-effective, falling prey to all sorts of pathologies, afflictions, and disease states. We're inexplicably confused about our nature and our potential.

This amnesia may well sound like an insignificant quirk of the human mind, a neurological annoyance, something akin to forgetting your phone number or where you left your car keys. But this is a very real affliction, just as dangerous as any virus. Not only does it weaken us as individuals, but it also puts our entire society and biosphere at risk. When people lose contact with the power and immensity of nature, they're moved to compensate and look for power elsewhere—in social status and wealth, and in ever-more-powerful and Earth-hostile machines, tools, vehicles, and weapons.

In this sense, our entire ecological crisis may be understood as a consequence of our collective forgetting. If we truly felt the power of the biosphere coursing through our bodies, a simple walk in the woods would be more than enough.

The essential thing to understand is that life on Earth is a singular force. The plants and animals around us appear to be many, diverse, and separate from one another, but in fact, they are part of a unitary process of generation, a biological tsunami that has swept across the globe in a three-billion-year wave of outrageous creativity. Rachel Carson put it perfectly:

> To understand biology is to understand that all life is linked to the Earth from which it came; it is to understand that the stream of life, flowing out of the dim past into the uncertain future, is in reality a unified force, though composed of an infinite number and variety of separate lives.

So how would our confused superhero feel if she suddenly woke up to the immensity of biological evolution flowing through every cell in her body? To use a wildly overused word in a perfectly appropriate context, it would be *awesome*. Our superhero would be transformed, awake, energized. No longer isolated in an epic struggle against the forces of evil, she'd feel the power of the entire biosphere in every cell. Every living thing would be an ally, every ecosystem a partner. With the totality of biological evolution at her back, she'd be a surfer on a magnificent, living, blue-green wave.

In theory, every living thing should feel this power in every minute of every day, but modern humans generally don't. So what gets in the way? How could we have become oblivious to something so vast, so vital, so ancient, and so deeply embodied? How could we have come to such a point that nature is considered an alien power, separate and outside ourselves? How could we possibly feel so powerless?

In part, this radical forgetting is a product of the nervous system itself. When something in our world is familiar, we pay less attention, which, in the context of evolutionary history, is exactly as it should be. New things grab our attention because they might be dangerous; familiar things are less likely to chase us down and eat us. And so the paradox of our amnesia: immense power lives in our bodies at all times, but because it's been with us in every moment, we forget to notice it or feel it.

But an even bigger obstacle is the distraction machine we call modern culture. Everywhere we go, we're constantly under siege by marketing, advertising, and a million blips, chirps, flashes, and tweets. Noise is everywhere, stealing our attention away from the primal processes that sustain us. And who can possibly feel the power of the biosphere when every waking moment is obscured with "buy now" and "donate now" messages?

Add to this the failure of the medical profession to take our continuity with life seriously. To the typical physician, medicine is little more than measurement, test results, and the administration of specific therapies. These methods serve a limited clinical purpose, but they don't come anywhere near to connecting the patient to the powerful, health-promoting processes that sustain our lives. At best, this is a missed opportunity to promote the patient's welfare; at worst, it's a waste of everyone's time and resources.

So how does our confused superhero wake up to her power? How does she remember the incredible life force—the original medicine—that flows through every fiber of her being? A few possibilities spring to mind: The first is experiential. This is where we feel our power through active, physical engagement with movement in habitat. Hiking, climbing, backpacking, surfing, and biking all offer this potential, especially when we take our attention off competition and put it onto what really matters.

Or we might find the connection through meditation and imagination. Sit down, focus on your breath, your body, and the power that flows from the biosphere into every cell. Feel the awesome history of life; you are part of this. Feel the life that surges through oceans and rain forests; you are part of this. Feel the vitality of every plant and animal in the world; you are part of this. Slow down and feel; you are a participant in something outrageously creative.

Or we can take a cognitive approach. Refresh your study of Big History and biology. Read the science about the origins of life and the immense reaches of biological time. Study the work of Humboldt, Darwin, Stephen Jay Gould, and Richard Dawkins. Learn about the tree of life, the great extinction events, and the great flowerings of biodiversity. Once you grasp the staggering depth and power of our biological drama, you'll be amazed and forever changed.

As we stand on the brink of ecological collapse, most of us are swamped by a sense of powerlessness, and the commonly recommended solutions don't really help. Recycling seems pale and vaporous. Voting for sane, green candidates is obviously worth doing, but even this doesn't feel like much. In contrast, radical remembering is something all of us can do, and even better, it's something with truly transformative potential. When we feel the life flowing through our bodies, we become engaged at the deepest possible level. If even a small percentage of our human population turned their attention away from distraction and toward the living world, the ripple effects would be profound.

This understanding also tells us something vitally important about the job description for the world's trainers, coaches, teachers, therapists, and health professionals. We all have content to share—practices, information, knowledge, and methods—but underneath it all must be a single imperative: to remind our students, clients, and patients of their continuity with all of life on Earth. This is the primal teaching and, without question, some of the most important work on the planet. We might even call it sacred.

CHAPTER 26

JOB QUALIFICATIONS

> I pledge allegiance to the soil of Turtle Island,
> and to the beings who thereon dwell one ecosystem
> in diversity under the sun
> With joyful interpenetration for all.
> —Gary Snyder

So you want to lead our country, our nation, our community? Well, we might ask, what are you bringing to the table?

In conventional circles, experts tell us that if we want to succeed in politics, it's a good idea to start with law school. In fact, this is often seen as the primary ticket for admission. If nothing else, lawyers at least know the rules of the game and will be able to navigate the complexities of constitutions, contracts, civil disputes, and criminal matters.

But how did we ever get to this point? How did we come to assume that graduation from law school makes a person qualified to lead us through the morass of modern life and a biospheric emergency? After all, the language of the law, noble as it often is, is simply a modern, recent, and arguably abnormal way to organize and manage human relationships. For the vast majority of human history, there were no written laws, and even more to the point, tribal leadership depended on an entirely different set of qualifications.

It must have been different in every tribe, but we can well imagine that our early leaders must have gained stature by way of charisma, physical presence, and the respect of others, earned through authentic experience, on the ground and in service of the tribe. Specifically, the tribal elder would have been expected to know the lay of the land, the ways of plants and animals, and the subtle qualities of the local bioregion. This much would have been completely obvious, and in fact, no one would have bothered to boast about it. No one would have put forward a résumé to brag about their knowledge of local flora and fauna. In the Paleo, everyone was a naturalist.

But today, we hire and elect leaders with absolutely no knowledge of or even interest in biological life on the ground. Knowledge of one's bioregion is never even considered as a job qualification for political office. If you happen to know everything about constitutional law, contracts, or the criminal code, you're considered a powerful applicant, but if your area of expertise is watersheds, plants, or animals, voters just shrug. It's safe to assume that no modern candidate for office ever bragged about their knowledge of ecosystem dynamics. And in some circles, knowledge of regional biology might even be considered a negative qualification and a liability—a marker of dangerous liberal politics.

All of which should be an enormous red flag to anyone who's interested in a functional future. It also suggests a simple, practical way to evaluate candidates and applicants for public office and leadership positions. Knowing basic legal concepts might well be desirable, but it's nowhere near sufficient for actually taking the reins in a wickedly complex, biological world.

In this spirit, we might imagine town hall meetings with potential candidates. Instead of asking prospective candidates about their law school careers or their entrepreneurial successes, we'd do a lot better to ask about their contact with the living planet:

"What are your biological qualifications?"

"How well do you understand the flora and fauna of our bioregion?"

"What do you think about the state of our watershed?"

"How do you feel about dissolving the artificial political boundaries that divide and fragment healthy ecosystems?"

If these questions strike him or her as absurd, maybe it's time to find another candidate.

CHAPTER 27

COGITO ERGO DUMB

> If you have a body, where is the spirit?
> If you're a spirit, what is the body?
> This is not our problem to worry
> about. Both are both.
>
> —Rumi

As legend has it, the young René Descartes aspired to be a great philosopher and was determined to get to the ultimate root of human knowledge. He resolved to doubt everything and even went so far as to doubt his own physical sensations. After all, he mused, there might be an unseen evil demon at work, pumping false sensory information into his brain—and how would he ever know? His brain might very well be floating in a vat of liquid, subject to the inputs of a mad operator with a hidden agenda; there was simply no way to tell.

So for Descartes, sensation was off the table as a reliable source of knowledge. And because the body was not to be trusted, all that was left was the mind, and in turn, this became his ultimate touchstone and identity. "I think, therefore I am," he famously declared. The body became irrelevant, except as a life-support system for his prodigious feats of cognition.

Descartes's work was profoundly influential in his day, and he eventually became an icon of Western civilization. We have thoroughly incorporated his philosophy into our culture and our institutions, and today we honor the mind while neglecting the body. We think, therefore we are; we are physical, therefore we are not. In effect, Descartes amputated the body and the emotions from the human experience in what physicians might call a "bodyectomy." In this paradigm, the body is little more than a locomotor device for the head. As Sherlock Holmes put it, "I am a brain, my dear Watson, and the rest of me is a mere appendage."

But indigenous people would have found Descartes's ideas to be not just strange, but abhorrent. Why would anyone ever want to doubt the sensations coming from his or her body? What good could possibly come from such an exercise? The body is our primary connection to habitat and survival; it would be folly of the highest order to doubt one's physical sensations. On the contrary, the whole point of practice in hunting is to sharpen your sensitivity and learn to trust what your body is telling you. In a Paleo setting, Descartes would have been laughed out of the tribe in short order.

And so, in spite of the fact that he's been dead for over three hundred years, Descartes remains the biggest man on the university campus. We honor the students of the mind and devalue those who study human physicality. We accept and promote an outdated mind-over-body caste system handed to us centuries ago, a system that now appears increasingly archaic, unhealthy, and even absurd.

Unfortunately, there's a huge price to be paid for this value system. When we put the body at the bottom of our hierarchy, we shouldn't be surprised to find a sedentary population completely out of touch with their physicality. We shouldn't be surprised to find an epidemic of physical apathy and psychological distress. The mind and the body want to be one thing, but when this is denied, trouble is bound to follow.

Even worse, the values of the university cascade downward through the rest of our educational system: high schools mimic colleges, elementary schools mimic high schools. In the process, the body becomes devalued across the board. If resources are tight and something needs to be cut, PE is always the first to go. Test scores are vital, we're told, but the body is expendable.

This ranking system plays out all across the health and medical landscape. Most of our modern lifestyle disease epidemics—heart disease, diabetes, depression, and obesity—are at least somewhat preventable, and yet we take almost no preemptive, upstream action. Instead, we wait for physical conditions to grow into full-blown diseases and then hand the problem off to the medical Cartesians at the top of the pyramid. When they succeed, we heap praise upon their heroic measures, but when they fail, we write it off as an intractable social problem.

The tragic irony is that Cartesian dualism has been soundly refuted by one hundred years of solid research into mind–body relationships. We now know without question that the mind and body are indivisible. The conversation between tissue and cognition is complementary; the mind drives the body, and the body drives the mind.

Neuroscientist Antonio Damasio describes this integrated relationship in *Descartes' Error*:

> The human brain and the rest of the body constitute an indissociable organism, integrated by means of mutually interactive biochemical and neural regulatory circuits (including

endocrine, immune, and autonomic neural components) . . . The organism interacts with the environment as an ensemble: the interaction is neither of the body alone nor of the brain alone . . . The physiological operation that we call mind is derived from the structural and functional ensemble rather than from the brain alone: *mental phenomena can be fully understood only in the context of an organism's interacting in an environment.*

Because of the tight interrelationship between mind and body, it is folly to put one above the other. Mind and body ought to be studied and enjoyed in equal proportion, as yin and yang. Rather than a totem pole with hard science on top and PE at the bottom, we ought to imagine a circle, with mind and body in intimate conversation with one another.

Our conventional academic hierarchy makes even less sense now that the "dumb-jock" myth is finally being laid to rest. Hundreds of research studies have proven beyond question that vigorous physical movement is good for the brain and, in turn, intelligence. Far from being dumb, people who move their bodies do better across a wide span of cognitive challenges. In short, movement makes us smarter.

Some will continue to cling to the dumb-jock mythology, of course, but the prejudice is getting weaker every day. We now know that physical movement promotes neurogenesis, the birth of new brain cells, and synaptogenesis, the growth of neural connections. Vigorous movement also promotes the production of brain-derived neurotrophic factor (BDNF), sometimes described as "Miracle-Gro for the brain." Vigorous movement also reduces the corrosive effects of stress hormones, which in turn preserves the function of the hippocampus, the brain's essential memory center.

ALTERNATIVES

As we ponder the long reach of Cartesian dualism and its pathological effects on human health, we might well wonder how different our world would be if Descartes had been an athlete, a dancer, or a hunter-gatherer. Instead of doubting his senses, he would have learned to trust and sharpen them. His attention would have gone out into the world, and in turn, his philosophical writings would have been more integrative. He would have emphasized relationship and connection.

And so we imagine ourselves teaching and coaching the young René, getting him out of his office and out onto the land. We'd have him run the trails and climb the mountains of Europe. We'd teach him to develop and trust his sensory capabilities. We'd give him lots of multiplane movement to stimulate fresh connections in his nervous system. We'd drag him out of the library and into the open air and help him see the magic of human physicality.

It was not inevitable that Descartes would mistrust the body and choose to identify with the mind. Given a different life experience or a creative coach, he might have come to entirely different conclusions:

"I feel, therefore I am."
"I dance, therefore I am."
"I move, therefore I am."
"I create, therefore I am."
"I love, therefore I am."
"I am physical, therefore I am."

Just imagine how different the world would be today.

CHAPTER 28

THE PHYSICAL LIFE

> I am not one of those who neglect the body
> in order to make of it a sacrificial offering
> for the soul, since my soul would thoroughly
> dislike being served in such a fashion.
> —Rilke

> The body says what words cannot.
> —Martha Graham

Exercise is dead. It's a product of the modern industrial revolution, something we can tell just by looking: gyms that look suspiciously like factories, treadmills and machines in perfect rows, people tracking every rep with digital devices.

Most of us are accustomed to such settings, but in fact, this is all profoundly abnormal. Prior to the industrial age, people simply didn't exercise. In general, they got plenty of physical movement in the course of their daily lives. First hunting and gathering, then dance, agriculture, and walking and occasionally running to get around. For the vast majority of our history, we've been moving our bodies, entirely without the help of gyms, machines, trainers, loud music, or protein shakes.

The same holds true for nonhuman animals. We never observe other mammals doing anything resembling exercise. They hunt, gather, graze, mate, play, fight, and flee, but never do they perform repetitive movements for the sake of "staying in shape." They move their bodies for pleasure, to explore, or to stay alive, but otherwise, they eat or rest.

This suggests a broader view and a new appreciation for context.

When we exercise, we engage in a physical specialization, but when we move, we put ourselves back into community with every animal that's ever lived. Instead of isolating ourselves in specialized facilities with specialized machines, we're sharing in a common experience with every primate and every mammal, a deep heritage that goes back more than a hundred million years. When we move our bodies, we celebrate our kinship with the natural world and make ourselves part of something much, much larger than ourselves.

And it's movement, not exercise, that keeps us healthy. Across the board, research shows that all forms of physical movement are health promoting and that exercise is only one possibility among many. This realization leads us to a powerful general principle: when it comes to maintaining health, exercise is optional, but movement is essential. No one ever died from a lack of exercise, but a lack of physical movement is absolutely dangerous to health. As long as we're getting vigorous movement during the course of our days, we might just as well skip the exercise altogether. Instead of setting aside big chunks of time to perform stereotyped exercise in specialized facilities, our challenge is to weave movement back into the fabric of our daily lives. If we can make our lives more vigorous, our health will largely take care of itself.

LEAPFROGGING

We also miss the point in modern educational settings when we train our students in isolated movement specialties, otherwise known as sports. Sports, like exercise, are fundamentally unique in human history. Athletic advocates like to point to the Olympic games of ancient Greece, but this is really part of modern history and, as such, is not really very ancient at all. To get the complete picture, we need to see the entire scope of human history, and in this world, the primary movement challenges were always hunting, gathering, walking, running, and more recently, dance.

This gets right to the heart of our modern problem with the human body and physical education programs. That is, we ignore our history, our ancestry, and the ultimate nature of our bodies. We act as if the body simply fell from the sky one fine day, out of shape and in desperate need of conditioning. Even worse, we fail to prepare our young athletes with developmental training. Instead, we set them up with dreams of stardom and intensive, professionalized programs. It's no surprise that so many of today's young athletes get injured.

This is not to say that sports have no value; they often do. But it is to say that sports should come later, after a primary movement curriculum of walking, running, climbing, jumping, and other functional movements. Starting a training program with sports is very much a case of putting the cart in front of the horse.

Likewise, we might well ask what function sports serve in our ambiguous and uncertain new world. Is there any relevance here at all? How might the ability to throw a ball serve us in a world of ecosystem collapse and social chaos? Today, it's becoming increasingly difficult to make the case that sports are of much use or value to anyone besides the fans, owners, and occasionally, the players. When the adversity hits the fan, what we really want are physical generalists, people who are strong and athletic but capable of functioning in any kind of setting. Sports may well be fun and exciting, but we're going to need more than fun and excitement if we're going to build a functional future.

Not only that, but professionalized sports training tends to be elitist, built on a sorting process in which weaker participants are relentlessly weeded out by competition. In the end, this gives us a small crop of incredibly talented athletes but leaves everyone else in the dust. It's good for spectators and the elite athletes themselves, but it doesn't work well for a society that aims to be inclusive. Can't we devise a system in which all the people get to play?

DO SOMETHING YOU LOVE

Movement is the way to go, but many of us are inclined to wonder what kind of discipline is best for our bodies and our health. With hundreds of options to choose from, it's easy to get confused, but the short answer is that it's all good. Every movement discipline, from the most meditative tai chi practice to the most explosive gymnastics, tends to promote health. Personality and preference have a lot to do with our choices and our success, but ultimately, it comes down to the actual doing. That's why more and more public health specialists advise us to "Do the thing that you'll actually do" and "Do something that you love." Try a bunch of disciplines, and when something turns you on, stick with it.

All the movement arts are good, but for best results, it's important to keep your eyes on function. Ditch the mirrors and the camera and stop thinking about how you look. Ultimately, it's our ability to move powerfully, gracefully, and effectively that counts. For this, the simplest human movement patterns are actually the best: basic locomotion patterns of walking and running, especially on naturally diverse outdoor terrain, along with climbing, lifting, carrying, and dancing.

Above all, concentrate your attention on challenges that are relevant to your daily life in the real world. Machine training is only appropriate if your goal is to get good at using machines. Free weights are best because they mimic actual objects that we are likely to lift: children, boxes, tools, construction materials, ladders, and furniture. Don't get distracted by the details of obscure methodologies or esoteric training programs. Instead, focus on what makes sense in relationship to the life you're living.

Also, don't get distracted by the concept of mandatory "workouts." Like exercise, the workout is an invention of the modern, industrial mind, a concept that has no precedent in human history. A better idea is to practice frequent "movement snacks," short periods of movement, repeated often throughout the day. These modest efforts won't turn you into an Olympian, but they will keep you happy and healthy.

In any case, there's no need to get fancy with any of this; practice the moves that you want to do for the rest of your life. Imagine your life ten or twenty years from now: What kind of activity do you want to be doing? Your answer will inform your practice.

Above all, the essential ingredient is not the number of sessions you do or the specifics of your training. Rather, the essential element is your connection with your physicality. Refresh your memory, again and again. When was the last time you felt the vitality coursing through your body? Do whatever it takes to sustain your vitality and your wildness.

BUILD THE RELATIONSHIP

Ultimately, our success or failure as physical beings depends on our relationship with our bodies, but sadly, this quality is mostly ignored by conventional culture. We obsess over techniques, substances, celebrities, and all manner of diets, hoping that we'll wake up one day in good condition. And in modern medical practice, it's almost unheard of for a physician to ask relational questions or teach relational orientations. As a consequence, people's relationships with their bodies are often reactive, driven by culture.

There are two dominant styles in popular circulation, both of them abnormal: In the adversarial relationship, we see the body as something to be punished into condition. This is most obvious in elite training programs where athletes push themselves to the brink on a regular basis. This is where we hear all manner of tough talk and dark humor: "Pain is just weakness leaving the body." Athletes pride themselves in driving their bodies to the outer limits of exertion, and in this, the body is treated as a distinct "other." The duality is obvious.

At the other end of the spectrum is the apathetic relationship. In this, the body is simply ignored. This is a life of minimal exertion and minimal engagement; physicality is something to be avoided. Even worse, there's no real curiosity about what the body is capable of. Armed with modern transport, power tools, and conveniences, the body can safely be disregarded until such time as something breaks. The body is a distant, even irrelevant, "other." Once again, the duality is obvious.

Clearly, the relational sweet spot lies in the middle, in what we might call a "conversational relationship." In this state, we're in intimate participation with our physicality, driven by curiosity and celebration. We push when we need to push, but it's all in collaboration. We move often and vigorously, but always listening and paying attention. The body is not *other*; it's our most intimate and powerful ally.

This, far more than the details of diet and exercise, is the priority that we ought to be sharing and developing with our students, clients, and patients. Once we get the relationship right, most other things will tend to fall into place, but if we get the relationship wrong, nothing else matters.

CHAPTER 29

THE KINDERGARTEN MODEL

> The goal of life is to make your heartbeat
> match the beat of the universe to
> match your nature with Nature.
>
> —Joseph Campbell

Once again, it's time to remember our lives in prehistory, long before the first hoe, before the first fences, plows, tractors, and fossil fuels. Imagine that you've been sleeping out with your tribe, clustered around the campfire, dreaming of animals and roaming the spirit world. As the first light appears in the sky, you awaken, and someone tells you it's time to move. The elders have decided that today, you'll join a hunting party to explore a distant valley on the other side of the river. It's going to be a big day.

Your party leaves camp at a brisk pace, traversing a familiar wash that you've explored many times before, but by midday, you're on new ground, alert for predators, scanning for tracks, scat, and any other signs that will tell the story of animal life. As the afternoon unfolds, you've crossed miles of open ground, including some hilly terrain, and forded a crocodile-infested river. By the time the sun reaches the horizon, you realize that you're going to be out that night and all day tomorrow as well. You're feeling strong, but the exertions are beginning to draw down your reserves.

It's three long days before you finally circle back to camp. The hunt was successful, and you return with a small antelope, some scavenged meat, and a new understanding of your bioregion. You're excited to be back in camp, but after the welcome, some stories, and a feast, you're feeling the effects. Your feet are tender, your legs are sore, and you've got a nasty bruise from when you slipped on the river crossing. Now you're ready to relax.

Which is exactly what you do. For the next three or four days, the whole tribe takes it easy, lounging in the shade, sleeping as much as possible, gossiping, eating, and observing the world. There's no urgency to do anything, and there's plenty of time to just rest. Your body takes full advantage of the lull and begins the work of repairing damaged tissues and replenishing energy stores. After a few days, you're ready to head out once again.

In their 1988 book *The Paleolithic Prescription*, anthropologists Eaton, Shostak, and Konner described this oscillating pattern of hunting and resting in native people as the "Paleolithic rhythm." Without question, this pattern of serious exertion and deep rest is the norm for human beings. Our bodies thrive on this kind of rhythm. If we're going to restore our vitality, this would be a very good place to begin.

ATHLETIC RHYTHM

Not surprisingly, we also see the power of rhythmic engagement in modern athletic training. If you're a professional athlete or serious amateur, you know the formula for success: when you're training, hit it really hard, but when resting, rest really deep. Go to the gym, the track, or the pool and put in your best possible effort for a couple of hours, then spend the rest of your day listening to music, napping, and lounging. Your body will love it.

Athletic coaches recognize this pattern as an ideal way to build and repair tissue and reorganize the body's nervous system for maximum performance. The body thrives on this kind of oscillation, and the higher the contrast, the better. To put it in technical terms, challenge plus rest promotes "supercompensation," the process by which the body remodels tissue in anticipation of similar future challenges. Typically, we think of muscle tissue, but supercompensation takes place throughout the body: bone, connective tissue, and nervous system circuits all become more robust with oscillations of effort. When we keep this beat, our bodies respond by giving us more of what we need.

HABITAT RHYTHM

But that's just the beginning. The body thrives on all sorts of rhythmic contrast. For example, the temperature oscillation in the natural outdoor habitat pumps our tissue, increases circulation, and makes us feel good. Hot, then cold, and repeat. We see this in various home remedies and hydrotherapy practices, but it's also a normal feature of an ancestral environment. Life on the grassland was always a high-contrast experience: hot during the day, cold at night, always changing, always promoting circulation and adaptation. This is also why going to the mountains is so incredibly health-promoting; the alpine environment is constantly pumping our bodies.

This is also why modern air-conditioned dwellings and workplaces are health-negative. When the air temperature is constant for weeks and months on end, the body has no incentive to adapt. Our tissue just doesn't get pumped by temperature change, and in turn, metabolism stagnates. The end result is sluggishness and lethargy, even psycho-physical afflictions such as apathy and depression.

We even see the power of rhythm in the world of high-intensity cognitive and professional labor, where performance experts recommend a high-contrast pattern for success. Engage completely with focused effort, then disconnect. Just like muscle tissue, the nervous system needs time to rest and reenergize.

Tony Schwartz, author of *The Way We're Working Isn't Working*, puts it this way: "Don't manage your time, manage your energy." Instead of grinding out long, chronic sessions of partial engagement, focus on your work with the maximum possible intensity, then step away. It may feel less productive in the short term, but your body and your brain will function at a much higher level. Think of it as a kind of cognitive athletic training. Work hard, then rest deep.

THE KINDERGARTEN MODEL

Rhythmic effort is something that children understand instinctively: play hard for a few hours, rest deep, then repeat. No instruction required. This primal rhythm is powerfully anabolic for their bodies and their nervous systems. If they can maintain this pulse throughout childhood, there's a good chance that their bodies will grow strong and capable. But if the rhythm is disrupted by invasive adults and regimented, artificial programs, things are likely to go astray.

Call this the *kindergarten model*, if you will: play and explore, then take a nap. Students of all ages need this, and it ought to be built into our culture, our programs, and our institutions. If we were truly serious about crafting education that is consistent with what we know about human neurobiology, our schools would look entirely different. Not only would school start later in the day, but there would also be more breaks for both students and teachers alike. We'd also pay more attention to seasonal rhythms. Do the academic work indoors in the wintertime, but when the weather gets better, it's time for everyone to go outside.

The Paleolithic–athletic–childhood rhythm is a proven formula for physical training and health, and we'd do well to assume that it works for artistic creation as well: music, painting, photography, drawing, sculpture. Dive in with your most concentrated effort, sustain it as long as you can, then back off and rest deep. Naturally, there will be plenty of individual variation here, but the rhythm should still hold. Short bouts with long rests, or long bouts with short rests. Try to feel what your body wants and go with it.

The same must be true in the world of activism. It makes no sense to bang your head against the power structure day in and day out; you'll just burn out. Instead, engage, then regroup. Fight the fight with as much intensity as you can muster, then retreat to the comfort of your home. Speak truth to power, then pamper yourself. You're in this for the long haul, so take care of yourself.

UNITED STATES OF ARRHYTHMIA

All this talk about the power of rhythm makes perfect sense, but it's becoming harder and harder to find a natural, rhythmic life in the modern world. The problem goes back to the dawn of the industrial revolution, especially the introduction of the steam engine and the power loom in England in the early eighteenth century. Local communities suddenly found themselves up against a massively disruptive force as the normal flux and flow of village life were forced into a regimented pattern of factory life and workforce capitalism. No longer could people work at a leisurely, rhythmic, organic pace that enhanced their health. Instead, they were forced to work at factory speeds, machines taking priority over human bodies and human lives. The Luddites rebelled, but they were eventually defeated by a corporate–government alliance. The capitalists won, and the body lost.

Likewise, the introduction of artificial light further eroded our experience of organic rhythm. By the end of the seventeenth century, many European cities had some form of artificial light, and darkness has been under assault ever since. Today it's no exaggeration to say that we're suffering from a very real darkness deficit. According to the World Atlas of artificial night sky brightness, two-thirds of the world's population no longer experiences a truly dark night, and eight out of every ten children born today will never see the Milky Way.

The problem intensified in the early twentieth century when management consultant Frederick Winslow Taylor introduced a series of "time and motion" studies into the workplace. As he calculated it, a worker could move so many shovels of coal in an hour, and this became the performance standard that workers were expected to adhere to. Taylor's methods were widely adopted, and by the late twentieth century, a twenty-four-hour global economy led to an always-on work style and the near obliteration of natural human rhythms. There can be no question that this trend contributes to widespread disease in the human body and spirit. In other words, our destruction of natural rhythm constitutes a massive public health crisis.

BE YOUR OWN COACH

So how are we supposed to function rhythmically in a modern flatline world? We can't expect much support from established institutions or programs, so we've got to take matters into our own hands. Be your own coach and map out your highs and lows as best you can. Plan your high-intensity efforts and your deep rest. Resist the workaholic pressures of our age and keep your own creative pace. Be ambidextrous and flexible. Don't get trapped into any single psycho-physical mode or value system. When working, hit it really hard; when resting, let it go.

Contrast is the key. Keep to the kindergarten model and you won't go too far wrong.

CHAPTER 30

NIGHTLIFE

> Even a soul submerged in sleep is hard at work
> and helps make something of the world.
> —Heraclitus

For most of our history on Earth, sleep has been a simple pleasure, a mystery, and a fundamental part of the human experience. Throughout the Paleo, people went to sleep when they felt the need, and no one seemed to fret over the details. It's impossible to say precisely how old sleep is, but we can be sure that the roots go deep. All of our mammalian ancestors slept, and it's probable that dinosaurs slept as well. Paleontologists have recently discovered several fossilized skeletons of dinosaurs in what look like sleeping positions. Even jellyfish, some of the oldest creatures on the planet, show sleeplike behavior.

Without question, sleep is an integral part of our physiology and something we ought to honor and respect, but in the modern world, we simply don't. Today we live in an achievement culture where human value is measured by the ability to produce. People are considered worthy if they can get a lot done, and in this environment, sleep is considered a nuisance and even an adversary. We idolize people who claim to get by with less sleep, and in many circles, people who do sleep are considered slackers, a point of view voiced most notably by Thomas Edison, who declared sleep to be "a criminal waste of time."

To make matters worse, our modern environment is distinctly sleep-hostile. Our homes are often plagued by noise and light pollution, and hotels are commonly located next to freeways, and the rooms themselves are rarely dark or quiet. Even campgrounds in the mountains are no longer refuges for sleep; late arrivals and partiers keep the noise going until the small hours. It seems there's no place left that's truly dark, quiet, and safe to rest our heads.

THE STATE OF SLEEP AND DREAMS

Our problems with sleep began hundreds of years ago, with the advent of artificial light, a trend documented in powerful detail by Paul Bogard in *The End of Night: Searching for Natural Darkness in an Age of Artificial Light*. By the end of the seventeenth century, many European cities had some form of artificial light, and darkness has been under assault ever since. As Bogard tells it, we're now suffering from a very real darkness deficit. Most people are so awash in artificial light that their eyes never make a complete transition to night vision.

Not surprisingly, a substantial body of research concludes that most people in the modern world are substantially sleep-deprived. In general, most of us go to bed too late and get up too early. A Gallup poll found that the average number of sleep hours per night dropped from almost 8 in 1942 to 6.8 in

2013. And as the world warms and nights become hotter, sleep is projected to become even shorter.

The consequences of sleep deprivation are no laughing matter: poor memory, increased impulsiveness, poor judgment, decreased creativity, weight gain, muscle atrophy, suppressed immunity, and increased stress have all been linked to inadequate or poor-quality sleep. In 2005, the National Sleep Foundation found that 75 percent of American adults experienced sleep problems at least a few nights per week. According to Rubin Naiman at the Arizona Center for Integrative Medicine in Tucson, sleep disorders are arguably "the most prevalent health concern in the industrialized world."

But our problem goes even deeper. Research suggests that rapid eye movement (REM) sleep—the period of our most powerful dreaming—is vital to learning and creativity, but as sleep gets shorter, we also suffer an epidemic of REM sleep loss. "We are at least as dream-deprived as we are sleep-deprived," says Naiman. In essence, we're depriving ourselves of a free, easy form of cognitive and spiritual renewal.

Compounding the problem is the fact that alcohol, marijuana, and antidepressants are REM suppressants. The popularity of these substances no doubt contributes significantly to an epidemic of dream-deprivation and, in turn, our struggles in adapting to the modern world. We have no idea what the ultimate consequences of population-scale dream-deprivation might be, but it's unlikely to be a pretty picture. In days to come, we may well consider dream-deprivation to be a public health crisis in its own right.

WHY SLEEP IS VITAL

Contrary to the popular, modern belief, sleep is not an indulgence; it is absolutely vital for everything we want to do in our lives. Sleep is a heightened anabolic state—a time for the growth and rejuvenation of the immune, nervous, skeletal, and muscular systems. Certain restorative genes are turned on only during sleep, brain function and memory consolidation are enhanced, genes promoting myelin formation are turned on, creativity increases, and synapses are strengthened. Not surprisingly, sleep, learning, and mental well-being are tightly linked. Some researchers have even taken to describing sleep as "overnight therapy." If sleep came in a bottle, it would—along with physical movement—be the most powerful medicine on Earth.

Sadly, many of us are tortured by the popular belief that sleep must come in a single, unbroken block of roughly eight hours. If we fail to perform in this way, we conclude that we have something called a "sleep disorder," a label that mostly serves to increase our anxiety and, in turn, make it harder to actually sleep well. But in fact, normal human sleep is probably not monolithic and might well depend on culture and environment. The new thinking is that humans are naturally inclined toward a segmented form of sleep with two distinct phases.

In 2001, historian Roger Ekirch published a seminal paper revealing a wealth of historical evidence that prior to the modern era, humans slept in two distinct intervals. His book *At Day's Close: Night in Times Past* explores the sleeping behavior of people in the Middle Ages, before electric lighting. He found a common pattern: a "first sleep" from roughly 8:00 p.m. to midnight and a "second sleep" from 2:00 a.m. to sunrise, separated by a period of wakefulness that included socializing, quiet time, conversation, and sex. No one expected to sleep through the night.

This pattern probably held for much of human history but began to disappear with the advent of electric lighting. People began to stay up later in the evening as the night became fashionable, and as the industrial revolution took hold, sleep gradually morphed into the single block we know today.

Of course, few of us are willing to go to bed at 8:00 p.m. or adopt a segmented sleeping style, but this history tells us that being awake in the middle of the night may not be a disorder at all. More likely, it's a simple expression of our animal nature. As sleep psychologist Gregg Jacobs put it, "Waking up during the night is part of normal human physiology." The new understanding also tells us that sleep is flexible and that there's probably no single "right" way to sleep.

In fact, we're also beginning to suspect that individual variations in sleep patterns probably served an important evolutionary purpose. This is precisely what Elizabeth Marshall Thomas described in *The Old Way*. In the wild, the Bushmen (and women) of the Kalahari didn't all go to sleep at the same time or sleep for the same duration. At any given time of the night, someone would be up, tending the fire and minding the camp. Some went to sleep early, others late, and people napped whenever they felt the need. Most importantly, sleep was never stigmatized.

Far from being a problem, this staggered pattern was actually vital to survival. Individual variation meant that someone was always up and vigilant, ready to spot predators and spread the alarm. Today we no longer worry about being attacked by lions in the middle of the night, but this story of individual variation does put our minds at ease. If your sleeping pattern doesn't happen to fall into line with the modern, conventional standard, maybe that's just your personal variation at work. In another era, your sleeping style would have been a valued asset. If you happen to be awake in the middle of the night, you're simply playing out a normal evolutionary pattern; you probably would have fit right in with a tribe of ancestral hunter-gatherers.

This view of sleep is liberating. We are now free to think of our insomnia not so much as a disease or an affliction, but as a normal human variation. Above all, it's not something to be ashamed of. The fact that you're awake in the middle of the night may simply be an expression of an ancient physiological inclination. You're awake because the tribe needs you to check the fire and watch for lions. In all likelihood, there's nothing wrong with you or your brain.

It's also important to remember that most of human history took place in equatorial regions that were often pretty warm, if not outright hot. In this kind of world, people would have risen early for hunting, gathering, and exploring. Then, as temperatures warmed into the afternoon, they would have sought out shade and slept for a few hours. When things cooled off, they'd be active once again. This "biphasic" or "siesta" pattern is common in many traditional cultures. In other words, napping during the day is probably a pretty normal human behavior too.

SLEEP ACTIVISM AND REFRAMES

By now, we've all heard the tips and suggestions for better sleep: no caffeine after noon, make sure your room is dark and cool, and cut back on the screen time before bed. If you're drinking alcohol, do it early and in moderation. These sleep-hygiene suggestions are sound, but our biggest problem with sleep may well be the way we frame it. If we continue to think of sleep as a selfish act of indulgence that takes us away from our work and family, sleep will continue to be an adversary, and we'll feel guilty about getting the sleep we truly need.

In *The Sleep Revolution*, Arianna Huffington calls for a new sleep ethic and declares that "sleep is a basic human right." This is a step in the right direction, but even better, it's essential to recognize that sleep is actually a prosocial act. It's a gift to everyone around you and our world as a whole. When we're rested, we're simply easier to get along with. We're more stress tolerant and resilient, and we're probably more sensitive to big-picture views of the world. In this sense, sleep is not just pro-health; it's also pro-future. When you head for the couch or off to bed, you're not being lazy and selfish; you're being smart and altruistic. So do us all a favor and give sleep the respect it deserves.

Likewise, we might do well to reframe our insomnia. In spite of our best efforts and our new understanding of historical sleep patterns, many of us feel cursed to wake up in the middle of the night. We're craving sleep, but our minds race, and the anxiety comes in waves. Vicious spirals of mental energy feed on themselves, making the night a special kind of torture.

It might seem like we're stuck, but all is not lost. From a Buddhist perspective, we might say that insomnia is one thing and our resistance to it another. By itself, insomnia is just wakefulness, but insomnia plus resistance equals suffering. It's one thing to be awake in the middle of the night, but it's another thing to curse the fact that you're awake. You may not have any choice about the fact that you've woken up, but you do have a choice as to whether to resist the experience. You may well prefer to be asleep, but your body has chosen wakefulness, so make something of it. Treat your wakefulness as raw material for something pleasant or creative. And above all, trust your body. Give it the time it needs, and it'll go to sleep when the time is right.

And remember, you're not alone in your effort. When your head hits the pillow, pay attention to your breath and think about all the people and animals on the planet who are sleeping at this very moment. Billions of creatures, fully absorbed by the sweet comfort of darkness and immersed in the world of dreaming. Taken together, this amounts to a vast, incredibly powerful experience that's sweeping across the planet every twenty-four hours. Think deeply about this and allow yourself to participate. Feel their sleep; feel their bodies and their breath. Sink in and join the sleepers. You are not alone.

PALEO DREAMS

As for what goes on when we're asleep, we might want to reconsider our thoughts about dreaming as well. In the modern world, we tend to think of dreams as nothing more than ghostly by-products of neural activity, chemicals and neurons sorting out their circuitry and consolidating memories. In other words, dreams are considered random and mostly meaningless—nothing more than secondary epiphenomena.

But historically speaking, this is an abnormal, sterilized way to look at it. In the Paleo, dreams were considered vital to the success of the hunt and the very survival of the tribe. People believed in dreams and savored them whenever possible. Some cultures even believed that the dream state was the real world and that wakefulness was just an interlude between the real action at night. Some tribes gathered every morning for what we would today call a "dream report."

So maybe the Old Way is better. A culture that's curious about dreams and respectful of their power simply has a more integrated experience of life. Research has little to say on this matter, but it makes sense. When we bolt awake every morning and cast our dreams aside like some kind of irrelevant neural noise, we are literally rejecting part of who we are. It's impossible to say what the health and life consequences might be, but we can be sure of one thing: the body knows the difference.

So try respecting your dreams. Use the night sky as a canvas for your imagination. Dream of the stars and the planets, of animals, vistas, the waters. Dream of people, your tribe. Dream of the hunt. Dream of passionate sex. Dream of your breath and your powerful animal body. Dream of the Earth.

CHAPTER 31

FOODSTUFF

> The shared meal elevates eating from a mechanical process of fueling the body to a ritual of family and community, from the mere animal biology to an act of culture.
> —Michael Pollan
> *In Defense of Food: An Eater's Manifesto*

The human animal has to eat, and for our Paleolithic ancestors, the enterprise was pretty simple. Hunt, gather, prepare. Eat what habitat provides. And even well into the age of agriculture, food remained simple and straightforward. People lived in coherent cultures built around food that was grown and prepared regionally and according to tradition.

But today, the situation is a thousand times more complex and chaotic. Food comes to us at the speed of modern transport, cultures overlap, experts argue about the details, and in the meantime, our confusion grows. In this respect, modern agriculture has actually given us a bumper crop of ambiguity and doubt. As Michael Pollan has put it, we're the first people in history who don't know what or how to eat.

Without question, our modern food environment is profoundly abnormal. For the last few centuries, we've developed ever-more-intensive systems for turning habitat into calories. Every link in the chain is now streamlined and optimized. From vast, industrial-scale farms to the restaurant table, we've eliminated every possible source of friction. This has given us a huge oversupply of cheap food, and today, most of us are surrounded by food, or more precisely, food-like products.

The problem is that much of what we eat in the modern world isn't, strictly speaking, food. Chemists and food scientists have learned how to tweak formulas (not recipes) to manufacture (not cook) a vast array of highly profitable and addictive food-like products. Advertisers assault us with nonstop images of these products, stimulating our appetites around the clock. None of this is historically normal.

To make matters worse, even our basic, real foods are changing in parallel with climate. Rising CO_2 in the atmosphere increases the speed of photosynthesis, but it also stimulates plants to produce more carbohydrates at the expense of other nutrients we depend on—protein, iron, calcium, potassium, zinc, and iron. Over the past three decades, the overall concentration of minerals in agricultural crops has dropped by 8 percent on average.

This would all be plenty bad enough, but we're also distracted by our modern obsession with single ingredients, a trend described by Michael Pollan as "nutritionism." Ever since 1747, when the Scottish surgeon James Lind discovered that citrus foods (vitamin C) helped prevent scurvy, we've gone all-in on the promise of isolated ingredients. Every day brings some new claim about the merits or dangers of some particular substance, and for many people, eating is all about ingredients. No longer do we say, "I'm hungry." We say, "I need protein," or

"I need carbs." Likewise, we don't say "I'm thirsty," but "I need hydration."

In the process, food has now become a potent source of anxiety and a battleground of competing claims. Some people simply give up and eat whatever comes, whereas others become afflicted with orthorexia, a psychological disorder defined as "an extreme or excessive preoccupation with avoiding foods perceived to be unhealthy." Likewise, our relationship with food is often saturated with religious overtones. Advocates of various diets are quick to moralize about what people should be eating, and zealots evangelize about food selection and even attack those who are eating "forbidden foods." Some people are considered heretics, some have been successfully converted, and some have fallen from grace.

FOOD IN TWO DIMENSIONS

One useful way to cut through the confusion is to look at food in two dimensions: content and context. *Content* refers to the actual ingredients of our food, the macronutrients of protein, fat, and carbohydrates, as well as various micronutrients, hormones, antibiotics, and toxins. *Context* refers to the setting and environment that surround our food: the way it's grown, produced, transported, prepared, shared, and consumed. Most importantly, it's about the meaning that comes along for the ride.

Without question, the lion's share of modern conversation about food and nutrition is about content; we treat food as a substance, independent from both habitat and people. But in fact, food has larger meanings that speak directly to our happiness and our health. In a normal ancestral setting, eating was a powerful experience that brought people and habitat together. Every bite told a story of land, water, plants, animals, and the people who hunted, gathered, or farmed there. Every meal reminded people who they were and where they came from. Food was grounding.

But today, food is nothing more than fuel, a substance with a certain chemical profile. We overlook the fact that food has powerful meanings, including powerful placebo and nocebo effects. Cartesian nutritionists like to focus on the chemical effects of specific ingredients, but for meaning-sensitive people living in vivo, context might even trump content. The lesson: pay attention to not just what's in your food but also what's around it.

This suggests another useful distinction: "Earth food" has a clear connection to the land and the people who grew it, gathered it, or hunted it and prepared it. You can source it. You've got some sense of what kind of habitat it was raised in and who was involved in getting it to your table. "Space food," on the other hand, has no visible connection to the land or the people who produced it. It simply shows up in your life, ready to be consumed.

Food is about more than chemistry. The space food that arrives on your doorstep from an online merchant may well be technically perfect in every biochemical detail, and the space food that arrives at your restaurant table may well have an ideal nutritional profile. But if you really want to eat in a meaningful way, you need to know the history of what you're eating, the habitat it came from, and the people who made it possible. Otherwise, it's just a bunch of molecules. And humans do not live by molecules alone.

PLANTS, ANIMALS, RESPECT

As for the debate between vegetarian versus carnivorous diets, the facts are mostly old news. Without question, plant-based diets are generally good for our bodies, and it's also clear that modern meat production is morally abhorrent. Plant-based diets are also a lot easier on the Earth: less deforestation, less fertilizer runoff, less freshwater use, and less methane production from livestock.

But at the same time, there's a strong case to be made that humans need at least some meat for basic physical health. Meat consumption has been a feature of most human cultures for most of our history, and it's safe to assume we're wired to seek it out, enjoy it, and benefit from eating it.

Unfortunately, there aren't many good work-arounds for this dilemma. To be sure, we can eat less meat and source what we do eat more humanely. We can stop consuming meat that is morally compromised and shift more of our consumption to wild fish and game, if we can get it. But these are only partial solutions, and for the time being, we're stuck with a system that is simply unsatisfactory.

What we can do is pay our food—carnivorous or vegetarian—the respect it deserves. We may not be able to access the Earth food we desire, but we can at least pay attention to its source, its history, and its meaning. This is the real problem with our modern fast-food environment—when something is fast, easy, cheap, and plentiful, we're not inclined to pay much attention to its meaning, history, or consequences. Whatever the ingredients might happen to be, it's hard to see much significance in something you can get with the push of a button. Why should we respect something that just appears through a car window?

But it's really a marvel that we can eat the way we do. The modern supermarket holds the collective bounty of a thousand square miles of land, condensed and refined by the labor of thousands of people, powered by thousands of gallons of fossil fuels and nitrogen fertilizers. By all rights, we ought to be in awe of the supermarket every time we visit.

So rather than stressing over the ingredients and biochemistry of our food, maybe we'd do better to pause before we eat and think about all the things that had to happen to make it possible. Think about the habitat, the people, and the labor that went into the process. Then, appreciate it.

TO-DO LIST

In spite of all the noise in the system, the path to health and nutritional sanity is actually pretty clear: Start by getting over the focus on single ingredients. Stop thinking in terms of "diet," and start thinking about whole, minimally processed food that ties people to habitat and to one another. Humans are flexible omnivores who can thrive on a wide variety of diets. Likewise, stop worrying so much about biochemistry and the therapeutic effects of specific nutrients. The whole food is the nutrient. As Dr. David Katz of the Yale School of Preventive Medicine puts it, "The active ingredient in broccoli is broccoli."

The next recommendation sounds ridiculously obvious but bears repeating: focus on a food-based diet. Humans have coevolved with real food for millions of years, and our bodies are intimately, microscopically adapted to whole, natural foods. Every detail of our digestion and biochemistry is the way it is because of our history in wild habitat. Above all, learn to distinguish between real food and "edible food-like substances." When in doubt, choose the simple options.

Focus on quality, not quantity. This too may sound obvious, but it's backed up by research, specifically a 2018 study published in the *Journal of the American Medical Association*. Researchers found that people who cut back on added sugar, refined grains, and highly processed foods while concentrating on eating plenty of vegetables and whole foods—without worrying about counting calories or limiting portion sizes—lost significant amounts of weight over the course of a year. In other words, it always gets back to the basics.

It's not just what we eat, but also when. For many, the last meal of the day comes late in the evening, a practice most nutritionists now consider a health negative. Late eating spikes our blood sugar just as the body is winding down into inactivity and sleep. In turn, this allows glucose to circulate in the blood and probably contributes to obesity, high blood sugar, and acid reflux. By eating dinner early, we give the digestive system a chance to rest completely each night. These mini-fasts allow the system to completely metabolize the day's food and clear away by-products and inflammation. This also allows the body to divert more of its resources away from digestion and back toward tissue healing and fighting infection. Try for a solid twelve hours between dinner and breakfast. Likewise, if you're drinking, do it early.

Above all, learn to cook. Cooking puts us into an intimate relationship with the process and the substances we consume; it turns space food into Earth food. By learning to cook, you can get exactly what you want, in the quantities you feel are best for your body. While you're at it, cook big. Find something that works for you and your tribe and cook a big batch of it. Have a feast, then save the rest. That way, you won't be tempted to junk out; you'll be pleasantly surprised tomorrow when you open the fridge to find some really good stuff.

FOCUS ON THE POSITIVE

Ultimately, it's all about relationship. In the world of nutrition recommendations, we're often told to avoid a long list of "bad foods" that, according to the narrative, will destroy our health. There may well be truth to such claims, but this focus on the negative can backfire and trigger our lust for "forbidden fruits."

This is why diets usually fail; they're all about restriction, deprivation, and absence. As soon as the dieter commits, he instantly becomes aware of all the things he's not supposed to eat. In this way, prohibition inspires the very thing it's intended to prevent.

Instead, we'd do better to focus on the positive. Reject the "glow-in-the-dark" food products, of course, but pay more attention to those foods that are rich and flavorful. Hunt down the Earth foods that are really dense in color and flavor. The modern supermarket may well be stocked with an astonishing number of disease-promoting substances, but it's also bursting with real foods that will make our bodies healthier. This focus on abundance by itself is health promoting. When you see yourself living in a world of nutritional plenty, you can celebrate at every meal.

CHAPTER 32

PAUSE

> Between stimulus and response there is a space. In that space is our power to choose our response. In our response lies our growth and our freedom.
> —Viktor Frankl
> *Man's Search for Meaning*

Throughout history, spiritual leaders and tribal elders have counseled the benefits of patience and reflection in the face of demanding challenges. Give it time, they tell us. Sit with the dilemma, go for a walk, and let the body do its work. Feel what you're feeling, and then, when the process has run its course, act with courage and resolve.

But sadly, the modern world is relentless and merciless in short-circuiting this process and driving stimulus and response ever closer together. Never before in the history of humanity has there been so much pressure to act fast.

In the first place, there's the nagging, incessant pressure to produce and, above all, get it done. We're constantly encouraged to work fast, gather information quickly, and generate some kind of profitable product or service in the shortest amount of time. The body wants to metabolize experience, but the marketplace demands action.

A general ethos of speed is baked into our culture at large. In the world of athletics, for example, most modern events are measured against the clock. For some reason, going faster is assumed to be better; it's encouraged, rewarded, and glorified. Fast running, fast driving, fast eating, fast working, fast thinking. Whatever it is, just do it faster and someone will give you a like or a thumbs-up.

Even worse, the marketing industry has evolved into a highly efficient machine for squeezing stimulus and response together into a single reflexive, impulsive act. Advertising has become neurologically sophisticated, and commercial websites are intentionally constructed to ease the path from initial contact to the "Buy Now" click. Everywhere we turn in the modern world, someone is pushing us to swipe our cards, open our wallets, and complete the "call to action." In a historical sense, this is all profoundly abnormal, not to mention hugely destructive to wise action in the face of complexity.

The end result is that we, as a people, are becoming progressively more impulsive and automated with each passing day. As stimulus and response are pushed ever closer together, we become increasingly robotic in our behavior and our relationship with the world. We may well become efficient, but along the way, our humanity and sapience are left in the dust. And this comes precisely at the moment when our planetary predicament demands a new level of reflection.

DON'T TAKE THE BAIT

Obviously, we need a new, or rather, an old approach, something that gives us a chance to breathe into the space between stimulus and response, something to dampen our reactivity. This is where it helps to remember our ancestral, Paleo way of life. Imagine having all the time you need in each day, a sense of temporal affluence, moving and living at the pace of habitat. On the grassland, there are no deadlines. This is the normal condition for the human experience.

Patience will come with age and experience. Just because there's a stimulus doesn't mean you have to act on it. Just because someone or something is poking at you doesn't mean you have to respond impulsively. You don't have to take the advertising bait that's dangled in front of you. For that matter, you don't have to take *any* bait that tries to manipulate you into fast, impulsive action.

Above all, stop worshiping speed for its own sake. Faster is not necessarily better, and often, it's really destructive. There are times to go fast, but these are rare events in the average human life. Instead, stretch out the interval between stimulus and response. Get comfortable in that space. Slow down and take a breath. Take a walk. Let the body have its way with the stimulus. And then, only then, act.

CHAPTER 33

LET IT BE

> To give way now is to conquer by and by. A fountain gets muddy with but little stirring up, and does not get clear by our meddling with it but by our leaving it alone.
> —Baltasar Gracián
> *The Art of Worldly Wisdom*

Imagine you're sitting on a hill in East Africa, tens of thousands of years ago. You're out with your hunting party, and you've been observing the animals for most of the day. It's an incredible scene: thousands of wildebeest migrating, birds by the millions, carnivores resting up, elephants and hippos bathing. And it's just another day in your life.

If you'd time traveled to this point, you'd be awestruck, not just by the vista of plants and animals before you, but by the silence. No vehicles, no aircraft, no construction crews, no car alarms, no leaf blowers. The only sounds are the voices of your friends, the calls of the animals, and the wind on the grass. Inevitably, you'd find this silence calming in a profound way.

In obvious contrast, today, we live on a planet of noise, only some of it acoustic. The modern world has become a twenty-four-hour distraction machine, a conspiracy against focused attention, every day a blizzard of beeps, buzzers, hypernormal colors, and flashing lights, all intruding on our lives at almost every moment. All of this presents an unprecedented challenge to our cognitive capability and our ability to pay attention. If you add up all the books, podcasts, radio shows, posts, tweets, and advertisements we're exposed to each day, it amounts to vastly more cognitive load than we've had to deal with before in human history.

YOUR LIFE ON COMPLEXITY

This acoustic and cognitive onslaught is a serious threat to our health, our happiness, and our ability to create a long-term relationship with this planet. As noise escalates, it becomes harder to hear and appreciate the essential signals in our lives—signals from habitat, relationships, and the people around us. Over time, our overconsumption of cognitive content depletes precious neurological resources and drives us into a state of nervous exhaustion.

This mental and spiritual overload is bad for both individuals and society as a whole. According to psychologist Daniel Kahneman, "People who are cognitively busy are more likely to make selfish choices, use sexist language, and make superficial judgments in social situations." Willpower is also depleted, which, of course, leads to all manner of poor behavior and impulsive decisions.

We try to keep up with it all by multitasking, but most of us have gotten the memo from the neuroscience community by now. That is, the brain only attends to one thing at a time. When we attempt to manage multiple tasks simultaneously, the brain simply increases speed in switching from one point of attention to another. In moderation, we can manage it, but this rapid alternation of attention eventually takes a toll on the whole mind–body. Over the course of months and years, we become increasingly vulnerable to stress and, in turn, depression.

THE POWER OF NOTHING

Overwhelmed by modern life and frustrated with conventional approaches, many of us turn to meditation for relief. Research suggests that regular practice reduces inflammation; lowers levels of the stress hormone cortisol; and reduces anxiety, depression, anger, and fatigue. It also stimulates the vagus nerve, a powerful player in the autonomic nervous system that helps us with healing, tissue repair, inflammation control, and psycho-physical rejuvenation.

The list of benefits is impressive, but it's important to frame our discussion in the right way. In our highly individualistic culture, meditation is often presented as a means to self-improvement, but this perspective may actually be a step in the wrong direction. The very act of trying to improve ourselves strengthens our sense of self, which in turn sets us up for more duality and, in turn, conflict and anxiety. A better approach would be to think of meditation as a practice of nonself. We aren't trying to make ourselves better; we're trying to let go of our ego and merge ourselves with the world. When we succeed, we experience less self, less duality, and in turn, less suffering.

In any case, meditation gives us a chance to step outside the complexity of our normal daily lives and observe exactly what we're up to. In the process, it gives us an increased understanding of our bodies and our experience. When we allow the chattering, judgmental mind to come to rest, we begin to actually feel what we're feeling. As we let go of the noise of the modern world, we begin to feel the life coursing through our bodies, via the breath.

From a mind–body point of view, the power of meditation lies in the experiential proof that we can coexist with ourselves. We sit quietly for a while, and behold—nothing bad happens. Our minds might get distracted, and we might waste some time ruminating on the dramas in our lives, but these things tend to fade away. In turn, it begins to dawn on us that it's not really necessary to spend every waking moment running away from ourselves or our predicaments. It's not really necessary to surround ourselves with distraction and compulsive activity. It's OK to just be. This is a liberating insight.

The beauty of regular meditation practice is that it takes us deeper into the human experience. Some teachers say meditation is all about being in the present moment, but we might also say it's like going back in time, all the way back to the preliterate, preverbal days of deep history. Once we let go of our verbal soundtrack and mental ruminations, we return to our primal, ancestral experience. We return to the Great Integrity, the Tao, the time before words. We return to our normal, aboriginal state of mind.

The experience is calming, but it's far more than even that. When we abandon our internal chatter and focus on our bodies and our breath, we reunite with the totality of life on Earth and all the power that goes with it. When we relinquish our compulsive narration about life and our troubles, we're left with a direct experience of a body that's literally millions of years old and continuous with all life. This takes us out of our isolation and back into integration. In this sense, the medical benefits of meditation pale in comparison. Reducing your blood pressure is undoubtedly a good thing, but even better is the chance to unite with the totality of life itself, all the way back to LUCA (the Last Universal Common Ancestor).

LET IT BE

Unfortunately, meditation is often presented as a complex, daunting practice that takes decades to master. There are dozens of styles, hundreds of books, thousands of teachers, and according to some, layer upon layer of sophistication. This diversity makes for some interesting conversation, but it also distracts us from the essential simplicity we're trying to nurture.

In fact, there's no wrong way to do it. Just sit still in one place for a while. Turn off the phone and abandon your concerns about work, your to-do list, and all the things nagging at your mind. Forget about proper posture, breathing technique, attention, mindfulness, compassion, and loving kindness, at least for the moment. Keep it as simple as you can. As one meditation teacher puts it, "Just sit down, shut up, and pay attention." If you can do this, you're halfway there.

Now, let things settle. Take a few good breaths and imagine a glass of muddy water. As you relax, the particles of dirt will sink to the bottom of the glass, and you will become calm. As you settle, focus your attention on your breath, the vital spirit that animates our bodies. Breath is your most intimate ally, a safe and reliable friend that will show you the way to equanimity and calm.

Of course, if you're anything like a normal human being, your attention will begin to wander, and this is the moment of truth. If you try to strong-arm your attention back to your breath, you'll simply produce more noise and wind up even further away from your target. But passivity also fails. If you simply allow yourself to be swept up in whatever thoughts and imagery your mind cooks up, you'll never learn how to stabilize your attention. You'll simply have a nice daydreaming session. The tricky part is that distraction feeds on itself. We drift off our focal point, and each thought generates another association, memory, or image. Before we know it, we're light-years from our original intent.

The solution, as the Buddhists point out, is compassion. There's nothing to be gained by abusing yourself for getting distracted. Every time you drift off target, you get another chance to practice.

Stick with it. When distraction intrudes on your experience, relax. Don't try to change anything. As Pema Chödrön, author of *When Things Fall Apart*, advises, "soften and stay." Relinquish effort, but maintain focus. Note the pain, the distraction, and the emotion, then return to your breath. Observe the way your mind goes on journeys into the past and future. Observe the chatter, the commentary, and the random images that appear as if from nowhere. Observe all this, and return your attention to your breath.

Whatever you do, keep it simple. In the popular imagination, many people suppose meditation is a path to some kind of higher, altered state of consciousness, and some of us seek it out precisely for this reason. We want the special thing, the extraordinary state of awareness that will take us to a new level of experience. Just as with almost everything else in the modern world, we want the exceptional, the incredible, and the elite.

But we've got it entirely backward. Meditation is not an altered, exceptional state; it's our normal state. It's our frenzied, modern condition that's the altered state. When we meditate, we simply return to our historically normal, Paleo condition of mind and body. In other words, the meditative state—being still and feeling the breath—is the baseline, the reference point. It's a safe home base. It's who we are.

So instead of reaching for something rare and astonishing, maybe we'd do better to reach for something modest. Don't worry about sophistication, advanced techniques, or mystical experiences. Stick with simplicity. It's reliable, accessible, and effective.

Of course, most of us claim to be too busy to bother with any of this. The practice takes time and produces no immediate payoff, so we simply avoid it in favor of more impulsive activity. But seen from another perspective, this makes no sense whatsoever. After all, we seem to have plenty of time for activities that bring noise, confusion, and complexity into our lives. Why not something that's proven to give us a sense of clarity, depth, and equanimity, if only for a few minutes each day? It's worth a try.

CHAPTER 34

HARDENING OF THE SELF

> In an individual, selfishness uglifies the soul; for the human species, selfishness is extinction.
> —David Mitchell
> *Cloud Atlas*

Once again, think back to your time in the Paleo, deep in the semi-wooded mosaic grasslands of ancient Africa. Your life was simple and consisted mostly of hunting, gathering, gossiping, standing around the fire, and wondering about the lives of the plants and animals in your bioregion. Otherwise engaged, you probably didn't spend a whole lot of time thinking about yourself or your appearance. You might have caught a glimpse of your reflection in a pool of water, but such an experience would have been rare, amusing, and not particularly impactful.

All that began to change in the nineteenth century with the invention of cameras and the widespread production of mirrors. Almost overnight, people in modern economies could see themselves frequently throughout each day. Each of these encounters would have been a reminder of the self, an abrupt jolt out of world consciousness into self-consciousness. Over the course of the next century, human attention was radically transformed, narcissism began to rise, and culture began to morph into what *New York Times* columnist David Brooks has called the "Big Me."

The consequences have been radically disruptive for our species. Today it's considered perfectly normal to obsess over one's self: the way we look, dress, talk, perform, and behave. Even our language reflects this new obsession, and an entirely new self-based lexicon has taken shape:

- Self-consciousness
- Self-awareness
- Self-acceptance
- Self-confidence
- Self-esteem
- Self-help
- Self-assurance
- Self-realization
- Self-actualization
- Self-mastery
- Self-control
- Self-love
- Self-care
- Self-worth
- Self-improvement
- Self-sufficiency
- Self-talk

Likewise, entire industries are now devoted to optimizing the self: personal training, personal wellness, personalized diets and medicine, genetic testing, personal shoppers, and personal branding. But in a historical sense, none of this is normal. And from a Paleo and indigenous perspective, this is absolutely self-indulgent, which is to say, it's bad manners, even shameful. In a Paleo setting, people who talked this way might even be thrown out of the tribe.

The psycho-spiritual consequences of this self-focused orientation are easy to understand. As we take our eyes off the world and focus more intently on our own personal dramas, we begin to feel increasingly isolated and, in turn, anxious and then depressed. And yet we persist in doubling down on the self, certain that the cure for our unhappiness must lie within.

Even worse, we amplify our self-consciousness with a culture of individuality and "rugged individualism." Bodybuilders stand on stage to demonstrate their perfect shape while adventure athletes embark on audacious solo ventures, crossing major oceans and polar ice caps without support. All of which reached its epitome with Alex Honnold's incredible and profoundly disturbing 2017 solo climb of El Capitan in Yosemite Valley, vividly depicted in the movie *Free Solo*.

To compound the problem further, we glorify the solo entrepreneur, the coffee-shop millionaire who writes his own code and sells it to the highest bidder. We tell our young people to strive for financial independence (sometimes called "fuck you money") so that they'll never have to depend on anyone else. This is all profoundly abnormal. What has gotten into us? Perhaps we can trace some of this back to Adam Smith, the founding father of capitalism, who suggested that self-interest is the path to a functional society. Or maybe Ayn Rand had a hand in it with her books about the glory of individual agency, especially *The Virtue of Selfishness*.

In any case, it's all delusion and dysfunction. Biology teaches us clearly that human beings are not stand-alone organisms. Not only are we completely dependent on habitat and other humans for our survival, but even our individual bodies are massively networked with the microbial life that exists in us and on us. The two million unique bacterial genes found in each human microbiome make the twenty-three genes in our cells seem paltry by comparison. Tom Insel, former director of the National Institute of Mental Health, sees enormous implications for our sense of self. As he sees it, "We are, at least from the standpoint of DNA, more microbial than human." In other words, our obsession with an independent self is a violation of everything we know about how the natural world actually works.

So maybe it's time to ditch the mirrors, the cameras, and the radical acts of solo individualism. Our self-consciousness isn't doing us much good, and even worse, it distracts us from the primal relationships that sustain us. It also makes us less effective in creating a functional future.

So look around. Put your attention back where it belongs—on relationship. Stop thinking about yourself and your body for a while and you'll feel a whole lot better.

CHAPTER 35

ANIMAL MAGNETISM

> Human beings are discourse.
> Everything is conversation.
>
> —Rumi

When you live in a culture that emphasizes individualism, it's easy to imagine yourself as an independent, stand-alone organism. *Live free or die!* we say. I have my own ideas, and I make my own decisions. I am a rational actor in the world, and I do as I please. This, of course, is nonsense. Humans are not just social; we're radically connected to one another via sensation, tone of voice, gesture, body movement, and language. In other words, our social nature isn't just a bunch of talk; it's fundamentally physical. Words are important, but the real action is taking place at a deeper level. Our bodies are highly sensitive emotion-detection instruments that gather and express social information in every waking moment. We are literally continuous with one another, but we forget.

THE LANGUAGE BEFORE WORDS

As hypersocial primates, our most important communication is via the body and what author Derrick Jensen calls "a language older than words." As hyperverbalists of the modern world, we may find this a strange idea, even nonsensical, but it makes perfect sense in the Big History perspective. We can't say precisely when human speech first coalesced, but there's no question that our primate and hominid ancestors were "talking" in physical forms long before the first words.

This is something that actors know full well. This is how people *really* talk to one another, with their bodies, their gestures, and their expressions. Actual words are, in many cases, an afterthought. And we can be sure that in many conversations, the specific words that are spoken carry far less weight than the body's tone and posture.

But sadly, modern education leapfrogs over this entire preverbal reality. Administrators like words that can be nailed down onto the page or a computer hard drive. In particular, we like words that we can measure, track, evaluate, and test. In contrast, the language of the body can be slippery, elusive, and not particularly testable. And so, the reality and immensity of our nonverbal lives get pushed into the background. Our bodies have important things to say, but in the modern classroom, no one is listening.

THE RESONANCE CIRCUIT

In *The Neurobiology of We*, psychiatrist Daniel Siegel describes a "resonance circuit" that mediates this preverbal continuity between people. In a drastically simplified form, it goes as follows.

As we observe the movements, postures, eye gaze, and microexpressions of other people's bodies and faces, we become sensitive to the pace of their conversation and their tone of voice, intonation, stress, and rhythm, the so-called prosody of communication. This information is processed by mirror neurons in the cortex of the brain, then relayed downward into the limbic, emotional brain centers. From there, this emotional content flows deep into the observer's body, where it's experienced as gut feeling and a sense of what others are experiencing.

In effect, this circuitry allows us to run simulations of what other people are experiencing. When the system works properly, we get to feel what others are feeling, and conversations tend to unfold smoothly. We understand and we feel felt. But when this resonance circuit atrophies through disuse or we neglect to listen to its messages, trouble is sure to follow.

PHYSICAL RAPPORT

For those of us living in the modern world, spending our days on electronic devices, we may well have forgotten this essential life skill. Our ability to sense one another through the body may be compromised by lack of training, distraction, or stress. In all likelihood, we may need some remedial education in this art.

So how do we refresh our memory and experience the rapport between our social bodies? One good way is a physical game called "animal magnetism."

The concept is perfectly simple: Define a point of contact between people, then stay connected in movement. Face off with a partner and set up with contact at the wrist, shoulder, or hip. (Wear a mask as appropriate.) To begin, don't do anything at all. Just feel your body and your partner. Feel their posture and the overall tone of their physical presence. Take your time.

Now take a breath and begin some easy, subtle movement in any direction. And here's the crux: no matter where your partner moves, stay sticky at the point of contact. The idea is not to move in some particular way, but to feel. Slow down and sense. What is my partner saying with her body? This is the physical experience of rapport.

To make things interesting, you can designate one person as "coach," the other as "athlete." Once contact is established, the coach moves as desired, taking the athlete through a series of fluid movements. Athlete follows with sticky contact. Or both parties can simply move as desired, keeping the connection intact.

For an advanced variation, you can set a distance between players, with the same intent. For example, establish a six-inch gap between two people and then start moving. Wherever your partner goes, maintain a sense of contact across space.

Animal magnetism is a fun game and is valuable on its own merits, but what's really important is the metaphor of continuity, connection, sensation, and what we might call "physical listening." No matter how your partner moves, pay attention and maintain contact. This is precisely how we ought to be living with one another in relationship.

BREAKING RAPPORT

The physical game tells us a good deal about connection and rapport generally. When our partners are paying attention and the rapport is strong, we feel safe. This is an ideal situation for a hypersocial primate.

But notice how it feels when someone abruptly breaks rapport, either by withdrawing or by moving in a way that's random, unpredictable, or jerky. It just feels wrong. You might even experience a wave of anxiety as your partner violates the physical agreement and rhythm that you've established.

This is precisely what's happening in the modern social world, where conversation is falling apart and distraction is becoming the rule rather than the exception. We establish rapport with our friends, family, neighbors, customers, and lovers, only to break it moments later when an electronic message comes in. Multitasking in every waking moment, we flit from one idea to the next, ghosting one another with abandon, never settling down, never feeling one another. Rapport, once a regular feature of human social life, is in danger of disappearing altogether. It's no wonder we feel so anxious, nervous, depressed, and fragmented.

In our high-tech world, we seem to believe that the essence of human communication is textual, factual, or numerical information—in other words, data. If this content is "delivered" as spoken words or text, we consider our communication successful and move on to other things. But this "hit-and-run" style of interaction can hardly be described as communication at all. That's because the vital, essential elements in human communication are actually attention, focus, and authentic presence. Animal magnetism is the key, one body talking and listening to another. And like it or not, this takes time.

We see a similar problem in our widespread inability to tell and listen to one another's stories. Some of us talk nonstop, others flit from one subject to another without the slightest transition, and still others can only talk about their pet issues. So where's the rapport? To enjoy a sense of continuity in relationship, there has to be careful, concentrated, and attentive listening. We need to hear and feel the trajectory of a person's story and the meanings that go along for the ride. Otherwise, our conversations are reduced to a series of jagged non sequiturs and desperate lurches for connection.

HEALING RAPPORT

Our rapport in the modern world may be fragmented and tenuous, but all is not lost. In fact, it's really pretty understandable. Even in ideal circumstances, breaks in rapport are common. It takes time to learn the movements and inclinations of those around us, so it's no surprise that we often fail to sync up. All of us are guilty of inattention, insensitivity, and outright ignorance of our partner's words, stories, and movements. Awkwardness in social communication is not just common, but it's probably a human universal.

Recognizing this must be the first step. Yes, it feels terrible when rapport is broken, but we can start the game over. Exercise some understanding and compassion. Rapport is a fine art, and most of us struggle to get it right. So try it again and listen more closely this time. Then try it again.

Once you've refreshed your memory with some practice, keep the idea of rapport alive as you go through your day. Your partner is a model for the world at large. How's your rapport with your neighbors, your workplace, your culture? Listen, feel, then listen some more . . .

CHAPTER 36

IT'S ALL CONTAGIOUS

We never think alone.
—Steven Sloman and Philip Fernbach
The Knowledge Illusion

If you really want to understand human social behavior, it helps to revisit the Paleo predicament, deep in prehistory, somewhere on the mosaic grassland of Africa. Imagine that you're part of an ancient hominid band, not yet fully human but highly intelligent and capable. The past few generations have been a time of prosperity and relative abundance, the climate has been friendly, the hunting and gathering have been good, and there's plenty of protein to go around. It's good news for everyone's health, but there's a surprising downside. As brains and heads have grown larger over the generations, childbirth has become increasingly dangerous, and sadly, many women and children have perished.

But you are one of the lucky ones. Your brain and head are large, but by the luck of genes and a few mutations, your mother goes into labor early. Strictly speaking, your body isn't really ready for prime time, but there's no fighting the process, and suddenly you've arrived in the world, premature and incompetent, but ready to make a go of it.

At this point, you've got some serious limitations. You can't walk, hunt, speak, or perform any of the functions necessary to make your way in the world. If left on your own, your life expectancy would be mere hours, so you've got to get some social life support right away. Specifically, you've got to attach to a caregiver as soon as possible. Ideally it's Mom, but any warm, caring human will do, someone who will keep you safe from danger, touch you, feed you, and keep you alive until you're fully developed. Attachment, in other words, is absolutely vital for your survival and development.

Back in today's modern world, you probably haven't given much thought to the premature nature of your birth, but your need for attachment remains and will have profound consequences that will reverberate for the rest of your life. Secure attachment to a caregiver isn't just important in infancy; it's a major predictor of how successful you'll be as an adult. If you're securely attached as a child, you have a good chance of going on to have a successful career, good health, and strong social relations.

A powerful body of research, beginning with British psychoanalyst John Bowlby and validated by American psychologist Mary Ainsworth, demonstrates that secure attachment is a better predictor of success than conventional measures such as IQ. And of course, insecure attachment goes the other way: children who grow up without secure attachment are more likely to fall into dysfunctional behavior and disease in adulthood.

In short, attachment is a critical fork in the road for the developing human body, mind, and spirit. If the process is successful, the young animal body concludes that the world is mostly friendly and switches on a host of metabolic and growth functions that continue throughout life. But if attachment fails, the body concludes that the world is unfriendly and prepares for defense. Brain centers go on red alert, and the mind crosses over into a state of vigilance or even hypervigilance. The body prepares for a life of danger and immediate action.

These findings confirm what indigenous people have known for thousands of years. Life on the grassland was dangerous and demanding, and personal survival was intimately linked to the welfare and functioning of the tribe. The tribe was a lifeboat on a perilous sea of wild land, open space, and hungry carnivores. Of course your body would be extremely sensitive to the attention of the people around you. Of course native people would go to great lengths to sustain tribal function and integrity. It would be bizarre if it were any other way.

HYPERSOCIAL BODIES

In the wild, attachment was truly a matter of life and death, and so it's no wonder we find loneliness and isolation intolerable. When we're alone for long periods, we're separate from our circle of life support, and in this sense, our lives are literally in danger. It's no surprise the body experiences rejection and isolation as genuine physical emergencies. This is also why solitary confinement is rightly classified as torture.

Given our survival predicament in the Paleo and our utter reliance on tribal life, it comes as no surprise to discover that our bodies are tightly linked with one another, down to the deepest levels. A sense of tribal belonging is essential not just for social amusement and friendship, but for the deep functioning of our bodies, brains, minds, and spirits. In fact, an enormous body of research in the fields of social neuroscience and interpersonal neurobiology has revealed astonishing levels of social sensitivity embedded in our bodies. We are so hypersocial, in fact, that our bodies are, for all practical purposes, continuous with one another. In a very real sense, our bodies and our lives are made of people.

CONTINUITIES

Our social nature is far more than a simple desire to affiliate; it is deeply, fundamentally physical. Tribe is etched into the very tissue of our bodies and reflected in the deep structure and function of our brains. In *The Neuroscience of Human Relationships*, psychologist Louis Cozolino classifies the brain as a "social organ" and even goes so far as to suggest that "there are no single human brains." We are so inherently social, so dependent on one another for our very cognition, that it makes little sense to view brains in isolation from one another. Even without digital technology, we are massively networked. As Robert Sapolsky put it in *Behave: The Biology of Humans at Our Best and Worst*, "No brain is an island."

In essence, our bodies are highly sensitive emotion-detection instruments that absorb and express social information continuously. As modern Cartesians, many of us like to think our mental activity is autonomous and self-contained, but the body is always getting into the act. The process is generally unconscious, but it's an extremely powerful force that's impossible to turn off. As job interview consultants sometimes put it, "Your body cannot *not* communicate."

Realize it or not, we are incredibly adept at reading one another's faces and bodies. A study in the *Journal of Nonverbal Behavior* found that study participants only had to watch about four seconds of basketball or table-tennis games to recognize—from the looks on the athletes' faces—who was winning and who was losing. Participants were also able to quickly surmise whether the game was close or a blowout.

Likewise, our bodies are quick to resonate with one another. According to a study published in the *Proceedings of the National Academy of Sciences*, holding hands with a loved one in pain not only synchronizes your breathing and heart rate but also causes brain-wave patterns to couple up. And that's just the beginning. Children who dance together are more cooperative in subsequent games. Adults who march, sing, or dance as part of a church, army, or community group are more likely to work for the good of their group than those who don't. And when two people bop to a steady beat, they are more likely to rate the other person's personality as similar to their own than do couples who move out of time.

Our hypersocial nature goes all the way to the deepest levels of our brains, where remarkably, social pain and physical pain are processed by the same circuits. This suggests that from the body's point of view, social contact is vital for survival and that social rejection is just as much a threat to our lives as physical injury. Similarly, in both humans and nonhuman animals, social contact reduces physical pain. Experiments summarized in the journal *Physiology & Behaviour* suggest that when given a choice of physical pain or isolation, social mammals will choose the former.

Even the odors that waft off other people's bodies can affect us. Researchers took armpit swabs from two groups: one that had just completed an easy, fun run and another that had just parachuted out of an airplane. Subjects who sniffed the parachute sample showed increased activity in the amygdala, a bigger startle response, and increased sensitivity to angry faces. Likewise, a study of dental students suggests that dentists can smell when a patient is anxious, making them more likely to make mistakes and perform badly. Our fear, in other words, gets around.

Even our stress is contagious. A 2018 study reported in *Nature Neuroscience* found that stress transmitted from others can change the brain in the same way real stress does. Working with mice, a research team removed one mouse from a pair and exposed it to a mild stress before returning it to its partner. They found that the networks in the brains of both the stressed mouse and naive partner were altered in similar ways.

Incredibly, even our health habits and physical condition rub off on one another. Researchers have found that body weight within couples is highly interdependent. Spouses often enter marriage at a similar weight status and mirror each other's weight trajectories over time. When one spouse develops obesity, the likelihood of the other spouse developing obesity increases significantly. There is also evidence that weight loss can spread within couples. A study from the University of Connecticut showed that if one party in a couple is trying to improve a health outcome—in this case, body weight—it is likely that their partner will have a similar outcome, even if they had not intended to do so.

Similarly, it comes as no surprise to learn that our long-term health outcomes are tightly linked to the quality of our social relations. This is the finding of the Harvard Study of Adult Development, a landmark seventy-five-year study of what makes us happy and healthy. Researchers followed 268 men who entered college in the late 1930s through war, career, marriage and divorce, parenthood and grandparenthood, and old age. The most recent leader of the study, psychiatrist Robert Waldinger, summed up the results this way: "Good relationships keep us happier and healthier. Period."

In short, social influence is turning out to be a much bigger factor in human health than previously realized. Biomedical specialists have long been inclined to view the body in isolation, and until recently, most medical professionals believed that social standing had almost nothing to do with health and disease. But our understanding has matured in recent decades, and we now know that the "social determinants of health" are incredibly powerful.

Work by epidemiologist Michael Marmot and others has shown conclusively that "health follows a social gradient." For hypersocial primates—especially humans—being high in the hierarchy gives a sense of power and control, but low status carries the threat of exclusion and the stress of having to scramble to make a living. The effect is so powerful, in fact, that one's position in the hierarchy may be just as important for health as more familiar factors such as diet and exercise.

The implications are wide ranging and highly inconvenient for culture-as-usual. In an indigenous, egalitarian culture, hierarchies were flat (or nearly so), and feelings of inclusion would have dominated the human experience. But in today's highly competitive environment, the pyramid is steep, and exclusion is an ever-present threat. In this radically unequal world, disease is essentially built into the system. This is how inequality kills. We can talk all we like about the dangers of sugar, refined food products, and sedentary living, but unless we correct these inequalities at the root, public health will continue to decline, and people will continue to suffer.

I SEE YOU

When it comes to satisfying our primal need for secure attachment, all of us have a deeply seated desire to feel seen, heard, felt, understood, respected, and appreciated. This need is a true human universal. People of every age, culture, origin, and status need and crave this experience. Even the Na'vi, the indigenous people of Pandora depicted in the movie *Avatar*, address one another with the honorific "I see you."

This need for human recognition is not a "nice-to-have" experience, nor is it "frosting on the cake" to be layered on top of other content or educational experiences. This is rock-solid biology that goes all the way to the deepest levels of physiology and nervous system function. Our need to feel felt is as real as our need for food and water.

When the body feels recognized and appreciated, the organism feels safe, and in turn, the autonomic nervous system goes into action, repairing tissues and opening up our cognition and creativity. Without question, this experience is a powerful and inexpensive form of medicine in its own right.

But sadly, the experience of feeling felt, heard, seen, respected, and appreciated is rapidly disappearing from our modern cultural landscape. In the very domains where we would most desire and expect it—education and medicine—it's often absent, eclipsed by administrative and technical urgencies. As we race from one task to another, our communications become increasingly superficial, and we neglect this most fundamental human need. Tragically, many students, clients, and patients go years without feeling felt, and some of us never experience it at all.

As a culture, we've lost sight of the primal, human fundamentals. Perversely, we take something that is (or was) intrinsically human and professionalize it. We wrap it up in technical language and hand it over to an expert class of psychologists and therapists. Today, if you really want to feel felt, you might have to pay an expert to do something that an average, nonexpert person should be able to do without any training whatsoever. This professionalization of our humanity is sometimes presented as a solution to our mental and spiritual distress, but it's really a reflection of our alienation and our failure to master the fundamentals of being good social animals.

In any case, there are two fundamental lessons here. First, look for these essential qualities in your interactions with others: "Do I feel felt, heard, seen, appreciated, and respected?" This should be the gold standard in evaluating personal and professional relationships. If the answer is no, an adjustment is in order.

Second, give these qualities to others as often as possible, to everyone in your world. This is a primal interpersonal gift, far more valuable and consequential than any physical object. When we take the time to see, hear, and recognize one another, we're actually giving a gift to their bodies and their lives. We're giving them medicine.

Give this gift to everyone, but especially people you disagree with. Make it both explicit and implicit. Paraphrase and repeat back your partner's concerns; make it clear that you're trying to understand. But even more important, slow down and show your willingness to sit and listen. When your body says, "I'm taking the time to listen," your conversational partner is going to relax. And quite likely, this recognition is all your partner really wanted in the first place.

CHAPTER 37

UBUNTU

You can't be human on your own.
—Desmond Tutu

As sophisticated modern people, we like to imagine that our bodies are self-contained and end at the outermost layer of our skin. First and foremost, we are individuals. We might occasionally identify with a team, a school, or a nation, but mostly, life is about our individual selves. We have friends and lovers, but mostly we're just ships passing in the night.

All of which is historically abnormal. In fact, for the vast majority of human life on this planet, identification with tribe was a fundamental priority. People understood their lives primarily in terms of affiliation. To be was to be a part of the group.

This prosocial identification shows up in many indigenous and Eastern cultures but is most conspicuous in the African philosophy of *ubuntu* (pronounced uu-boon-too). According to *ubuntu*, there exists a common bond between all human beings, and it is through this bond that we discover our own human qualities; we affirm our humanity when we acknowledge the humanity of others.

For native people, identity is not independent; it is interdependent, intimately connected to the life and welfare of the tribe, the family, the community. People define themselves not as individuals but as participants in a larger social order. As the Bushmen of South Africa put it, "We are people through other people," and "I am what I am because of who we are." This theme is common, if not universal, among native and indigenous people.

A BIG *UBUNTU*?

To our modern ears, this all sounds refreshing, good, and true. But what are we to do in a world of eight billion people? When alliances and organizations are in a constant state of flux? When your "tribe" is scattered across the planet, and the only source of contact is on-screen? Can we really identify with everyone simultaneously?

Sadly, the neuroscience suggests otherwise. Social interaction is neurologically demanding and, as they say in the world of computer science, "processor intensive." This means that the human brain can only manage so many interpersonal relationships. The legendary "Dunbar's number" tells us that the human neocortex is only capable of processing and maintaining a hundred or so human relations, roughly the same number as a typical Paleolithic tribe of hunter-gatherers. Going beyond that number puts us under an enormous cognitive load, and not surprisingly, most of us naturally avoid becoming too social.

In other words, our situation is unprecedented and calls for social, philosophical, and spiritual creativity on a scale never before seen on this planet. This fact alone takes us to the first step: compassion. Everyone shares in this predicament. All of us are confused about how to live in one small tribe, in the midst of one immense mega-tribe. No one knows how to do this, so forgive us our awkwardness. Forgive us our stupidities. Forgive me when I step on your toes, and I'll try to do likewise. We're all beginners in this one.

STOP BREAKING THE CIRCLE

A sense of big *ubuntu* feels elusive, but at the very least, we can stop breaking the circle. For example, we might well stop focusing on subdivisions of humanity—race, gender, age, or national origin—at least for the moment. Obviously, there are plenty of human groups who deserve a larger share of our attention, prosperity, and justice. But we need to be careful in our activism. Every time we promote the interests of a particular group, we run the risk of creating division. When every group has its own advocacy program, we tend to lose sight of the whole.

Likewise, the time has come to revise or, better yet, abandon the competitive, exclusionary model that's common in nearly every modern school. As it stands, most programs are built on a scarcity model and a grading system that guarantees, right from the outset, that only some fraction of students will advance. Or to put it another way, the bell curve of academic grading tells students, rather explicitly, "Some of you are going to fail and will be rejected." Obviously, it's hard to think about tribal identity and *ubuntu* when you're living under the constant threat of exclusion.

In fact, critics are right to charge that the modern school system isn't really about education at all. It's simply a method for parceling out precious social opportunities to selected individuals. It's built on a refinement metaphor that goes all the way back to the dawn of agriculture, winnowing the wheat from the chaff. If you throw away all the lesser athletes, lesser students, and lesser performers, you'll eventually wind up with a stellar group of exceptional individuals who can go on to achieve even more greatness. But you'll also produce a radically unjust society that's bad for everyone.

BIG HISTORY AND BIOLOGY

A better approach is to keep our attention focused on Big History and the totality of the human experience. We're more alike than we are different. Every human being shares similar hopes and dreams. United by common DNA and a shared predicament on a small, fragile planet, we're all striving for the same things: security, attachment and acceptance, meaning and love.

Once again, Big History keeps our vision intact and reminds us of our common humanity. If all we see is the short history of a single country or group, we're likely to lean toward defense, vigilance, and xenophobia. But when we grasp the essentials of the big human story, we're far more likely to see our commonality and our shared future.

The solution here is to stop thinking of Big History and biology as conventional academic disciplines. Instead, start thinking of them as tools of spiritual and social awakening. You might even think of them as Trojan horses. Bring these studies into the classroom under disguise, then let them do their work. Show your students the immensity of geologic and evolutionary time and the magnificence of Darwin's "copiously branching bush." Show them the simple fact that all of humanity has come from the same common ancestor, the same evolutionary root: LUCA (the Last Universal Common

Ancestor). Explain that the differences between peoples, races, and nationalities are in fact trivial. Then, let them come to their own conclusions.

Likewise, focus on human universals, the features and qualities of the life experience we all share. Donald Brown and other anthropologists have done great work on this score, some of which appears in his 1991 book *Human Universals*. According to common estimates, there are sixty-seven human universals, but you don't have to be an anthropologist to guess what they might be. Every human culture ever studied includes language, abstract symbolism, art, music, play, food preparation, and other activities we would all recognize no matter where we come from. Everyone sleeps, dreams, wakes, eats, talks, mates, fights, and makes up. This is common human ground.

But even more important is our common experience of simply being alive in this impermanent and mysterious world. No matter where we're from or what culture we inhabit, we're all faced with the same ambiguous predicament. Everyone is surprised by life, and everyone fears death. Everyone fears abandonment and longs for attention and attachment. Everyone wants to learn and achieve a sense of mastery and control. Everyone loves a story and longs for an explanation of why we're here. And most of all, perhaps, everyone needs to feel felt.

CHAPTER 38

THE DARK SIDE OF US

> The greatest crimes in the world are not committed by people breaking the rules but by people following the rules.
>
> —Banksy
> *Wall and Piece*

As hypersocial animals, it's easy to romanticize the warm, fuzzy benefits of tribal affiliation. We talk a good, seductive game about belonging and inclusion, and we love the benefits that come with secure attachment, social acceptance, *ubuntu*, and the "tend-and-befriend" response. But there are some dark sides to tribe, and we'd be fools to ignore them.

Consider the now-famous hormone oxytocin, often celebrated in the popular press as the "love hormone" or the "trust hormone." Advocates call it an *empathogen* and point to its many virtues: It promotes trust, relaxation, social bonding, and affiliation. It decreases fear and anxiety and even decreases inflammation and promotes wound healing. Just the idea of oxytocin makes us feel good.

But there's more to the story. While oxytocin does produce the trusting, prosocial effects we hear so much about, it also stimulates some nasty out-group behaviors. In *Behave: The Biology of Humans at Our Best and Worst*, Robert Sapolsky describes research showing that when interacting with strangers, oxytocin actually *decreases* cooperation: "Oxytocin makes us more prosocial to Us and worse to everyone else." In other words, it sharpens our in-group, out-group distinctions. When we're under the influence of oxytocin, we're all about Us, but we have little interest in the welfare of Them.

Then there's obedience, famously described by Stanley Milgram in his legendary *Obedience to Authority*. Seeking to understand the atrocities committed in World War II, Milgram recruited volunteers to participate in a fake experiment of "social learning." Subjects were instructed to administer tests to "learners" located in another room. If the learners answered incorrectly, the "teacher" was to administer increasingly painful shocks. Individuals who questioned the process were pressed by an authority figure in a white lab coat who ordered, "The experiment must continue."

The findings were profoundly disturbing: a substantial percentage of volunteers submitted to authority and continued shocking the learner, even going so far as to administer (fake) lethal doses of electricity. In this "agentic state," the subject gives up his own judgment and sense of responsibility and becomes an instrument of authority. If enough people lapse into this condition, atrocity becomes increasingly likely.

Equally troubling is the problem of conformity, famously explored by Solomon Asch in the 1950s. His experiments demonstrated that a sizable percentage of people are willing to adjust their personal sensory perceptions to fit the dominant estimates of the group. In other words, a lot of us are willing to reject our own judgment for the sake of getting along.

Closely related is groupthink, a process by which ideas tend to coalesce within a group. When we're under the influence of groupthink, we avoid raising controversial issues or alternative solutions, and as a consequence, individual creativity begins to disappear. Like obedience, groupthink can also lead to dehumanizing and violent behavior against others. Irving Janis, an early pioneer on groupthink theory, warned:

> The more amiability and esprit de corps there is among the members of a policy-making ingroup, the greater the danger that independent critical thinking will be replaced by groupthink, which is likely to result in irrational and dehumanizing actions directed against outgroups.

These findings force us to confront a monstrous dilemma for effective living: tribal affiliation is essential for keeping us happy and healthy, but mindless obedience, conformity, and loyalty are a recipe for atrocity. The dark side of tribe isn't just unpleasant; it holds the seeds of disaster, for both people and the Earth. Tribalism nurtures us, but it can also destroy our future.

In this sense, historian Howard Zinn might well have been speaking on behalf of the biosphere when he wrote, "Civil disobedience is not our problem. Our problem is civil obedience." When rich corporate interests hold the biggest megaphones, the dangers of conformity and groupthink are multiplied a thousandfold. When advertising becomes omnipresent and neurologically sophisticated, we're under the influence almost constantly. We go along to get along, and before you know it, we're doing as we're told, mindlessly destroying the future on command.

LOST IN THE HOMOSPHERE

Obedience, conformity, and groupthink are bad enough, but our hypersocial nature has another monstrous downside—our almost maniacal fascination with *Homo sapiens*. We absolutely love to watch, critique, and judge one another's appearance, language, and behavior. We might even call this tendency *homo hypnosis*, the inclination of modern humans to focus so intently on their own dramas that they forget the rest of the living world.

In his book *Wild Law: A Manifesto for Earth Justice*, author Cormac Cullinan describes this incestuous circle of self-fascination as the *homosphere*, an exclusive club dedicated to humans and human interests. Lost in the homosphere, many modern humans are functionally oblivious to our impact on the natural world. Obsessed with ourselves, we go blind to the suffering of nonhuman creatures and the destruction of our life-supporting systems. Seen in this way, the alpha issue of our day is not carbon in the atmosphere or the plastic in the oceans, but humans' inability or unwillingness to look away from their own immediate concerns.

The lesson is to adjust our vision and break the trance of *homo hypnosis*. Give up the obsession with human-on-human drama and look at the wider world for a change. The prescription here is not misanthropy, but *lessanthropy*. Humans are interesting creatures, to be sure, but if we can't look beyond our immediate interests and self-fascination, we are well and truly sunk.

CHAPTER 39

FIRST, DO NO MEDICINE

> Modern medicine is a negation of health. It isn't organized to serve human health, but only itself, as an institution. It makes more people sick than it heals.
>
> —Ivan Illich

For the vast majority of human history, the body was naked to the world. Like all wild animals, we were exposed to the elements and vulnerable to heat, cold, trauma, and predation. Serious injury or illness was an ever-present danger, and medical care as we know it today was unimaginable. It's no surprise that our hunting-and-gathering ancestors were strong and resilient. They had to be.

But beginning in the modern era, medicine became increasingly effective, and a new mindset began to emerge. Physicians became increasingly confident in their powers and began to apply the medical model more broadly, and before long, almost every human condition and experience became a candidate for medical interpretation and intervention: childbirth, athletics, minor afflictions, mood swings, aging, wrinkled skin, and of course, death.

This process of creeping medical intervention in human life is known as *medicalization*, famously described by social critic Ivan Illich in his landmark 1976 book *Medical Nemesis*. His idea was simple: as modern medicine extends its reach into more and more areas of human life and hands more responsibility for the body over to an expert class, it takes away our sense of personal power and control. We enjoy some obvious benefits, but the existential and experiential costs are immense. Illich described this process as the "expropriation of health."

Today, medical and health professions lay claim to every cell in the body and almost every aspect of the human experience. Most obviously, we medicalize exercise: "Before beginning an exercise program, see your doctor" goes the ominous warning. But that's just the beginning. Today we attempt to medicalize nutrition, sleep, meditation, stress, family and social time, work–life balance, music, travel, and even education. If it touches the body or human life in any way, we attempt to track it, diagnose it, treat it, and of course, profit from it.

The rise of medicalization is reflected in the wave of overtesting, overdiagnosis, and overtreatment in clinics and hospitals across America, and the industry has taken on a life of its own. A 2007 essay in the *New York Times* put it bluntly: "What's Making Us Sick Is an Epidemic of Diagnoses." Similarly, *Times* columnist Gina Kolta has written about the rise in "disease mongering" and concluded, "If you've got a pulse, you're sick."

As a patient population, we've grown accustomed to visiting experts and professionals for every ache and pain. We've become dependent upon their expertise, methods, machines, and prescriptions. The end result is that while some of us get better, many of us are doing worse. As Illich put it:

> [D]ependence on professional intervention tends to impoverish the non-medical health-supporting and healing aspects of the social and physical environments, and tends to decrease the organic and psychological coping ability of ordinary people.

When used in excess, modern medicine becomes a kind of prosthetic, an artificial prop for people who may not truly need the help. When every ailment is treated, people no longer need to fight their way through difficult or painful experiences. And when there's no fight, there's no adaptation. When the challenge disappears, the body has no incentive to reorganize itself to a higher level of function. In this way, modern medicine can deprive us of the very stimulus our bodies need to find their own solutions.

As medicalization has become pervasive, it's actually altered our popular understanding of health itself. Today we think that healing comes from substances, procedures, products, and providers. In the process, we've forgotten the ancient and immensely sophisticated regenerative power that lives in every cell in our bodies. In fact, animal bodies have been actively healing themselves for hundreds of millions of years, and this legacy still lives in our history, our tissue, our relationships, and our experiences.

Medicalization turns our powers upside down and confronts us with an inconvenient truth. That is, medicalization may well constitute a significant public health problem in its own right. In other words, maybe what we really need is less medicine, not more. Maybe what we really need is more challenging physical experience, especially in natural outdoor environments, along with real food, more sleep, and meaningful work.

To be sure, modern medicine does provide a valuable service, and we can be grateful it works as well as it does. The discoveries of germ theory, antiseptics, anesthesia, and antibiotics surely rank as some of the greatest advances in human history. But at the same time, medicalization stands as a real threat to our health and personal power.

So, to borrow an idea from medicine itself, perhaps the solution lies in getting the dose right. Physicians often speak of a dose–response curve for various drugs and medical treatments. This simply means effectiveness varies, sometimes dramatically, depending on the amount administered. As toxicologists often tell us, "The dose makes the poison." Likewise, "The dose makes the medicine."

We can say the same thing about medical care itself. A small amount can be extremely helpful and a moderate amount even more so, but after a time, the returns begin to diminish and even reverse themselves. The trick for maintaining our health and personal power is to focus on our innate powers first, then turn to the medical system as needed.

Obviously, there are plenty of perfectly valid reasons to make use of wonder drugs, technologies, and knowledge that can make our bodies whole again. But in the main, our goal should be to use modern medicine as little as possible and to shift the challenge of adaptation back onto our bodies.

Of course, it's always a judgment call. When you're suffering a minor injury or illness, it's tempting to go straight to the health care professional and get the fast-acting substances that will make the unpleasantness go away. But there's value in fighting the fight and delaying the medicine as long as possible. Keep your body in the adaptation game as long as you can, and give it the opportunity to do what it does best.

If you really want to sustain your health, the fundamental art lies in fighting the fight with your intrinsic powers first. This means demedicalizing your life as much as you possibly can. Not only should we cut back on excessive use of medical care, but we should also stop thinking of our bodies and our lives in medical terms. Do we really need medical supervision to tell us what to eat and how to exercise? Do we really see ourselves as chronically sick and in constant need of medical expertise? What happens to the human experience when we start from an assumption of illness and imminent disease?

Not only will this demedicalized approach benefit your body and your resilience, but it will also benefit society as a whole. By using less medicine, we reduce the load on our already overburdened health care system. If everyone leaned a little more toward their own powers of adaptation, the entire health and medical system would work a lot better. This would be a dramatic win-win.

The trick is to trust our history and our almost unlimited powers of adaptation. In fact, our bodies are far more powerful and creative than we've been led to believe. If we're going to create a functional future, it's essential we stop thinking of ourselves as perpetual patients. Stop interpreting every sensation and experience in medical terms. Above all, trust your body to adapt. It's done it before and it can do it again.

CHAPTER 40

WORLD OF WOUNDS

> It may well be that more and more of what people bring before doctors and therapists for treatment—agonies of body and spirit—are symptoms of the biospheric emergency registering at the most intimate levels of life. The Earth hurts, and we hurt with it.
> —Theodore Roszak
> *The Voice of the Earth*

Can you feel it? Can you feel the destruction of the biosphere in your body—the continuing degradation of habitat, the loss of biodiversity, and the chaos in our social systems? If you can, you're probably a normal, sensitive person with an extended sense of your body in the world. And in turn, there's a pretty good chance that you're in pain.

The statistics are staggering: According to the Centers for Disease Control and Prevention, an estimated 20 percent of US adults had chronic pain in 2016. A 2011 Institute of Medicine report titled "Relieving Pain in America" found that some one hundred million Americans are burdened by chronic pain. And in recent years, the opioid epidemic has killed thousands of people and shows little sign of abating. Chronic pain may well be the greatest psycho-physical epidemic in human history.

PAIN IN THE PALEO

It didn't used to be this way. To be sure, our hunting-and-gathering ancestors no doubt had their share of acute injuries and even chronic conditions, but the status quo was always robust health. Physical bodies suffered insults, but it's also safe to assume that most of our ancestors were generally pain-free. They were sensible, after all, and smart enough to rest in camp when injured.

But in the modern domain, our pain is far more complex and intractable. We might even think of it as an entirely new kind of pain, a wicked, complex condition that's massively bound up with the larger psychological, social, and ecological crises of our day. And sadly, our medical professions are almost entirely unequipped to deal with it.

When we're suffering in this way, tissue inflammation is only a minor part of the problem. As we've seen, contagion is the rule among hypersocial animals. Stress, social strife, and fear for the future ripple through society like wildfire, touching everyone, whether we realize it or not. And as cortisol levels soar, minor physical injuries begin to feel pervasive and permanent. Inevitably, our pain is bound up in context: the Earth hurts, society hurts, and we hurt with it.

We're desperate for relief, but no amount of nonsteroidal anti-inflammatory drugs (NSAIDs), opioids, alcohol, massage, or CBD will do the trick. We try to distract ourselves with entertainment; we deny reality and get lost in trivia. We shrink back from engagement in life, and we get depressed. But all these efforts only seem to make things worse. Our suffering, it seems, is baked into our predicament. Our pain is physical, but it's also situational, inextricably tied to larger realities of modern human life.

In order to truly cure ourselves, we'd have to cure the world first. We'd have to ease the suffering of the natural world and the people in our communities. But this seems beyond us, and in the meantime, we are left with our aching backs, necks, knees, and hips. We feel stuck.

STOP RUNNING

At times like these, some Buddhist wisdom might be helpful. We've all heard the classic observation that "All life is suffering," sometimes translated as "All life is impermanent, therefore unsatisfactory." Teachers advise us to accept this condition, and in turn, things may become easier.

This leads to the paradoxical prescription recommended by Pema Chödrön in her book *The Wisdom of No Escape*. In short, stop trying to run from the pain. When you're living in a culture that treats the biosphere and people as nothing more than resources to be exploited and monetized, of course you're going to feel pain. When you live in a hyperpolarized society that denies basic dignity to enormous numbers of people, of course you're going to feel the hurt. It comes with the territory. But trying to deny reality or wish the pain away only makes it worse. In fact, it's our resistance to the experience that really digs us into a hole. As they say in the meditation world, "Pain plus resistance equals suffering." The pain may well be nonnegotiable, but the resistance is optional. Give up the resistance, and you just might feel better.

THE LAW OF LIFE

In a sense, pain seems to be woven into the human experience. No matter what we do, we'll eventually lose our possessions, our friends, our families, and our health. As the Buddhist writer Pico Iyer put it, "Loss is the law of life." The path to peace lies in relinquishing our attachment and our expectation that life ought to be a certain way. If we can let go, we can transcend our suffering.

This all sounds right, and yes, with reflection, we can learn to accept the prospect of our own personal loss and eventual demise. Yes, we'll admit, all is insecure, death is coming, and there's no escape. We can breathe, relax, and come to peace with our inevitable reckoning. Our bodies are falling apart, our friends and families will perish, and death is on the calendar.

But there's another layer to our suffering. It's one thing to accept our own personal demise, but the death of the biosphere by our own species feels like an entirely different kind of catastrophe. It's not just our personal suffering and death anymore; it's the very fabric of life that's at stake.

Buddha was an astute observer of the human condition, but even he would have been shocked to learn the scale, magnitude, and pace of today's assault on the biosphere. He would have been taken aback by reports of climate crisis, habitat destruction, ecological overshoot, and the sixth extinction. But then, after a period of adjustment and reflection, he would have nodded peacefully. "Yes, of course it would be so. All that striving for permanence could only lead to a deeper and more profound predicament. Are you not surprised? It's your fear and continual striving for permanence that is making your world ever more insecure. If you could give up your obsession with security in all things, you might be able to find some equanimity."

WORLD OF WONDER

In any case, the wounds are real, and the pain is both contagious and acute. This much is undeniable, but maybe there's relief in the other direction. If we turn our minds around, we begin to remember that the biosphere is immense in her powers and awesome in her ability to rebound after injury and disease. She's done it many times in the past and will no doubt do so again in the future, and no matter what kind of wounds we inflict on her body, she's going to be OK. The injuries that we're inflicting on the planet are acute, but not mortal. She will rebound.

In his classic *A Sand County Almanac*, Aldo Leopold famously observed that "one of the penalties of an ecological education is that one lives alone in a world of wounds." And it's all quite true. For those of us who care enough to learn the facts of ecological destruction, the suffering is pervasive. How could we do this to life and to ourselves? How could we be so foolish, so ignorant, and so selfish?

These laments are all on the mark, but knowing what we know about the resilience and grandeur of the natural world, we could very well rephrase Leopold's observation another way: "One of the benefits of an ecological education is that one lives together in a world of wonder."

Forget the destruction and the stupidity for the moment and focus your attention on the immensity, subtlety, and wonder of the natural world. Forget the tar sands atrocity, the dams, the pipelines, the deforestation, and the rape of the oceans. Instead, focus on the way that nature rebounds from disaster, the way that plants and animals regenerate into new forms at the earliest opportunity. Remember the way the biosphere has bounced back from asteroid strikes, volcanic catastrophes, and oxygen holocausts. Life will find a way.

This shift in attention won't be a cure for all that ails you, but it might well serve as a powerful analgesic and give you the relief you need to keep up the fight.

CHAPTER 41

THERAPY SESSION

> I think the concept of "species loneliness" has it right. Living in an economic system that regards nonhuman beings—plants, animals, ecosystems—as a mere stock of resources to be exploited leaves us on some subconscious level deeply troubled by the trauma of our separation.
> —Jason Hickel

For some mysterious reason, it usually starts with frogs, dead frogs pickled in formaldehyde. Squeamish high school students are directed to dissect the corpses into pieces and document their findings in detail. From there, the study of biology begins, and little by little, the vast scope of life on Earth is revealed. In theory, at least.

But sadly, biology is usually presented as yet another exercise in schoolwork, which is to say, the entire discipline is presented as an enormous pile of facts, names, and dates, all of which are to be memorized, assimilated, and tested at the end of the semester. What's missing is the fact that biology can actually be seen as a spiritual discipline and a powerful form of therapy in its own right.

Consider the story: when we take the big biological view, life is revealed as something both ancient and enormous—timescales that span millions of years, marked by the appearance and disappearance of millions of species, all in flux, all mutating, adapting, metabolizing, and reproducing. The immensity is mind-boggling. And of course, if you happen to be of the species *Homo sapiens*, you'll suddenly begin to feel very small and temporary in comparison. And so the obvious question: How does all this make you feel?

Reactions vary, but if you're like many, you might well find the whole thing rather unacceptable. You probably like feeling big and important, but this story goes the other way altogether. You might get angry, you might go into denial, and you might well reject the entire enterprise. Biology, you might well conclude, is for frogs and other slimy creatures, not for people.

Others may accept the grand story but find it depressing. After all, you've been questing after status and significance most of your adult life, and now the frog people tell you that you're really nothing more than a minor, possibly dysfunctional life-form with no particular standing. Just another animal, destined for extinction on the trash heap of biological history. Yuk.

But these reactions, understandable as they may be, miss the point. That is, biology succeeds as therapy precisely *because* it makes us feel small and insignificant. It's an antidote to our ego, our sense of human supremacy, our narcissism, and our delusions of grandeur. It takes us down not just a few notches, but all the way to biological ground zero. You're just another organism, my friend, no more consequential than any other primate, any other mammal, any other vertebrate. Even your large brain is nothing to brag about. In all likelihood, your kind will be extinct in a million years, or maybe even a few decades.

This is a powerful dose of humility, but there's actually an upside. To be sure, the big story of biology kicks us off our pedestal, but in so doing, it simultaneously puts us into kinship with an immense and unimaginably powerful band of associates, colleagues, and maybe even friends. There is exuberant, powerful life in this circle. In fact, this is precisely where our health and sanity come from.

It's easy to forget, but life on the pedestal was actually not that great to begin with. We assumed the position of superiority because our culture told us to do so, and as individuals, we feel immense pressure to "be somebody." But this is a stressful place to live, and it's destined to fail, especially when we succeed. The higher the pedestal, the greater the separation; the greater the separation, the greater the anxiety and fear of failure. We assume the throne, only to discover that it's a lonely, isolating place. If only we could play with our friends once again.

So maybe it's time to sit down with a biologist once a week. Lie on the couch, put your feet up, and share your tales of woe. In turn, she'll tell you a story of the grandeur of life, and by the end of the hour, you'll feel a lot smaller, a lot more powerful, and a whole lot better.

CHAPTER 42

THE ART IS LONG

> A physician is obligated to consider more than a diseased organ, more than even the whole man—he must view the man in his world.
> —Harvey Williams Cushing
> American neurosurgeon (1869–1939)

As we've seen, our cultural myopia has compromised our ability to see clearly and, in turn, create solutions that might lead to a functional future. Nowhere is this so apparent as in modern medicine, where the individual is now treated as little more than a medical object, a hairy bag of water, isolated from his or her life-supporting systems of habitat, tribe, and culture.

In this system, our diagnoses and treatments are all about the welfare of what we might call the "short body." We treat symptoms and syndromes with highly targeted therapies and procedures, but it's almost unheard of for a modern physician to ask a patient about the larger relationships that sustain his or her life. No one ever asks, "How often do you get into the outdoors?"; "How connected are you to your habitat and your community?"; "How's your social standing?"; "Do you have friends and loved ones in your life?"

There's no time for any of this because in today's paradigm, efficiency is everything. The greatest priority is to move patients along, and in the process, all other considerations get stripped away. If it doesn't have a direct bearing on the administration of biomedical procedures, it's simply rejected as "outside the scope of practice."

In other words, modern medicine has become a giant game of "let's pretend." Let's pretend that the world has no influence on health and medical outcomes. Let's pretend that society, race, habitat, income, class, stress, and sense of purpose have nothing to do with how people function and how their bodies heal. These are messy complications that interfere with the business of processing patients. Let's ignore these considerations and maybe they'll go away.

This small-health orientation is sometimes effective in its own way, and some of the results are even spectacular. But even as it succeeds, the side effects of this orientation are substantial, even catastrophic. Every short-body medical encounter leaves patients with an increasing sense of isolation and reinforces their sense of alienation. The explanation for their suffering usually hinges on some microscopic causal agent—a microbe or a virus, an offending tendon or ligament, or an insufficient level of some particular neurotransmitter. But rarely, if ever, does it connect to the larger, life-sustaining world. In other words, the modern physician is actually contributing to a psycho-spiritual illusion of separateness, which in turn leads to a deterioration of health. This is what Ivan Illich called *iatrogenesis*.

MEET THE LONG BODY

The solution is rather obvious, although not so easy to actualize. What modern medicine needs is a "long-body" orientation, a term that comes from the Native American tradition. In essence, the long body is simply the body plus its circles of life support. The operative principle is continuity. Appearances to the contrary, the human body—in fact, all animal bodies—is radically connected to the so-called "outside world." Instead of describing disease as an affliction that's exclusive to the individual body, we begin to speculate on injuries and diseases in relationship to society and culture. And in turn, we begin to think holistically.

The good news is that some physicians have proposed a more inclusive, systems-based approach. In a landmark 1977 article in the journal *Science*, psychiatrist George Engel called for a new "bio-psycho-social model." As a physician, Engel was disenchanted with the limitations of analytical biomedicine and believed that clinicians must attend simultaneously to the biological, psychological, and social dimensions of illness.

Engel did not deny the power of biomedical research but took issue with its narrow focus, especially its tendency to regard patients as broken medical objects. His goal was to reverse the dehumanization of modern medicine and the disempowerment of patients. His approach struck a resonant chord with many, both inside and outside the medical community, but as we can now see, even this perspective was incomplete, something that native people would recognize immediately. Yes, the biological, psychological, and social elements are all well and good, but where is habitat? And where is the continuity of health across generations?

For indigenous people, this would be seen as a glaring omission, a rookie mistake. Yes, it's laudable that some segments of medical culture have moved beyond the mechanistic view of the body to include mind and society, but that was simply an obvious step in the right direction. If we're really going to get serious about bringing together all the influences on human health, we need a six-part model of mind, body, spirit, land, tribe, and ancestry.

This more expansive view of the body reminds us of the philosophy described by Aldo Leopold in *A Sand County Almanac*: "The land ethic simply enlarges the boundaries of the community to include soils, waters, plants, and animals, or collectively: the land." In other words, we need to start thinking big about health, community, and the body.

STOP BREAKING THE CIRCLE

This all feels right, but the devil is in the details. How could any one practitioner or physician possibly address all the influences that bear on a patient's health? Such an endeavor would take an entire team and span immense amounts of time. And does it really make sense to address such a broad range of influence when a patient is suffering from a simple injury or illness that's treatable with conventional methods?

The average physician has her hands full as it is and can hardly be expected to go out and fix the entire world every time a patient presents with diabetes, heart disease, or an arthritic hip. But at the very least, the physician can stop reinforcing the isolationistic view of the body in the world. Yes, time pressures are real, and there are lots of technical details to keep track of in modern practice. But perspective is essential, and patient education is vital. It's not enough to simply prescribe a substance and make sure that the patient complies. Patients need to feel involved and integrated with the world at large.

Physicians need to be teachers and guides as well as technicians. And while it may not be possible to fix the entire world to cure every affliction, it *is* possible to show the way toward continuity and integration, to remind the patient of his or her connections to society, habitat, and ancestry.

Likewise, we can and should expect physicians to be vocal advocates for interdependence, planetary health, and the totality of their patients' welfare. In other words, health professionals should be activists and leaders, speaking out on behalf of the body–habitat connection, the body–culture connection, and the body–society connection. These are not mystical, vaporous ideas. They are just as important to human health as microorganisms, inflammation, and poor blood-sugar control. In other words, activism should be an integral part of medical practice. Hippocrates would surely approve.

CHAPTER 43

THE CREATIVE IMPERATIVE

> This is precisely the time when artists go to work. There is no time for despair, no place for self-pity, no need for silence, no room for fear . . . Like failure, chaos contains information that can lead to knowledge—even wisdom.
> —Toni Morrison

These days, it's easy to be angry. Surrounded by destruction, injustice, and chaos, we resolve to act. We protest as best we can, bringing the fight to the street, the workplace, and cyberspace. We speak truth to the pyramid.

But while our resistance to destruction and injustice is necessary and honorable, it is not sufficient. As Naomi Klein has put it in her book *No Is Not Enough*, outrage, indignation, and protests are good first steps, but by themselves, they don't go very far. We must stand in the way of bad policies and bad behavior, but we've also got to build something of value. Buckminster Fuller said much the same thing: "You never change things by fighting the existing reality. To change something, build a new model that makes the existing model obsolete."

ART FAILURE

This would be a good time to take another look at the nature of our planetary predicament. Most reasonable people would agree that something is dreadfully wrong. Some might call it a biological emergency, a social emergency, a humanitarian emergency, a relational emergency, or a failure of vision. These are all accurate descriptions, but we would also do well to see it as an *aesthetic emergency*. In other words, our predicament is an artistic failure on a vast, planetary scale—a triumph of economics, efficiency, and expediency over beauty and proportion.

In fact, we've produced a lot of ugliness in our quest to dominate the planet and one another: ugly methods, ugly processes, ugly products, and ugly ideas that violate our deepest sense of balance and relationship. And along the way, art has been demoted from a vital human universal to a minor pastime for children and romantics.

To describe our condition as an aesthetic emergency might sound soft, as if our planetary predicament is nothing more than a failure to get the right colors and shapes on a canvas. But in fact, this perspective gets to the heart of the matter and even offers a glimpse of how we might do better. So much of what plagues us today comes from our stubborn insistence that bottom-line values should take priority over context, quality, and harmony. By our way of thinking, profit is the most beautiful thing on the planet.

But if we had listened to the artists in the first place, things would be much different. And instead of putting art at the bottom of the academic totem pole—along with physical education and the humanities—maybe we ought to let the artists take charge for a while. Instead of basing all our decisions on financial feasibility, why couldn't we use beauty as the standard? To modern bean-counters, this sounds fundamentally crazy, but from a historical view, it's the financial model that's truly abnormal. We can be sure that the Paleolithic cave painters of Europe and Africa weren't making judgment calls based on economics and profit–loss calculations.

To be sure, not everyone agrees on what makes something beautiful, but we should be able to agree that some things are fundamentally, objectively ugly: poisoning our atmosphere with waste products, the relentless destruction of habitat, strip mining our future and leaving nothing for future generations. We don't need spreadsheets or experts to tell us these things.

In fact, it's no surprise that artists and activists are natural allies, exemplified in the emerging movement called *artivism*. In *It's Bigger Than Hip Hop*, M. K. Asante gives us a typical definition:

> The artivist uses her artistic talents to fight and struggle against injustice and oppression—by any medium necessary. The artivist merges commitment to freedom and justice with the pen, the lens, the brush, the voice, the body, and the imagination. The artivist knows that *to make an observation is to have an obligation*.

In modern society, we're conditioned to believe that art is something we do with paints and brushes, wood, metal, and glass, something that lives in museums, galleries, and gift shops. But for the artivist, art is all about the human encounter with life and culture. As Joe Brewer, the cofounder and research director of Culture2, a culture design lab for social good, sees it, "ALL of our problems arise through pathologies of culture." He advocates "culture hacking" with new rituals, new art, new writing, and new relationships. "If we want to design our way through this maelstrom of crises we will have to become culture designers who learn how to guide and shape the evolution of entire societies." Culture, in other words, is our canvas.

To be an artivist is to stand at the leading edge of culture and point the way to something better. It requires that we remain alert and awake to the meaning and consequences of our actions in context. Unfortunately, it's easy to fall into a state of reactivism. We wait for someone in power to do something abhorrent, then we strike back with venom, satire, or ridicule. But this kind of effort usually goes nowhere and accomplishes nothing. Even if our snark is right on target, we haven't really created anything of value.

Calls to action are all well and good, but what we really need are calls to cultural creativity. As we've seen, modern culture has yet to develop a curriculum for dealing with mismatch, lifestyle disease, social inequality, or a functional future, and it simply isn't delivering the kind of teachings we need to craft a long-term relationship with the planet. Activists must fight the good fight against planet-hostile and future-hostile actors, but even more important is the need to create curriculum. What can we teach each other about building a functional future? Can we show the way through the chaos to something that actually works?

As artists, we need to illuminate what's wrong, but even more importantly, we need to show what's better. Use your art to draw attention to bad actors, highlight foolishness, and speak truth to power, but more than all this, use your art to revive and extend our health and sapience. As always, the cure for bad ideas is better ideas.

CHAPTER 44

WICKED WAYS

> We cannot solve the problems we have created
> with the same thinking we used in creating them.
> —Albert Einstein

Hang around with people who work on large-scale social and ecological challenges and it won't be long before someone describes the matter in question as a "wicked problem."

It sounds like cool pop-talk, but there's actually a working definition in play. According to Jay Rosen, professor of journalism at New York University, wicked problems have these features:

> It's hard to say what the problem is, to define it clearly, or to tell where it starts and stops. There is no "right" way to view the problem, no definitive formulation. The way it's framed will change what the solution appears to be. Someone can always say that the problem is

just a symptom of another problem, and that someone will not be wrong. There are many stakeholders, all with their own frames, which they tend to see as exclusively correct. Ask what the problem is and you will get a different answer from each. The problem is interconnected to a lot of other problems; pulling them apart is almost impossible . . . It gets worse. Every wicked problem is unique, so in a sense there is no prior art, and solving one won't help you with the others.

All of which adds up to a really nasty state of affairs. There can be no question about it: all of our modern-day challenges—health care, social inequality, housing, education, and habitat destruction—add up to one monstrous cluster of super wickedness. It's no wonder that so many of us throw up our hands at the end of the day.

Unfortunately, modern education fails to recognize or teach for wickedness. The vast majority of conventional education is devoted to teaching linear problem-solving, which simply isn't up to the task of dealing with hypercomplex, nonlinear systems. In many programs, the whole idea is for students to get the "right answer" on an exam, but by their nature, wicked problems simply don't have "right answers."

And as for big science and big government, the common tendency is to double down on familiar measures that might have worked in simpler times. We count, measure, and track everything we can get our calipers on. We build bigger and faster computers and data centers, all in the hopes that one day, we'll get every process and detail locked down so that we can finally apply the right leverage and master the problem once and for all with a conclusive and enduring "right answer."

But this enterprise is destined to fail as well, or at least extend to the horizon in a never-ending grind of calculation. That's just the way it is with wicked problems; every success only seems to reveal another layer of complexity that no one thought of before. It's no wonder most of us are so exhausted.

WICKED ART, WICKED ACTION

Wicked problems may look and feel intractable, but they also suggest new forms of action, art, activism, and living. Wicked problems call for a paradoxical approach. Instead of doubling down on calculation and analysis, we own the wickedness, relish it, and celebrate it. Embrace the uncertainty, the doubt, and the ambiguity. Stop trying to nail everything down. In this sense, what we need are behaviors, ideas, and orientations that are themselves wicked, complex, nonlinear, and creative. Instead of looking for right answers, we look for wicked answers. Wicked problems, in other words, call for wicked activism and wicked action.

For creative people, art often feels like the only sensible response to the problems of our age, but what would wicked action look and feel like? This is where things really get interesting. The essence of wickedness is complexity, dynamism, and radical interconnection with other processes and systems. In this light, wicked action would have these characteristics:

- Wicked action seeks to influence entire systems. The goal is to touch the totality.
- Wicked action targets relationships, not objects.
- Wicked action works with meaning, story, and narrative.
- Wicked action is dynamic and flexible.

- Each wicked action is unique. There can be no standardizing wicked action.
- Above all, wicked action is human and humane. The idea is to bring the whole organism to the effort. This means using both sides of the brain, the gut, the heart, and above all, the body.

This all sounds promising, but does wickedness work in action? Is it powerful? Does it get results? Actually, these questions come from a conventional, linear problem-solving orientation and, in turn, miss the point. That is, the idea isn't to "solve" the wicked problem but to create something of value, even something beautiful. In this respect, wicked action is the ultimate work-around.

A WICKED CURRICULUM

So how would a wicked orientation fit into modern education? As it stands, we tend to focus on testable material, especially linear problems with right answers. We believe that it's best to keep things simple in the early grades and leave the complexity for later. Let the college students grapple with the really tough, systemic problems down the road.

But why not introduce wickedness right at the outset? To be sure, there are fundamental skills to be learned, but we already know how to do this: sets and reps with letters and numbers eventually lead to literacy and competence. So why not present wickedness to young children? Why not pose complex, interdependent problems and see what they come up with?

As always, it's about practice and specificity. Students get good at dealing with wicked problems by dealing with wicked problems. They get good at generating wicked answers by generating wicked answers.

It makes no sense whatsoever to leave these encounters to the end of the educational enterprise. Any coach or trainer would agree: if you want to become proficient in working with wickedness, work with wickedness.

To make this feasible, we need to teach art in an entirely new way. Instead of thinking of it as craft, elevate it to a universal orientation, one that applies to all levels of the human experience, from materials to relationships, to activism and policy. Art isn't about nice colors and shapes; it's about taking on the biggest challenges of our day. It's about creating a functional future.

Along the way, try these principles for wicked action:

- **Give up the physics envy:** We're never going to find certainty on wicked issues, nor should we try. Certainty doesn't exist, not in the real world. Give up the expectation that the wickedness can or should be reduced to something solvable.
- **Free your mind:** Don't let the predicament drive your thinking. Let go of your assumptions about the nature of the problem. Engage the beginner's mind, rest, then do it again. Think like a kid.
- **Create:** Remember, the goal is not to solve the problem. You may not be able to frame the issue in some "right" way, but you can frame it in a beautiful way.
- **Feel:** Use your whole body to understand and engage the process. Slow down and let your body metabolize the situation.
- **Keep moving:** Wicked problems are notoriously dynamic. Update your methods and your understanding frequently. No creation is ever finished.

Above all, remember this: wickedness is not the enemy. Radical interdependence and hypercomplexity are the way of life itself. Wickedness is woven deeply into human life as an unfathomable mystery. Far from being a problem, wickedness is actually the raw material for our art. Instead of looking at wickedness as a problem, see it as a gift.

CHAPTER 45

ESCAPE FROM THE DRAMA TRIANGLE

> I recommend that the Statue of Liberty on the East Coast be supplemented by a Statue of Responsibility on the West Coast.
> —Viktor E. Frankl

"It's all his fault!"
    "It's all their fault!"
    "I'm not to blame!"
    "Please come and fix me."
    "Make my life work again."

These refrains are common across the modern world, and we hear them hundreds of times each day in one form or another. They're so common, in fact, we might even suppose that they're normal, human statements. This is just how people talk.

But all these statements are symptoms of a dysfunctional attitude and relational pathology, first described by psychologist Stephen Karpman in 1968. Often used as a tool in counseling and psychotherapy, the "drama triangle" has powerful applications across the entire range of human experience.

The trouble begins when a person identifies himself as a powerless victim in the face of circumstance. According to the victim's narrative, the primary source of his unhappiness lies with other people, agents, forces, and events. He pins the blame for his predicament on a persecutor, or if that doesn't work, he goes in search of a rescuer, someone or something that will extract him from his predicament and save the day.

Of course, it's essential to remember there *are* genuine victims in this world and, just as obviously, authentic persecutors who deserve justice. Likewise, there are times when we can and should reach out to others for support. But the drama triangle is about attitude, identity, and orientations. What roles are we claiming in the world? Who is creating our lives? These are questions of agency and responsibility. By reflecting on our roles in the triangle, we gain a sense of clarity about our stance and our relationship to the world.

The drama begins when we stumble, get hurt, or fail to get what we desire. Looking for a way out of our unhappiness, we claim victimhood. We blame our parents, our genes, our childhood, our jobs, our bosses, and our partners. We blame modern culture, government policy, the opposition party, stress, and overwork.

These accusations may well contain some elements of truth, but all of this is beside the point. The real issue is our orientation. By claiming the role of victim, we give away our power. No longer are we acting in the world—the world is acting on us.

Going to the other point of the triangle—toward rescue—is not much better. In our unhappiness, we look for people,

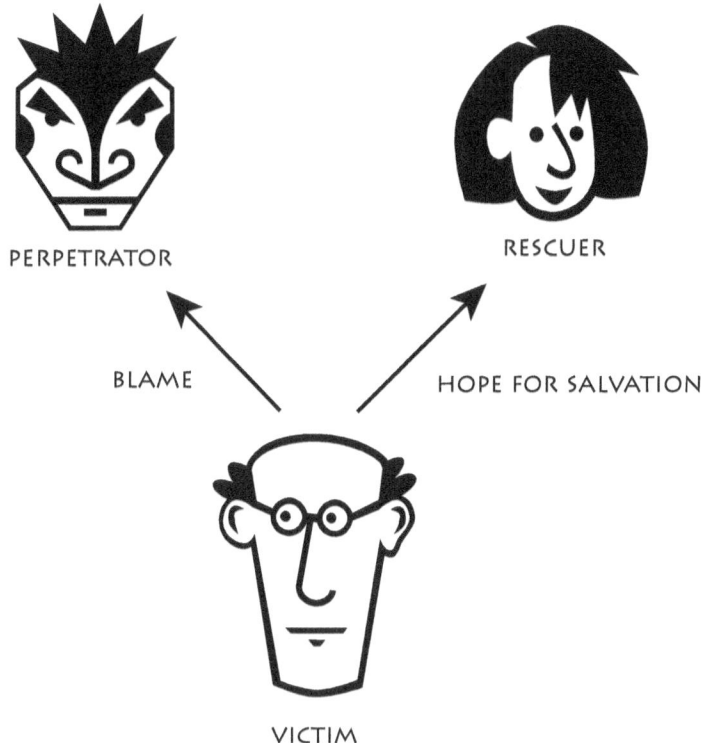

substances, ideas, or organizations to bail us out of our predicament, but once again, we give away our power. The more we seek to be propped up by the world, the weaker we become.

Many of us have heard this story before, and it's easy to assume that victimhood is something reserved for the dark underbelly of society; alcoholics, drug addicts, and criminals come to mind. But victimhood is alive and well at every level of society, and no one is immune. Donald Trump is the most notorious example in the modern era; his entire career has been nothing if not one extended rant of flamboyant victimhood—blaming, complaining, and making excuses.

Victimhood is an easy, seductive trap. There's always plenty of blame to go around, and excuses are always handy: The economy is in recession, our parents were flawed, our neighborhood was in turmoil. Bullies abused us, the schools failed us, the system didn't provide the kind of employment we deserved. That's why complaining has become a national sport, with entire media empires dedicated to around-the-clock finger-pointing. When things aren't going well, there's always a handy perpetrator we can blame, right across the aisle or down the street.

Not only does victimhood weaken our sense of power and agency, but it's also bad for our health. When we see ourselves as powerless agents in a sea of influence, we simply go along with whatever lifestyle choices are presented to us. We lose contact with the strength and vitality of our primal bodies and hand our fate over to the forces of marketing, advertising, and corporate culture. When we cast ourselves as victims, we give up the very qualities that would protect us from adversity. Ultimately, adopting a victim orientation may be even worse for our health than widely recognized behaviors such as smoking and physical inactivity.

Even worse, the attitude is contagious. When people see us blaming perpetrators and compulsively running for rescue, the behavior becomes normalized. We come to believe that that's just how it's done in human society, and before long, thousands of people are working the drama triangle. In turn, victimhood infects our politics and our culture, leading to the polarization and chaos we see today.

CREATE FORWARD

The way out of the drama triangle, as many teachers, therapists, and coaches have suggested, is the creative orientation. This is where we exercise responsibility and start building a vision of what we want to become. As we move beyond habits of blaming, complaining, excuses, and wishful thinking, life begins to open up into a world of opportunity, power, and freedom.

In this practice, we actually change our identity. Instead of blaming circumstance or hoping for a rescue, we ask a new set of questions: What can I do today, right this moment, to advance my creation?

Where can I exercise control? Where does my power lie?

At its core, activism is about escaping the drama triangle and taking responsibility for our lives. But the activist doesn't just take responsibility for her own life; she takes responsibility for the state of the entire world. When confronted by systemic challenges that afflict our world and communities, the victim's anthem is "It's not my job." In contrast, the creative personality takes responsibility for all of it: the climate crisis, habitat destruction, social injustice, racism, sexism, and every other abuse that people inflict on the Earth and one another. In short, she owns it all. In other words, "It *is* my job."

To be clear, the activist didn't cause these things, and she's unlikely to solve these problems in her lifetime, but this is very much beside the point. The activist isn't concerned about the specific causal chain of events that led to some particular problem, and she's not inclined to spend her time working out the fine-grained details of who's to blame for every human calamity. Instead, she concentrates on what's possible and, in the process, finds a wellspring of meaning and energy.

Not surprisingly, this willingness to accept responsibility is also the defining quality of our most popular leaders and superheroes, both real and imagined. These people are not complainers, nor are they seduced by rescue agents, substances, or ideas. They may well be fighting epic battles against powerful forces of destruction and injustice, but they keep their energy focused. It's hard to imagine Jackie Robinson, Martin Luther King Jr., Nelson Mandela, Mahatma Gandhi, Colin Kaepernick, or the men and women of Standing Rock blaming, complaining, or looking for a rescue. They're too busy creating the future.

Ultimately, it's all about our orientation. Yes, some predicaments are overwhelming and exhausting, but no matter the depth of the adversity, we are free to choose our interpretations. We're free to choose our stories. We're free to move beyond complaining, blame, excuses, and rescue. The creative path is not an easy one, but this is where the meaning lies. Ultimately, it's better to fail as a creator than to succeed as a victim.

CHAPTER 46

ALPINE STYLE

> Minimalism is an abundance of enough.
> —Torley

One of the most abnormal qualities of modern culture is our dysfunctional relationship with the material world. We buy too much stuff, own too much stuff, and no matter how big the pile gets, we always seem to want more. Buried under a mountain of things, we find it almost impossible to move, and in turn, many of us are stuck in a quagmire of our own creation.

This is where we can take some inspiration from the world of alpine climbing, a sport in which it's essential to have a good relationship with your gear. In the early years, Himalayan climbing was done strictly in expedition style, and it typically took months to plan an expedition, secure the material, and transport it all to base camp. From there, teams of climbers and sherpas would establish a series of camps and fixed ropes, climbing higher and positioning themselves for the final push to the summit. Climbing was a major work project.

But almost overnight, the game changed. Equipment got lighter and more functional, and suddenly it was possible to climb big mountains in a single, lightweight effort. No camps, no fixed ropes, no hauling loads—just climbing. This came to be called "alpine style." Famously advocated by Yvon Chouinard, the founder of Patagonia, the goal was to design beautiful, well-crafted tools and clothing to deepen the alpine experience and reduce the impact. As he put it, "He who dies with the least toys wins. Because the more you know, the less you need."

The beauty of this orientation soon became obvious to climbers around the world. Alpine style puts climbers in direct physical contact with the essential ambiguity of the mountain experience. No longer supported by fixed ropes and numerous camps, climbers were fully exposed to the dangers and beauty of the route, forced to rely on their skills, endurance, and wits. Less work, more sport.

This was a powerful win-win. There's joy in crafting, owning, and using simple, high-quality tools. There's power in this "creative subtraction." While expedition style asks, "How much stuff can we take with us?" alpine style asks, "How light can we go? Do we really need this extra stuff? Can we put ourselves into direct contact with the experience we seek?" If in doubt, leave it behind. Less is the new more.

But alpine style is far more than just an elegant way to climb a mountain; it's an incredibly valuable metaphor for our time and a practical answer to the problem of consumerism. It teaches us a fundamental, commonly overlooked life lesson: how to own things. It teaches us to savor experience over possessions, to value what we do own, and to reject the voices constantly shouting at us to buy more.

Moreover, alpine style teaches us to appreciate quality. As it stands, a common rap has it that modern culture is "too materialistic," but perhaps it's precisely the opposite. The reason we buy so much stuff is because we don't really value what we've got, and in this sense, we're not materialistic enough. If we really paid attention to the quality of the things we owned, we wouldn't have to go looking for more. If we took the time to savor good craftsmanship and prime materials, we'd be content. A few simple, beautiful possessions would satisfy us.

ESCHEW SURPLUSAGE

The practice of simplicity is, well, simple. We start by buying less, consuming less, and owning less. Does this thing add meaning to my life? Is it well crafted? Is it an appropriate use of technology? What meanings come along with it? If the item in question fails to bring meaning into your life, get rid of it. If it fails to inspire you by virtue of its quality, materials, and form, sell it or give it away. If you haven't used it in twenty years, it's safe to assume you're not going to need it.

To make this practice work, it's important to be wary of the tyranny of sunk costs. You may well have a lot invested in your stuff, and you'll be reluctant to take a loss, but remember, continued ownership also extracts a cost in the form of a cluttered mind and a cluttered life.

Better to cut your losses and live a richer, simpler life.

In the same vein, the time has come to rethink our cultural habit of giving material gifts on holidays. Most people already have enough stuff as it is, and there's a good chance your recipient is already trying to dig out from under his own pile of excess. In this sense, giving material gifts can actually be a burden. Better to give the gift of your presence and your time. Give some food, cook a meal, or make a contribution to a worthy cause in your recipient's name. Enough with the stuff.

MINIMALISM AS METAPHOR

The beauty of minimalism is that it suggests a way, a Tao, for conducting our entire lives. Trimming down our stuff inspires us to reduce complexity everywhere. Clear out the garage and the closets, clear out the mind and spirit. Author Greg McKeown calls this practice "essentialism," the disciplined pursuit of less. We're reminded of the teachings of Thoreau and the Zen masters. Keep it simple. Chop wood, carry water. Stay close to your core experience, and don't get distracted by complexity.

In this practice, we lean toward monotasking and single-focus activities. We set up our days to minimize interruptions and distractions. Scale back your ambition. Put one very important thing on your to-do list and do that thing. Don't try to master every skill, sport, or discipline. Survey the options, choose one, and make it your own. Likewise, focus your activism. Don't try to address every crisis or injustice in the world. Instead, concentrate your energies on one issue at a time. Precision activism, like precision living, is a powerful way to make a difference.

BIG MINIMALISM

It's one thing to choose minimalism in our personal lives, but what really needs to happen is a cultural transformation, and this means taking aim at the absurd belief that economies must grow for people to prosper. As it stands, we're hypnotized by the supposed need for economic growth. We measure it, track it, and in effect, worship it. A rising tide will lift all boats, we say, but even a child would recognize that this kind of system is unsustainable. Sooner or later, you're going to hit some limits. As the economic philosopher Kenneth Boulding put it,

"Anyone who believes that exponential growth can go on forever in a finite world is either a madman or an economist."

What we need is a shift in values and a culture-wide adoption of alpine-style living. It's a big ask, but just imagine the difference. Instead of bludgeoning one another to buy more and own more in every minute of every day, we'd have a built-in ethic of minimalism. In this kind of culture, people would value a small footprint because it's smarter, more elegant, less destructive, and ultimately makes us happier.

Remember, the alpine-style climber doesn't think in terms of depriving himself. Going light up the mountain isn't a form of self-denial. Rather, it's an expression of freedom, sensibility, and aesthetics. Going light is easier, faster, more elegant, and one hell of a lot more fun. This is not deprivation; it's liberation.

In an alpine-style culture, we'd frown on expressions of excess affluence. A big house filled with stuff would be an embarrassment, not a goal. Likewise, we'd end our practice of tying our social and political decision-making to gross domestic product (GDP) and similar economic measures. Instead, we'd look to actual human welfare as a measure of our success. Obviously, a de-growth economic philosophy is a hard sell in the modern world, where economic growth is widely considered sacred; any politician who advocates for lower economic growth is probably destined to crash and burn. Nevertheless, if we were to look at the grand sweep of human history, it would be obvious that people can live happy, successful, and meaningful lives with modest possessions. Nobody actually needs a big pile of stuff or perpetual growth to enjoy life.

But to do all this, we'd have to stop listening to economics-as-usual. Specifically, we'd have to stop listening to the incessant rap that tells us to do more, be more, and above all, consume more. Close your ears and your vision will become clear. As Chouinard himself put it: "If we could all come to see our consumer products as tools that help us to live our real lives—rather than as substitutes and surrogates for that life—we'd need many fewer products to be happy."

CHAPTER 47

TELL ME A STORY

> People think that stories are shaped by people. In fact, it's the other way around.
> —Terry Pratchett
> *Witches Abroad*

Faced with the epic challenges of mismatch, environmental destruction, and social chaos, we're struggling to find our way, and to make matters worse, we've got no master narrative to guide us. The dominant narrative of progress and infinite growth staggers on, but many of us no longer believe its promise. Religious narratives no longer carry the influence they once did, and an increasing number of young people identify themselves as "nones," which is to say, they have no affiliation or interest in the subject. Futurists try to whip up enthusiasm for a green technological utopia, but many of us remain skeptical of that narrative as well. Even science itself is running out of steam; the dominant narrative is powerful, but it's not really alive or spiritually inspiring. We are suffering, you might say, from a narrative-deficit disorder.

To put it another way, author Alex Evans says we're experiencing a "myth gap." As a former political adviser with the British government and the United Nations, Evans advises scientists how to be better storytellers and mythmakers:

> In this time of global crisis and transition—mass migration, inequality, resource scarcity and climate change—it is only by finding new myths, those that speak to us of renewal and restoration, that we will navigate our way to a better future. It is stories, rather than facts and pie-charts, that have the power to animate us and bring us together to change the world.

The problem with the myth gap is that it leaves us exposed to distraction, division, and toxic myths that erode our health, our lives, and our future. Without a functional story, we become vulnerable to whatever messaging happens to be making the rounds at the moment, putting us at the mercy of whoever's got the biggest megaphone. A culture without a unifying narrative is in big trouble.

To make matters worse, many of our traditional guiding narratives have been replaced by synthetic commercial narratives that have come to dominate modern consciousness. Today, we no longer talk about Paleo themes of habitat, hunting, or the spirits that inhabit the world—we talk about brands. We design stories to sell lifestyles to sell stuff. And in the context of human history, this behavior is profoundly abnormal.

In fact, today's synthetic narratives are so far removed from their original, organic form that they're best described as "plastic narratives" or "narrative products." Like food products, these narratives are refined, distilled, and stripped of their original nutrients and meaning. They're intentionally produced not to reveal, express, or enlighten, but to manipulate and exploit. The objective is to produce a certain kind of behavior in the consumer, usually in the form of clicking the "Buy Now" button.

But synthetic narratives don't just lure us into buying particular products and services; they also manipulate us into living in particular ways. Lifestyle narratives tell us whom to admire, what to eat, what to aspire to, and how to succeed in life. And above it all is the master commercial narrative that tells us that we can buy our way to beauty, happiness, power, and control. Health, adventure, romance, and transcendence can all be yours with a click or a swipe.

Just as excess consumption of food products eventually compromises our health, the chronic consumption of synthetic narratives ultimately degrades our ability to think clearly and exercise our own judgment. The threat is subtle and insidious. Narrative products sound like real stories and are highly palatable, maybe even tastier than the real thing, but the danger is real, to individuals and to our culture as a whole. Try to get by on a diet of synthetic narratives, and you'll eventually lose contact with your identity, your history, and your purpose. You'll simply exist as a character in someone else's story. In the process, you'll degrade your personal health and our chance for a functional future.

So what kind of stories should we be telling ourselves about our moment on Earth? What narratives will lead us out of the myth gap and into a functional future? Can we make our narratives healthier in the same way we make our bodies healthier?

Narrative health may well sound like a new thing. In the modern world, our inclination is to listen to stories and rate them for their entertainment value. We like or dislike stories, but rarely do we hear a movie reviewer claim that a film was driven by a "healthy narrative" or a "diseased narrative." But given the power of the story–body connection and the ability of narrative to shape our culture and our future, this orientation makes perfect sense. If we can make our stories healthier, we can make our lives and our culture stronger.

In fact, given what we know about the power of language to shape our sense of reality and the function of our bodies, narrative hygiene is probably just as important to our health as our more familiar practices of diet and exercise. Get the story right and your body will flourish. Get the story wrong and no amount of cardio, strength training, or kale smoothies will save you.

BIG, HEALTHY NARRATIVES

Healthy narratives bring us closer to the wellsprings of life: our habitat, our bodies, our imagination, and one another. Diseased narratives move us further away from the things that sustain us. Healthy narratives move us toward unity and integration with the biosphere and one another; diseased narratives move us toward division, fragmentation, fear, and chaos. Healthy narratives show us a path to a meaningful future, but diseased narratives drag our spirits and our bodies down. They sap our sense of meaning and leave us empty, unable to take the next step into a functional future. Healthy narratives emphasize continuity, connection, and courage in the face of ambiguity and uncertainty; diseased narratives leave us stranded and disconnected or, worse, put us on a path to polarization, cynicism, nihilism, and destruction.

Throughout history, our great spiritual leaders have given us healthy, integrating narratives that stressed the unity of humankind and the universe, but biology tells a similar story. Many of us have come to believe that science and religion are mutually exclusive domains and that it's necessary to choose sides, but from another perspective, the two are natural allies. Fundamentally, the core message of LUCA (the Last Universal Common Ancestor), deep ecology, and planetary health is no different from the teachings of Jesus, Buddha, Mohammed, or any of the Old Way elders. It's all one thing. We all breathe the same air and share the same ancestry. We're united by DNA, human universals, a collective unconscious, and now, a shared planetary fate. The whole world is kin, and the time has come to start acting like it.

STORIES ARE REPS

Story is the most underrated power on the planet today. Everyone loves to be entertained, but most of us believe stories are nothing more than fleeting collections of words and images that tickle our minds and emotions and then disappear into the ether. But in fact, the story effect is just as real as any other encounter with the world. Every time we hear or tell a story, our bodies are literally transformed. The effects are microscopic and subtle but immensely consequential. When synapses and circuits change under the influence of story, so too does the trajectory of our lives.

As we've seen, the human nervous system is constantly remodeling itself as it attempts to adapt to the world around it. In every moment, millions of synaptic membranes are becoming more or less permeable to stimulation, and millions of nerve fibers are becoming faster or slower by way of living myelin wrappings. Likewise, the cortex of the brain is continually remapping itself to manage new sensory and motor demands.

Stories play right into this process. Every story we tell or hear—especially those with emotional impact—produces a distinct neuroendocrine response in the body and the brain.

With every telling, the brain becomes more receptive to the meanings that come with the story, and this becomes the beginning of a watercourse. With each retelling or rereading, human attention becomes more likely to follow along and deepen those grooves, for better or for worse.

In this sense, repeated tellings and listenings are no different from the reps we perform with dumbbells in the gym. Listen to a story once and you might be momentarily moved, but listen to that story a hundred times and your body actually begins to change. In turn, your transformation will touch the bodies and minds of people around you and even be passed from one generation to the next. Stories don't just carve grooves in your body and brain; they also carve grooves in the future.

Even in folklore, we have an understanding of this process. We say, "The hand that rocks the cradle rules the world," but we might well put it in terms of story: "The voice that tells the earliest narratives rules the world." The implications go far beyond the lives of individuals; the effects are literally intergenerational. The attention we pay today may well be flowing along grooves and ruts laid down by storytellers in our distant past. Likewise, the stories we tell today are carving grooves in the nervous systems of our descendants.

Sadly, the modern educational system has largely abdicated its role in telling unifying, healthy narratives that can lead students into a functional future. Instead we teach mountains of facts and disconnected subjects with no unifying theme. And then we test those mountains of facts, as if this will tell us something meaningful about student achievement. Perhaps our educators need to go on a vision quest and spend a few weeks or years in retreat and come to a consensus as to what kind of story might unify the curriculum. This would be a story worth telling, and even better, we wouldn't have to torture one another with an endless cycle of administration, testing, and evaluation.

In any case, the meaning here is clear. Storytellers—all of us—have an immense responsibility. Every time we open our mouths or put our fingers to the keyboard, we're shaping people's bodies and, yes, the future of the human race. Many of us complain about being voiceless and powerless, but if you can tell a meaningful story, you can make a difference.

CHAPTER 48

BELIEVE IT OR NOT

> There's more to biology than biology.
> —Daniel Moerman
> *Meaning, Medicine and the 'Placebo Effect'*

Here in the modern world, we're accustomed to thinking of stories as entertainment. A good story keeps us engaged and maybe even distracts us from the demands of our daily lives. But story also has powerful effects on our bodies and the trajectory of our health, most notoriously by way of the placebo effect.

When we think about placebos, most of us are quick to imagine inert sugar pills given to unwitting test subjects in medical trials, but our popular view is far too narrow. In fact, *every* health and medical procedure carries a placebo effect. Surgery, physical therapy, orthotics, even stents—the mesh devices placed in coronary arteries to relieve chest pain in heart disease—have a measurable mind–body influence. Even the most disciplined, scientific, evidence-based treatments bring powerful meanings along for the ride. There's meaning in the stethoscope, the white lab coat, the magnetic resonance imaging (MRI) machine, and the framed diplomas hanging on the wall.

Placebos can improve just about any dimension of human experience and capability: athletic performance, intelligence, creativity, memory, compassion, gratitude, and probably happiness as well. And of course, nocebos—substances or experiences coupled with a negative expectation—take us in the other direction entirely. The power of expectation and belief in human life is almost boundless.

Even our beliefs about exercise are influential. Alia Crum, the head of the Mind & Body Lab at Stanford University, studied hotel workers and primed them with story. Some were told that housekeeping is exercise—this group went on to show statistically significant improvements in their biomedical profile. In a similar study, Crum's team examined a database that tracked people's beliefs about how much they exercised and how long they lived. They found a strong correlation between people's early deaths and their belief that they were relatively inactive, even if they were getting as much exercise as others in their age group.

A summary of research into the placebo effect tells an amazing story of human susceptibility:

- Large pills work better than medium-size pills.
- Blue pills make better sleeping pills.
- Red and black pills are perceived to be the strongest.
- Very tiny pills are perceived to be highly potent.
- Prescription drugs are assumed to be more powerful than over-the-counter medications.
- Pills work fine, but shots work better.

- Surgery works even better, even when it doesn't actually do anything.

Likewise, an ingenious study found that "placebo sleep affects cognitive functioning." Sneaky researchers brought people into a sleep lab in the evening and put them to bed. In the morning, one group was informed that they slept well; the other group was told that they slept poorly. Both groups were subjected to cognitive tests, and those who believed that they slept well performed better.

As vulnerable humans in an uncertain and ambiguous world, we're always on the alert for signals that might give us a hint of where our lives are headed. Placebos, nocebos, and omens live in relationships, experiences, technologies, and casual conversation. Every time we turn around, our bodies are scanning the world for clues that might tell us about the nature of our lives and how we might fit in. We're hungry for meaning, and we'll take it wherever we can get it.

In fact, some observers have suggested we need to refine our definitions. In *Meaning, Medicine and the 'Placebo Effect'* Daniel Moerman suggests that it's time to abandon the term *placebo effect* and replace it with the more accurate *meaning effect*. From this perspective, we're no longer limited to studying the mind–body effects of inert sugar pills. We can start looking for placebos and nocebos across the entire scope of human life.

This is why language and story are so important in creating a functional future. The nuts and bolts of law, government, and policy are obviously important, but narrative is where the real action is. The stories that we tell and shape go on to influence people's minds, bodies, and behavior. Just as a fake sugar pill can change human physiology for better or for worse, so too can the words we use.

THE POWER OF MEANING

So if placebos, nocebos, and omens are everywhere, and if humans are in fact deeply irrational animals, what does this mean for our health and experience in the modern world? The life lesson here may be obvious or unexpected, depending on your history: our lives are saturated with meaning, and that meaning has tremendous power. Objects and experiences are rarely, if ever, neutral. We are constantly sculpting and being sculpted, led by what we believe.

And when it comes to matters of health and medical care, it's safe to assume that placebo effects are always at work. Like it or not, a substantial percentage of medicine—of any variety—is show biz. The linear, Newtonian causality that we expect in biochemistry and biomechanics can never be more than a partial explanation for anything. And at worst, such explanations can be a distraction from what's really going on with the whole organism.

If you're a health professional, teacher, trainer, or coach, take the time to find out where the meaning lies for your patients, students, and clients. Don't assume that your treatment or teaching is universally effective. And if you're just a regular person trying to make your way in the world, sharpen your focus on the meanings you experience and create. Don't settle for meanings that are destructive, unhealthy, boring, or disintegrating. In the end, meaning matters.

CHAPTER 49

THE ART OF THE REFRAME

> A Stoic is someone who transforms fear into prudence, pain into transformation, mistakes into initiation, and desire into undertaking.
> —Nassim Nicholas Taleb

For the narrative activist, the ability to reframe ideas and issues is vital. When we change the borders around an issue or perspective, we open up new possibilities for awareness, action, health, and even sapience.

Of course, reframing is as old as storytelling itself and can be used by anyone, for any purpose. Marketing, public persuasion, courtroom presentations, and political campaigning are all about framing. Most of our difficult conversations and arguments in daily life, romance, and family are about where to put the frame. All of us are reframers to some degree, although some are better at it than others.

The beauty of reframes is that when used wisely, they can move us toward a functional future. For example, when we reframe lifestyle behaviors like sleep and regular physical movement as prosocial and pro-future, we promote personal and public welfare simultaneously. Likewise, when we reframe a crisis as an opportunity, we change our experience in a fundamental way. Suddenly, our stress and fear feel less overwhelming, and our minds are free to pursue the possibility of creativity. Instead of thinking, "Adversity is a stressor," we can reframe the situation and say, "Adversity is a stimulus for adaptation." We can even reframe our injuries as opportunities to live and move our bodies in new ways. Pain is unpleasant, but it's valuable information that can lead us in new directions.

On a larger scale, "Conservation is health care" is an extremely powerful reframe because it shifts our attention to the human–habitat connection and illuminates our continuity with nature. Suddenly, we see the link between our bodies and the world.

In the world of activism, reframes can be particularly effective. In 2016, activists at Standing Rock declared, "We are protectors, not protesters." This kind of shift moved the focus away from militancy and toward the preservation of something universally valuable.

Bioregionalism is a powerful reframe because it inspires us to ask hard questions about the way we've been structuring our politics, our economy, our commerce, and even our relations with one another. It gets us out of the homosphere and forces us to look at the habitat and creatures that sustain us. Equally powerful is the Rights of Nature movement. Small but growing numbers of governments are now granting rights to various ecosystems, rivers, and watersheds. The beauty of this reframe is that it forces us to confront the contradiction that lies at the heart of our culture and our failure to give voice to the world that gives us life.

Another powerful reframe comes from the world of neurobiology. For most of human history, we've been quick to condemn people with bad behavior as "evil" or "stupid" or of "poor character." We put them in jail, exile them from our communities, medicate them, or kill them outright. But today, we're beginning to understand and appreciate the biological effects of adverse childhood experiences, trauma, concussions, combat, and disease. In this light, people who behave badly usually aren't bad people—they're people with neurological injuries, and they can be helped. This understanding moves us away from retribution and toward compassionate treatment.

Even the entire field of biology can be described as a reframe. Darwin's *On the Origin of Species* threw our human identity into question, and suddenly, humans went from being the greatest creation the world had ever known to just another animal. For a culture built on the assumption of human supremacy, biology is turning out to be one radically inconvenient idea—and one of the greatest reframes ever.

These reframes are just a beginning. No matter the issue or challenge, there's always another perspective that we can bring. For the narrative activist, this is the essential skill. Stay fluid and alert for new visions of old problems. There's almost always another way to see it.

CHAPTER 50

STRESS ME OUT

> The tipping point on Planet Earth may well come, not when the heat waves become unbearable and our ecosystems collapse, but when the noise in our own heads becomes unbearable and our psychosystems collapse—when mood disorders, distraction, and psychosis reach a point where we can't think clearly anymore.
> —Adbusters

Everyone feels it now: the maddening sense of urgency, the impending loss of control and the pervasive cognitive overload. Stress has become a ubiquitous, chronic, and even debilitating feature of the modern world. We all joke about it, but this is serious, even lethal business. Not only does stress wreck our bodies, but it also has extremely negative consequences for cognition and, in turn, our ability to create a functional future.

By now, most of us have heard the story of the autonomic nervous system, the deep, ancient wiring that controls the basic regulatory functions of our bodies and, in turn, our minds and spirits. Two branches extend from the brain, deep into the body, one devoted to action, the other to restoration and repair. These nerves regulate everything from breathing to digestion, cardiac function, arousal, and even the long-range trajectory of our health.

When we perceive a threat, the action branch of the autonomic system stimulates our bodies for vigorous physical movement—notably, fighting or running. Every organ and tissue in the body goes on alert; heart rate goes up, digestion is suppressed, blood pressure increases, and glucose is released into the bloodstream. Pain is dampened and immunity is stimulated. In short, the body prepares itself for a physical encounter with the world. This is the famous fight-or-flight response.

The repair system does the reverse. When the world feels friendly, heart rate and blood pressure go down, digestion picks up, and nutrients are delivered to the cells that need to be patched up. In popular culture, this is sometimes described as the *rest-and-digest* or *feed-and-breed* response. (When we're relaxed, we like to eat and have sex.)

But there's more to the stress response than a binary, on–off reaction to the world. In real life, the process unfolds along a classic inverted-U-shaped curve. On the left side, rising levels of stress hormones mean good things for the body and cognition. Metabolic fuels are released into the bloodstream to feed our attentive brains. At the same time, our brains secrete neurotrophic chemicals that stimulate the growth of new nerve cells, dendrites, and synapses. In this sweet spot, memory is sharp, and attention is focused.

As stress increases, benefits also increase, but beyond the tipping point, the effect reverses itself, and stress becomes destructive. Our cognitive, psychological, and spiritual resources begin to drain away, and our bodies are slower to recuperate from exertion, injury, and illness. In turn, this makes us increasingly

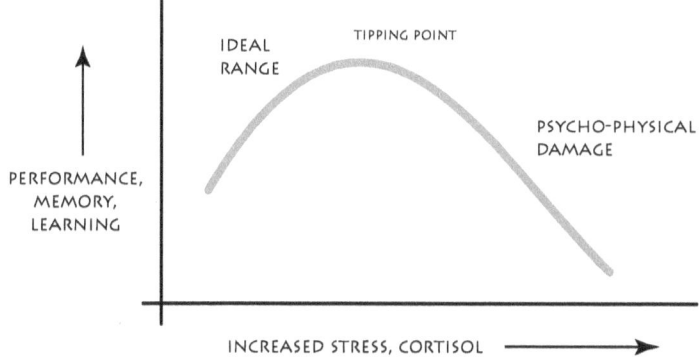

vulnerable to other stressors, even those we would normally weather without a second thought. Aches and pains seem worse than normal, and we begin to worry about the trajectory of our health.

Over time, chronic activation of the stress response inhibits the growth and connectivity of precious neurons and can even damage the brain centers involved in learning, memory, and impulse control. Key neurotransmitters such as dopamine become depleted, which leads to a loss of pleasure. If stress continues, our mood becomes increasingly serious, then grim. Our sense of humor declines, then disappears entirely. We stop laughing. We stop loving life.

At this point, we enter the dark world of disease, dysfunction, and depression. Stress hormones may become neurotoxic, endangering neurons and even killing them outright. Chronic exposure erodes the structure and function of the hippocampus, a crucial brain center involved in explicit, short-term memory and learning. In turn, this can lead to a host of neurological disorders, ranging from minor attention problems all the way to full-blown dementia. At this level, stress hormones become psycho-toxic, leading to impulse-control problems and substance abuse. We fall into a state called "learned helplessness" and begin to generalize our lack of control to other circumstances, even to those cases when control is, in fact, possible.

WARNING SIGNS

The inverse-U curve provides some powerful life lessons. In the first place, it teaches us that stress has real value. In moderation, it's essential for learning, performance, and a good life. So instead of trying to make our lives stress-free, the superior strategy is to seek an optimal level of stress: the right kind of stress, in the right intensity, for the right duration. In other words, look for precision, not eradication. Whenever possible, fine-tune your adversities. Expose yourself to stress strategically in service of your goals and purpose.

This objective should be built into every learning and performance environment, especially schools. As it stands, most of our teaching efforts are based on tradition. We present material and give exams not out of any consideration for the body or human biology, but simply because that's the way it's always been done. But we'd get far better results if we paid more attention to the stress status of our students. Where are they on the curve? Can we administer educational challenges in such a way as to keep them in the sweet spot? Someday, we'll measure stress hormones directly, but in the meantime, we can work with what we know. When giving exams or other educational challenges, take the body into account. If students are on the left side of the curve, keep the pressure on. But when they go past the tipping point, back off and give them a break.

The second lesson is to recognize the point of diminishing returns. As stress increases and people approach the top of the curve, be alert for these warning signs:

- Anhedonia (loss of pleasure)
- Neophobia (avoidance of new things)
- Perseveration (mindless repetition of established habit patterns)
- Increased reliance on familiar features of life
- Reduced ambiguity tolerance, increased extremism and black-and-white thinking
- Social withdrawal and isolation
- Cognitive distortions, especially overgeneralizing and small-picture, short-term thinking
- Physical lethargy, poor sleep quality, and decreased resilience
- Irritability, "making mountains out of molehills"
- Catastrophizing, going straight to the worst-case scenario
- Decreased sense of humor and play
- Poor concentration and attention span
- Impulsive behaviors and reduced self-control
- Decision resistance, procrastination, and impatience

If this sounds like an accurate description of your life or your students' lives, take heed. You're well on your way to going past the tipping point, and it's time to try a different approach.

STRESS US OUT

Everyone knows that chronic stress is bad news for our individual bodies and health, but we're now beginning to realize it's also bad for us collectively. As highly social animals, stress gets around fast. Humans are always on alert for signs of danger or safety, communicated through words, gestures, postures, and even odors. We're always wondering: Is the world friendly or not? If there's fear or anxiety in the air, we feel it. And obviously, the process is amplified by our always-on media environment. In turn, stress can generate a wicked, destructive cycle that feeds on itself and makes solutions increasingly difficult.

The effects are corrosive on a planetary scale. First, stress and fear make us more likely to "otherize" the world. Fearing for our welfare, we lean toward xenophobia. Our sense of continuity with the world dissolves, ego becomes dominant, and we become increasingly selfish, vigilant, and antisocial. In *Behave: The Biology of Humans at Our Best and Worst*, Robert Sapolsky summed up the research about moral decision-making after a social stressor:

> Stress made people give more egoistic answers about emotionally intense moral decisions; the more glucocorticoid levels rose, the more egoistic the answers.

Not surprisingly, stress also shifts our perspective away from abundance and toward scarcity. It feels like there's less of everything: less wealth, less time, and fewer resources to work with. We're more likely to see life and society as a competitive, zero-sum game. Hoarding behavior—by both individuals and organizations—becomes increasingly common. There's only so much to go around, so we'd better get what we can when we can.

Stress even affects our sense of time. When stress escalates, we begin to undervalue tomorrow and overvalue today. Stressed people aren't thinking about their health or the planet twenty years from now; they're thinking about the pleasure they can get today. They aren't thinking about the welfare of the seventh generation; they're thinking about the welfare of the first generation, right here, right now.

Stress also contributes to a siege mentality. It drives us into our bunkers and narrows our sense of tribe. The world is against us, so we must defend ourselves at all costs. Social trust declines, and we become increasingly risk averse. We cling to the conventions of Mother Culture and the status quo. Deviations from business-as-usual and culture-as-usual strike us as dangerous, inconvenient, and out of the question.

Likewise, stress also pushes our political inclinations to the right. In 2012, a research team found they could move people in a conservative direction by distracting them and putting them under time pressure. At the same time, stress also drives many of us to adopt a victim orientation. Instead of taking responsibility for our lives, we're more inclined to seek out rescue and/or blame perpetrators. In the process, we become less creative and less effective in moving the world.

Finally, stress erodes our willingness to participate in civic life. When the pressure becomes too extreme, many of us simply withdraw. American novelist John Dos Passos once described apathy as "one of the characteristic responses of any living organism when it is subjected to stimuli too intense or too complicated to cope with." This description, of course, is a dead ringer for life in the modern world.

In short, stress robs us of our humanity, drowns out our sense of awe, wrecks our communities, and diminishes our sapience. Social resources such as trust, reciprocity, and cooperation diminish at the very time we need them most. Even worse, the effect is intergenerational; waves of stress are passed from fathers to sons, from mothers to daughters. From this point of view, it becomes increasingly obvious that stress is a public health problem on a planetary scale.

This leads us to a vital reframing of the entire issue. In the popular view, stress is nothing more or less than a personal issue—get too stressed out and your individual health will suffer. But in the larger view, our own personal stress is very much a public concern. In other words, taking care of your life is a prosocial behavior. Turning down your stress isn't just good for you; it's good for all of us, human and nonhuman alike.

STRESS RELIEF: YIN AND YANG

The paradox of stress relief is that we can come at it from either direction. You can emphasize power and control (the yang arts), or you can learn how to relinquish, accept, and adapt (the yin arts). Each style has its place and time.

The yang arts begin with the recognition that all animals need a sense of power, control, and predictability. When nonhuman animals are placed in laboratory conditions that decrease their sense of control, they show biological markers of stress, but when control is granted, they do better—a rat that can turn off an electric shock does better than a rat that can't. Even fake buttons and levers that offer the appearance of control reduce the stress effect. Predictability helps too—a rat that gets a warning light before an electric shock does better than one that gets no such warning, even when the levels of stress are precisely the same.

In this sense, the solution to stress may lie not in relaxing and letting go but in focusing our attention on executing the work at hand. When our lives are in chaos, we need to accomplish vital tasks that will help us get a grip on our situation. In these circumstances, it makes little sense to imagine you're lying on a beach in the South Pacific, breathing in the fresh air and contemplating the gentle waves as they caress the shore. No, we've got to redouble our efforts and get the work done.

There's no real mystery here. It's all about task management and the fundamentals of modern living: planning your days and your weeks, using a calendar, budgeting your time, making to-do lists, and keeping your schedule in order. Do the planning, get the work done, gain a sense of control, and in turn, your stress will diminish. To put it simply, work works.

Naturally, and unfortunately, money helps. A fat wallet dampens uncertainty and gives us a sense of power and control. There is no question on this score: money is a powerful stress-relieving agent and even a form of medicine—it's no wonder we fight so hard to get it.

Likewise, having the right tools gives us a sense of leverage. Good tools—whether physical or digital—help us get our work done and, in turn, give us a feeling of mastery. Education also increases our sense of power and control, especially when it's relevant to actual circumstances on the ground. Knowledge gives us options and, in turn, makes the world seem less arbitrary and more predictable. Even physical strength training can give us a feeling of mastery. When we work our bodies against gravity and build our physical competence, the rest of the world begins to feel more manageable by comparison.

YIN

Power, control, and predictability are great antidotes to stress, but we also need to practice the art of letting go. Anything that creates an atmosphere of safety is a good place to begin. Massage is excellent. Meditation is perfect. Just sit and observe your breathing. Just be with whatever state your mind–body happens to be in. Don't try to change anything. Accept the world, accept your body, accept the turbulence in your mind and spirit. It's all OK as it is.

Progressive relaxation is also powerful. Lie down on the floor, and let yourself go limp. Allow the floor to do all the work of supporting you, then start with your breath. With each exhalation, let go of any holding or areas of tension. Now go system by system: Feel all the bones in your body, and let them go limp. Feel all the muscles in your body, and let them relax. Feel your heart and all the blood vessels in your body; let these relax. Let every cell in your body relax. Or go part by part: Feel your feet, and let them relax. Feel your lower legs, knees, upper legs, pelvis, and so on, all the way up to your neck, skull, face, and scalp. With every exhalation, relax a little more. Think of your hands as heavy and warm. Imagine all the space inside your body as large and expansive. Your chest and abdomen are as a vast chamber. And then relax some more...

Above all, get your mind and spirit in on the process. As your body relaxes, let go of whatever it is you're holding on to. Turn the quest for power and control around, and simply let the world be as it is. No matter the pain and confusion in your spirit, let your life be. Leave yourself alone. Forget the self-improvement and the to-do list. Relinquish your expectations, your grudges, your outrage, and your ambition. Forgive and let go. Breathe and let go. For this moment, at least, all is well.

CHAPTER 51

REALITY IS NEVER WRONG

> Life is a series of natural and spontaneous changes. Don't resist them; that only creates sorrow. Let reality be reality. Let things flow naturally forward in whatever way they like.
> —Lao Tzu

Ultimately, stress is about perspective. Sometimes we experience direct threats to our physical survival, but more often, our stress is a consequence of the way we explain reality to ourselves. When there's a mismatch between our story and reality, our bodies and minds begin to feel uneasy. This suggests a strategy: if we could just give up some of our expectations and judgment, we might feel and perform a whole lot better.

This is precisely what we see in the world of martial arts, where teachers sometimes advise their students to shift their perspective and remember that "the enemy is never wrong." This counsel may well sound preposterous to the beginner, but the lesson is sound. The idea is to remain fluid and adaptable—don't get wrapped up in some expectation about what your opponent should or shouldn't be. The enemy—the adversary, the situation—just is. Abandon your psychic resistance and your anger. Observe that reality and adapt accordingly. Fight for what you believe in, but don't get caught up in unnecessary judgment and evaluation. Don't be trapped by your own mind.

This is not to say we should simply accept everything about the enemy or world as it is. Of course the destruction of our biosphere is wrong. Of course the exploitation and domination of other people are wrong. Of course our narrative of human supremacy is wrong.

Rather, this is an argument for freedom and adaptation. It's an argument for letting go of expectation and working with the world as it presents itself. The fight remains essential, but the indignation and stress are optional. In the long run, "reality is never wrong" might well be the ultimate koan for stress relief and resilience, the ultimate expression of adaptive psychology.

Think of your favorite opponents, grievances, and pet peeves. Now imagine abandoning your judgment; these things and people simply are what they are. It's a powerful thought experiment that might just free you up, dissolve your stress, and put you in a position for more skillful action.

Outrage has its place, but there comes a time when the best course is to play the situation as it stands. Life is capable of anything. People are capable of anything. Humans are multilayered animals, struggling to live in an alien environment. We're driven by ancient impulses that sometimes bubble to the surface, leading us to behave in some strange and incomprehensible ways. Everyone is irrational.

We'd all like to have things a certain way, but our preferences are not the issue here. Our job is to create and re-create adaptations on the fly. When we get too wrapped up in the wrongness of people, organizations, or events, we become rigid and lose our sapience. We lose our ability to move and, in turn, become even more vulnerable. If we can let go of our indignation, we can start fresh and return to the encounter with a clear vision.

We all have expectations about reality and relationships, but it's essential to remember that the word *ought* is a product of the human imagination. For every other animal on Earth, and for the vast majority of human history, *is* has been the reference point for action. For every other primate and every other mammal on Earth, there is no *ought* and, thus, less stress. Life is what it is.

As a stress-relieving practice, this reframe is almost magical. As soon as we say, "Reality is never wrong," our minds turn around, and a lot of our angst simply disappears, at least for a while. The conflict and the danger may persist, but the anger and indignation lose their ability to tyrannize us. In turn, this frees us up to bring more of our resources to bear on doing what needs to be done. So whatever you do, keep your eye on the *is*.

CHAPTER 52

IS THE UNIVERSE FRIENDLY?

> Everything you can imagine is real.
> —Pablo Picasso

In essence, the human stress response is built upon Einstein's legendary question: "Is the Universe friendly?" If the answer is yes, the body activates its anabolic systems and prepares for exploration, affiliation, curiosity, growth, and learning. If the answer is no, it becomes vigilant and prepares for action and defense, fighting, or fleeing.

This is where things get interesting. Not only do we have the ability to sense genuine physical threats directly, but we also have the ability to imagine them in ways that are completely independent of reality. Mind, story, and culture are always getting into the act, interpreting the meaning of events at every turn.

Acts of imagination have very real physiological consequences; every thought, every mental image, every muse has a downstream physical effect. This is why stress researchers are careful to say that the trigger for the stress response is not a threat to the organism but rather a *perceived* threat to the organism. In other words, belief matters. If you believe some circumstance constitutes a threat to your life or your status, your body will buy your story. If you believe in the safety and friendliness of your world, your body will believe that as well.

Perception and interpretation are everything here. If we perceive our capability to be adequate for the challenge at hand, it's going to be an easy day. But if we judge our skills to be deficient, it's going to be a struggle, no matter the actual nature of our circumstances.

Work by June Gruber at Yale University has shown remarkable physiological differences between various kinds of stress events. When a stressor was perceived as a *challenge*, subjects showed increased cardiac output, increased diameter of circulatory blood vessels, increased blood flow to the brain, and increased cognitive and physical performance. All good things.

In contrast, when a stressor was perceived as a *threat*, subjects showed decreased cardiac output, decreased diameter of circulatory vessels, decreased blood flow to the brain, and decreased cognitive and physical performance. All bad.

This suggests a narrative strategy for dealing with potential stressors and big events on the horizon. Perhaps you're called upon to step up to speak in public, manage some chaos at work, or navigate the turmoil of a difficult personal drama. Instead of simply reacting to the pressure, try telling yourself this story:

> *This situation is simply a test of my adaptability. Fortunately, I come from a long line of highly adaptable animals that have been adjusting*

> to difficult and even life-threatening circumstances for millions of years. My body has a rich history of adaptation. My ancestors have found ways to live in outrageously challenging circumstances. If they can do it, so can I.

Interpretation is such a powerful driver of human experience and physiology that it even affects our long-term health outcomes. Stanford professor Kelly McGonigal describes a study conducted at the University of Wisconsin School of Medicine and Public Health in which researchers asked two very simple questions: "How much stress are you under?" and "Do you believe stress is harmful to your health?"

Years later, they compared death records and found a marked difference in mortality. Those who believed "stress is bad for you" were significantly more likely to die early than those who held a friendlier view. The authors concluded:

> High amounts of stress and the perception that stress impacts health are each associated with poor health and mental health. Individuals who perceived that stress affects their health and reported a large amount of stress had an increased risk of premature death.

In other words, the belief that stress is bad for your health is actually bad for your health.

Even worse, there's a bias at work here. When faced with a universe that's both friendly and unfriendly, many of us are inclined to lean toward the darker interpretation. As we see it, the world is a dangerous place, and the outlook is bleak. Evil forces are ruthless and out to destroy everything we hold dear. This is the National Rifle Association (NRA) vision of life, a world filled with adversaries, criminals, and bad guys with guns. In this world, the only solution is to "harden up" our schools, our world, and our lives.

The problem is that we don't see reality clearly. Our history as vulnerable bipeds in the predator-rich habitats of prehistory has skewed our attention toward vigilance, even hypervigilance. That rustling in the bushes could be anything, but if you interpret it as a dangerous predator on the prowl, you're more likely to live to see another day and pass your psychophysical disposition down to your descendants. Treat that rustle as something friendly, and you're more likely to wind up in the gut of a hungry carnivore. And so, even in a modern predator-free environment that's generally safe, we tend to see events and conditions as more dangerous and unfriendly than they actually are. In this sense, we're wired for paranoia.

The consequences are far-reaching. What was an asset in the Paleo becomes a liability in a modern world that's swarming with stimuli. When you're living in the bush, there's not much of a price to be paid for "false positives." If that rustle in the bushes turns out not to be a leopard, you can simply take a deep breath, laugh it off, and return to your walkabout.

But in the modern world, the false positives add up. Fears that are triggered by a news headline, social media post, or ambiguous social encounter may turn out to be unfounded, but when it happens often enough, the repeated activation of the stress response begins to feed on itself, corroding both our bodies and our cognition. Our vigilance intensifies, and the world begins to look deadlier than it really is. Our lives become filled with false leopards.

The good news is, once we understand this primal inclination toward vigilance, we're in a better position to think clearly about the world. Yes, there are genuine threats, but we almost always exaggerate. Our negativity bias tries to keep our bodies safe and alive, but in today's world, it actually makes our problems more intractable. We blow things out of proportion and turn molehills into mountains.

Knowing this, we can remind ourselves that things are probably not as bad as they seem. We can calm down, take a deep breath, and rest assured that things are probably going to work out.

This frees us up to see more of the friendliness around us. In recent years, researchers and therapists have pointed to the beneficial effects of gratitude, kindness, and the intentional practice of focusing on the nurturing qualities of the world. This advice bears repeating because for many of us, it just doesn't come naturally. Our ancient, slightly paranoid brains need to be reminded that, yes, there are plenty of things to celebrate, to savor, and be grateful for. Predators are real, but so too are the spectacular qualities of the natural world, the friendship and love of the people around us, and the richness of human culture. In this sense, we're actually swimming in a sea of friendship. Friendliness is the norm; unfriendliness is the exception.

Likewise, we're reminded of our creative responsibility. Everyone we meet is wondering about the friendliness of the world, scanning the environment for clues about danger and potential. We are part of that creation. We can sculpt one another's attention toward danger, duality, and hostility, or we can show people the friendliness that exists in almost every moment. This is not just a good thing to do; it's a smart thing to do. When the people around us see friendliness, they relax. They become more receptive and maybe even a little more sapient. Being friendly is far more than just being nice; it's a vital element of health activism.

To be sure, the universe has its share of dangers, but don't let that fact obscure your vision or your capability. Keep one eye on the beauty. The friendliness will sustain you.

CHAPTER 53

A WHY TO LIVE

> Life is not an easy matter. You cannot live through it without falling into frustration and cynicism unless you have before you a great idea which raises you above personal misery, above weakness, above all kinds of perfidy and baseness.
> —Leon Trotsky (1879–1940)

Viktor Frankl looked around his camp and saw suffering everywhere. Men were starving and freezing, and some were literally worked to death. There was pain and misery in every moment; everyone was suffering. Some of the men buckled under the strain and perished early, but others managed to live and even find fleeting moments of satisfaction in companionship. Frankl wondered, "Why do some survive while others weaken and die?"

His conclusion, as most of us now know, was that the survivors possessed a certain sense of meaning and purpose that animated their lives and helped them transcend their conditions. Frankl was fond of quoting Nietzsche: "He who has a why to live can transcend almost any how." Or, we might say today, "He who has a why to live can tolerate almost any stressor."

Quite naturally, this insight has a powerful appeal to those of us living in a hyper-stressed environment, and it even suggests that having a "why" might well be the single most important factor in our health and our ability to manage the complexity of the modern world. Suddenly, all our obsessive focus on diet, exercise, and the minutiae of health begins to seem rather trivial and even irrelevant. After all, none of the prisoners in Nazi concentration camps had anything resembling an optimal diet or exercise program. And yet, some of them managed to live and later thrive. Frankl himself lived to the age of ninety-two, animated, we can be sure, by his own powerful sense of why.

SMALL WHY, BIG WHY

For many of us, the fundamental problem of our lives is that we spend too much of our time chasing after small whys. Frantic and overwhelmed by information overload, stress, and distraction, we don't take time to reflect and, instead, go about chasing whys that are shallow and weak. Driven by impulse, we chase the whys that are given to us by commercial narratives and, in the process, become little more than good consumers. And sadly, these little whys do little or nothing to sustain us in the face of adversity.

Steven Cole at the University of California, Los Angeles, has spent years studying how negative experiences such as loneliness and stress can increase the expression of genes promoting inflammation and, in turn, disease. In 2013, he examined the influence of well-being and focused on two types: *hedonic*, that which comes from pleasure and rewards (think sex, drugs, and rock and roll), and *eudaemonic*, that which comes from having a purpose beyond self-gratification.

These two forms were measured by having participants note their well-being over the previous week, how often they felt happy (hedonic) or that their life had a sense of direction (eudaemonic). Although scoring highly in one often meant scoring highly in the other and both correlated with lower levels of depression, they had opposite effects on gene expression. People with higher measures of hedonic well-being had higher expression of inflammatory genes and lower expression of genes for disease-fighting antibodies, a pattern also seen in loneliness and stress. For people scoring highest on eudaemonia, it was the opposite. "There were surprises all around," Cole says. "The biggest surprise being that you can feel similarly happy but the biology looks so notably different."

Cole suspects that eudaemonia—with its focus on purpose—decreases the nervous system's reaction to sudden danger that increases heart rate, breathing, and surges of adrenaline. Overactivation of this stress-response system, as we see with chronic stress, causes harmful inflammation. "There may be something saying 'be less frightened, or less worried, anxious, or uncertain,'" said Cole.

There's a neurological explanation for how this might work. Focusing on something positive and bigger than yourself may activate the ventral striatum, which can inhibit areas like the amygdala, which usually promotes the stress response. Similar research shows that higher scores on a scale of purpose correlated with less amygdala activation. Other studies indicate that people with higher eudaemonic well-being have both increased activity in the ventral striatum and lower levels of the stress hormone cortisol. "Things that you value can override things that you fear," says Cole.

Sadly, it's beginning to look like sex, drugs, and rock and roll might not be the true path to health, stress resistance, and sustainability after all. What we need is a big why. And the good news is that we already know how to do this. It's a human universal to be moved by the big whys of family, community, country, justice, and the quest for a better future. Intuitively, we seem to understand that life just works better when we focus on something bigger.

Likewise, we begin to see that the self-focused why of modern culture is abnormal and historically deviant. "I'm working for me" just doesn't take us very far. The narcissistic why can drive us for a time, but it ultimately turns ugly, dysfunctional, and irrelevant. Frankl would surely recognize the poverty of this kind of thinking and would have predicted the demise of any self-focused prisoners in his camp.

Instead, we need to keep our attention extended, outside the self to the bigger circles of life. In particular, we need to connect our sense of meaning to the domain of ecosystems, the biosphere, and the seventh generation. These whys are important not just for the obvious benefits they bring to the systems and people in question, but because of the way they help us prevail in the face of chronic stress and uncertainty.

In fact, we might well take inspiration from the old Darryl Cherney protest song, "Earth First! Maid" (set to the tune of "Union Maid"):

> There once was an Earth First! maid
>   Who never was afraid
>   Of the chain saw boys and their phallic toys
>   And the bulldozers who cut the grade . . .
>   Oh, you can't scare me, I'm working for the forest . . .
>   I'm working for the forest . . .

CHAPTER 54

TEACH THE FROG TO FIGHT

> Of all the dangers we face, from climate chaos to nuclear war, none is so great as the deadening of our response.
> —Joanna Macy

Legend has it that frogs are pretty stupid. Put one in a pot of water, turn up the heat, and it'll just sit there until it's cooked alive. Stupid amphibians.

In actual fact, frogs are smart enough to jump out of the water, but never mind that for the moment; it's the metaphor that counts. The problem is that the human nervous system is fantastically good at adapting. Put a human in a novel predicament, and after a few weeks or months, that person will find a way to live, even in circumstances that are ultimately hostile to human health. This fact contains vital lessons for the way that teachers, coaches, trainers, and therapists approach their students, clients, and patients. The question is simple: How shall we treat, train, coach, and educate the human frog in context?

For example, consider a popular wellness-based approach for treating anxiety, depression, and related sufferings. Patients and clients are counseled to be receptive, accepting, tolerant, and at ease with their circumstances. "Just breathe," we tell them. "Surrender. Adapt, relax, and let it be."

This approach may well be appropriate in some settings and surely provides some temporary relief for some, but what if the ultimate source of the person's suffering lies not within the individual, but in their circumstances? Seen in this light, our advice seems entirely backward and counterproductive. Instead of improving the frog's situation, we actually drive its predicament deeper. The frog relaxes, comes to peace with its world, and ultimately gets cooked alive.

As in all things, framing and context are crucial. Every time we focus on personal attitude as the solution, we reinforce the notion that the ultimate source of the problem lies exclusively within the individual. According to this narrative, the frog is the one with the problem. If only it could relax and be more receptive to its life experience, all would be well. But this is a perilous path for all of us because it blinds us to vital bigger pictures.

This is precisely the point made by Ron Purser in *McMindfulness: How Mindfulness Became the New Capitalist Spirituality*. Purser's argument is that spiritual practices and self-care are now becoming tools for corporate compliance. One reviewer profiled the book with the headline "Why Corporations Want You to Shut Up and Meditate."

As Purser sees it, the problem with the mindfulness–wellness movement, especially at the corporate level, is that it places the onus entirely on the individual while simultaneously downplaying the importance of context:

> What's happening with corporate mindfulness is a complete denigration of critical thinking into the causes of stress, which are all privatized into the individual.
>
> There is also an implicit denigration of collective action and building solidarity . . . It's sending individuals a message that they are the problem, they need to be calm, and they need to regulate . . . the systemic and structural apparatus of the company is completely untouched and not called into question.

Exactly. The frog is counseled to give up resistance, adapt, and be at peace with her circumstances. Ignore the fact that the water is getting hotter with each passing moment. Ignore the systemic ills and the impending crisis. If you're feeling uncomfortable, that's *your* fault. How convenient.

Journalist Sebastian Junger takes a similar approach in his reporting on combat veterans with posttraumatic stress disorder (PTSD). As he sees it, the fundamental problem for vets is the challenge of returning from war to a society that's highly individualistic and not given to group cohesion. In other words, "The problem is not with them; the problem is with us."

MARTIAL ARTISTRY: LEARNING HOW TO FIGHT

To be sure, today's human frog does have a problem, but it's got little or nothing to do with a neurotransmitter deficiency or her failure to breathe deeply. Rather, the problem lies in her setting, predicament, and context. The frog is being forced to live in an alien, mismatched, perilous world, one that's often hostile to her health.

As teachers, trainers, and coaches, this puts our job description in a new light. Instead of teaching the human frog to feel better, we should be teaching her how to rebel against the life-hostile characteristics of the world she inhabits. In other words, stop thinking in terms of individual cures, therapies, prescriptions, and remedies. Instead, start thinking in terms of practical activism at a large, systemic scale. Stop adapting and start fighting.

Naturally, this suggestion will make many of us feel distinctly uncomfortable. We're accustomed to working with individual bodies, individual minds, and individual problems, not with widespread, system-level dysfunctions. And as a culture, we feel uneasy about the whole notion of fighting, rebellion, and activism. We're conditioned to thinking of fighting as a problem to be solved, not a solution to be embraced.

But the real problem is not fighting itself; it's our lack of training and skill in social and political engagement. The water is getting warmer, but even if our frog realizes the nature of her predicament, she is poorly equipped to make a difference. What she really needs is a fighting curriculum and a broad sense of martial artistry. As teachers, therapists, trainers, and coaches, our job is to teach these fundamentals: when to fight, whom or what to fight, and especially, how to fight. Judgment and skill are essential, but the good news is that these arts can be modeled and taught.

This proposal will strike many as "radical" in the extreme, but from the frog's point of view, this fighting curriculum is actually a conservative, life-preserving act. Save yourself by taking action. Jump out of the water, turn down the heat, and change the system that's killing us. This is not only prudent; it's ultimately a prosocial, pro-future act.

CHAPTER 55

IT'S THE CULTURE, STUPID

> There's nothing fundamentally wrong with people. Given a story to enact that puts them in accord with the world, they will live in accord with the world. But given a story to enact that puts them at odds with the world, as yours does, they will live at odds with the world. Given a story to enact in which they are the lords of the world, they will act as the lords of the world.
> —Daniel Quinn
> *Ishmael*

Who exactly are we? Listening to whispered conversations at the margins of our conventional, public lives, we hear a host of dark and cynical metaphors going around. Depending on whom you're talking to, *Homo sapiens* is either a virus, an invasive species, a cancer on the planet, or an asteroid on par with the impact that wiped out the dinosaurs.

All of these metaphors are pretty grim, and all of them might be described as "inverse human supremacy." We're a destructive force on a planetary scale, to be sure, but as far as that goes, we're still the best, the alpha pathogen, if you will. We always like to take center stage, even when we're destroying our own life-support system.

These images of human destruction are tempting and easy, but all of them paint the situation with an excessively broad brush, as if all humanity behaves the same way, holds the same values, and has the same impact. And this is obviously not the case.

In fact, the situation is nuanced. Not all societies hold the same values, and not all humans have the same impact on the biosphere. In fact, there are plenty of human cultures that have lived in rough harmony with the natural world and have done so for a long time.

Clearly, there are too many people on the planet, and in general, our impact is unsustainable, but the problem is not humanity itself. It's one particular value system, one particular narrative that's driving the lion's share of the destruction. This is the culture of human supremacy, advanced and supported by industrial and technological capitalism.

To the extent that we embrace this culture, we are the architects of our separation from the living Earth. We are the ones who inflict traumatic damage on our life-supporting system. We are the ones who hold the bottom-line values that allow us to sell off the future for short-term personal gain. Now, if you want to describe industrial-corporate culture as a virus, a cancer, or an asteroid, well, that's something we can work with.

This understanding is both clarifying and liberating. Even better, there's less reason to be depressed. After all, if humanity is the ultimate problem, why get out of bed in the morning? Why do anything at all? If our biological fate is sealed, why not just give up?

But when we identify a particular culture and value system as the problem, we've got something to focus on and fight against. We can have targets, strategies, and tactics for change. And in comparison, this is something that's actually doable. Just focus on the planet-hostile and people-hostile features of the culture in question, and you've got a starting point. This is where we can succeed. Cultural creativity can go where legal and policy measures cannot. Cultural activism can cross boundaries and touch minds at any level, provided you can get the message and the narrative in front of the right people.

Even better, this orientation gets us away from the politics of personal antagonism. In other words, the problem is not particular people or even particular parties but, rather, the ideas and values that circulate through a society. To be sure, there's no shortage of ignorant, anti-planet, and anti-future individuals in our midst, but there's not much to be gained by attacking them directly. Indeed, personal attacks are notorious for producing blowback and hardening positions. Better to ignore them and challenge the ideas, images, values, and aesthetics in question. Work the culture at every opportunity, and keep creating. This is powerful and vital work.

CHAPTER 56

ACTIVISM IS MEDICINE

> Resistance is not only about battling the forces of darkness. It is about becoming a whole and complete human being. It is about overcoming estrangement. It is about the capacity to love. It is about honoring the sacred. It is about dignity. It is about sacrifice. It is about courage. It is about being free. Resistance is the pinnacle of human existence.
> —Chris Hedges

In the popular imagination, medical practice and political activism are two completely different animals. Medicine is all about disease, infection, antibiotics, physical exams, diagnostics, and outrageous, inexplicable bills. Activism is all about politics, legislation, organizing, raising money, and messaging. They're two completely different domains with miles of empty space between them.

Or are they really? What if we're wrong about all of this? What if activism isn't just distantly related to medicine but is actually an integral part of health itself?

In recent years, lots of people have labeled various activities as medicine. We've heard that "exercise is medicine," "art is medicine," and "music is medicine." But if these activities have medicinal and health benefits for the human organism, why not activism? It hardly seems like a stretch, after all: acting on something you're passionate about almost certainly has an integrating effect on the human mind–body. When we look at it from this perspective, the connection begins to seem perfectly obvious.

As it stands, there isn't much research on the activism–health connection, but if we come at it from the opposite direction, some key insights are revealed. For example, we can say with absolute confidence that *in*activism is bad for our spirit and, in turn, our health. Across history and across the spectrum, writers and activists have taken note of the perils of apathy and nonparticipation:

> Edward Abbey: "Sentiment without action is the ruin of the soul."
> Eleanor Roosevelt: "When you cease to make a contribution, you begin to die."
> Martin Luther King Jr.: "The way of acquiescence leads to moral and spiritual suicide."

These elders are absolutely right: the failure to engage and participate is bad for our lives, and because everything in our lives and bodies is radically connected, it makes sense to suppose that inactivism will have some very real downstream consequences for our bodies. By the same token, acting and engaging with the world in the service of our meaning and purpose is likely to have some substantial health benefits.

In fact, a growing body of evidence confirms the power of purpose and meaning. In 2017, *New Scientist* summarized the findings:

> People with a greater sense of purpose live longer, sleep better, and have better sex. Purpose cuts the risk of stroke and depression. It helps people recover from addiction or manage their glucose levels if they are diabetic. If a pharmaceutical company could bottle such a treatment, it would make billions.

Likewise, Victor Strecher, a public health researcher at the University of Michigan and author of *Life on Purpose*, writes:

> Over the past 10 years, the findings about the health benefits of purpose have been remarkably consistent—revealing that, among other advantages, alcoholics whose sense of purpose increased during treatment were less likely to resume heavy drinking six months later, that people with higher purpose were less likely to develop sleep disturbances with age, and that women with more purpose rated their sex lives as more enjoyable. These findings persist "even after statistically controlling for age, race, gender, education, income, health status, and health behaviours."

The power of meaning is so vital to health that it ought to be included as a routine part of every medical exam. In the long run of a person's life, it's probably at least as important as body weight, blood pressure, and lab results. In fact, most of us can easily weather minor biomedical abnormalities, but when meaning is weak or absent, our resilience, stress resistance, and vitality are all compromised. In other words, lacking a sense of meaning and purpose is a genuine risk factor for disease. So why is it that we pay so little attention?

If modern medicine is to catch up with the times, it needs to make meaning a regular feature of practice. We might even look forward to the day when "sense of meaning" is given its rightful place as a diagnostic sign, recorded on medical records, and updated regularly. Hippocrates would surely consider this as a step in the right direction.

On the surface, it might seem that political activism doesn't have any of the familiar challenges that we've come to associate with promoting good health. Holding up a sign on a street corner doesn't burn many calories; filing a petition or writing a letter, even less. Go to a conference or testify in front of a committee—on the face of it, these things sound stressful, annoying, and even health-negative. Who ever heard of someone going into activism specifically as a health practice?

But the main value in activism lies in its integrating effect on the human organism. In this respect, activism is very much akin to vigorous physical movement, otherwise known as *exercise*. When we act, particularly in the face of ambiguity and uncertainty, we call on the body to gather its resources into a single, cohesive effort. This integrating effect is powerfully health promoting.

In the meantime, the message is obvious: get clear about your meaning and purpose, and start acting. Engage the world, bang the drum, speak truth to power, and do the important work as you see it. This will bring focus and integration to the systems in your body, stimulating them to work in harmony.

Your body will thank you.

CHAPTER 57

LIFE HAS STANDING

> Our governance systems are based on false premises. The core falsehood is that we humans are separate from our environment and that we can flourish even as the health of Earth deteriorates.
> —Cormac Cullinan
> *Wild Law: A Manifesto for Earth Justice*

People have rights, some of them. Corporations have rights, all of them. But in general, animals, plants, and ecosystems have no rights. In other words, from a strictly legal perspective, the vast majority of creatures on this planet are outlaws, outside the reach of conventional jurisprudence. So what's wrong with this picture?

In 1972, attorney Christopher Stone wrote a landmark legal essay posing the question, "Should Trees Have Standing?" This became a rallying point for the then-burgeoning environmental movement and launched a worldwide debate on the basic nature of legal rights. Today, small but growing numbers of governmental organizations are now granting rights to various ecosystems.

In April 2010, the Universal Declaration of the Rights of Mother Earth was adopted by the World People's Conference on Climate Change and the Rights of Mother Earth in Cochabamba, Bolivia. In the United States, the first rights-of-nature lawsuit was filed in 2017, seeking judicial recognition of the Colorado River as a person under the law. This followed similar legal actions in India, Colombia, Ecuador, and New Zealand. And in July 2018, a high court in northern India issued a ruling declaring, "Every species has an inherent right to live and are required to be protected by law."

HUMAN SUPREMACY 2.0?

"Rights of nature" sounds like a step in the right direction, but then again, it also strikes us as rather preposterous. In fact, from a strictly biological point of view, the entire proposal seems outlandishly homocentric and vainglorious. *Homo sapiens* is one species, a minor bit player in a vast and incomprehensibly complex, unimaginably ancient biosphere. In this world, no one species gets to grant rights to the entire system. It's like a fish granting rights to the ocean. It's like a single leaf granting rights to the tree that gives it life. From this perspective, the rights-of-nature movement might well seem like one more example of human supremacy run amok.

Then there's the thorny question of *who* is granting the rights. Some scholars have celebrated the expanding circle of rights that we've seen over the last hundred years or so. Emancipation of slaves, women's right to vote, some animal rights, gay rights, and so on. Worthy of celebration? Yes, but it also depends on where you're starting from. If your reference point is white, male, Eurocentric supremacy, then granting rights to other people or creatures hardly seems like much progress. The original power structure and perspective remain intact.

In this, the truly revolutionary question would be, "What gives *you* the right to grant *us* rights?" Those who grant the rights are laying claim to superiority, but this is only a consequence of history and even the luck of the draw, not of any intrinsic superiority. In a true Paleo society, this kind of thing would never be an issue; people understood the problems inherent in ego, supremacy, and declarations of superiority. When the entire world is alive and kin, everyone—humans, plants, animals, sky, and land—has the right to exist.

It would be fun to have this conversation around the campfire and debate the philosophical merits of the movement, but this might well be a waste of time. That's because, practically speaking, the rights-of-nature movement stands as one of the most promising developments on the planet at the moment. Already in its short history, the movement is beginning to catalyze change. It's a monkey wrench in modern legal theory, as well as modern, alienated human consciousness. It forces us to revise many of our pet assumptions about ownership of land, animals, and people, about human supremacy and what constitutes criminal behavior. It forces us to reinhabit the circle of life and start behaving with humility.

Even better, the movement dovetails perfectly with the Stop Ecocide movement, led by a team of criminal lawyers, researchers, and diplomats working to amend international criminal law. As it stands, the Rome Statute of the International Criminal Court (ICC) lists four crimes: genocide, crimes against humanity, war crimes, and crimes of aggression. Notably, these are all instances of human-on-human violence. Not mentioned is violence against life-supporting systems, which, seen from a normal, indigenous point of view, is largely indistinguishable from violence against people. The

Stop Ecocide movement seeks to add a fifth crime to the list. Unlike suing and fining corporations (which simply budget for this possibility), ecocide law would make individuals who are responsible for funding, permitting, or causing severe environmental harm liable and subject to criminal prosecution.

As with all legal projects, the rights-of-nature movement and ecocide law are going to take some time. Organizers are putting together teams of activist attorneys, and law schools are beginning to offer courses on these subjects, but progress is going to be slow. Nevertheless, there are things we can do to support these movements.

Most importantly, engage the conversation whenever possible, especially in schools. As it stands, most of our educational systems ignore the rights of nature, and in fact, many are complicit in promoting the idea that nature simply has no rights. The notion is baked into many curriculums to the point where the discussion simply never comes up. "Ecosystems have rights? Don't be silly."

But this can all change, starting with young children. Tell them the story that all life is kin, that animals and people belong to the same family—the normal, indigenous story. This will make perfect sense to them. After all, they haven't yet been indoctrinated with the dogma of human supremacy. Then, engage their imagination and pose the vital questions: "Who has rights?"; "Who gets to grant rights?"; "Are rights just for people?"; "And if animals and ecosystems don't have rights, why not?"

This will get them fired up and ready to move forward. They'll see the injustice and be moved to act.

CHAPTER 58

WHAT MOVES PEOPLE

> If you want to build a ship, don't drum up people together to collect wood and don't assign them tasks and work, but rather teach them to long for the endless immensity of the sea.
> —Antoine de Saint-Exupéry

When Greta Thunberg first arrived on the scene, her warnings were stark, bold, and unambiguous. As she famously put it, "Our house is on fire." People sat up and took notice. A *Guardian* cover story about youth climate activism made her point in dramatic fashion: "I want you to panic," it declared, leaving no doubt about the urgency of the situation.

About the same time, author David Wallace-Wells began writing articles and books about the "uninhabitable Earth." A *New York Times* story on his work was titled "Time to Panic. Fear May Be the Only Thing That Saves Us." A similar opinion piece declared that "Alarmism is the argument we need to fight climate change," and some climate activists have declared outright that "people should be terrified."

But this kind of messaging, appropriate as it may be, is not the only way to communicate the urgency of our predicament and, in fact, may even be counterproductive. Will people respond to apocalyptic warnings, or will they simply tune out and retreat into the comfort of familiar amusements, trivia, and entertainment?

A more reflective approach might be in order. Consider the spiritual teachings of legendary Yosemite climber Ron Kauk. As he sees it, the most important action we can take in this moment is that "people need to calm down" and "stop being so afraid." In his view, fear is coursing through our society and is making everything worse. When people are terrified, they become reactive and, even worse, blind to the essential wonders of the natural world.

Much as we love Greta Thunberg and respect the work of David Wallace-Wells, Kauk's teachings ring true. Yes, there are plenty of reasons to panic, and yes, many people need a cold-shower wake-up call, but for the already well informed, fear doesn't really help. We're already going at full tilt as it is, trying to patch the holes in the lifeboat. Remember Viktor Frankl's observation that "between stimulus and response there is a space. In that space is our power to choose our response." The problem with fear-based messaging is that it narrows that space. It makes us more reactive, which, in the context of a social environment that's already saturated with stress, is probably the last thing we need. People are already anxious and reactive enough as it is. If we can relax, take a breath, and let things be for a while, the body is more likely to generate something creative, meaningful, and effective.

Of course, it all depends on who we're talking to. We know full well that many people are oblivious to climate reality, and in fact, the term *climate change* gives a misleading impression.

Such soft language completely masks the blunt-force fact that "climate change" really means catastrophic trauma for millions of people and animals around the world: mass migrations, raging wildfires, collapsing ecosystems, poisoned aquifers, and social chaos. These people need a wake-up call, and for this audience, alarmism is perfectly appropriate.

On the other hand, there's another segment of society that's completely up to date on the apocalyptic facts of our predicament. They understand the gravity of the situation, and for this audience, heaping on another layer of fear really isn't going to help.

So what are we left with? Appeals to naked self-interest? Ethics and morality? Incessant nagging with numbers, facts, tweets, and posts?

PALEO MOTIVATIONS

One approach that doesn't seem to work is the rational, nonfiction narrative. Today, we're awash in research reports that are pumped into our inboxes every day, an endless stream of gory numbers, facts, and data, all of which adds up to an ever-bleaker prognosis. And while some people are moved by such a narrative, most are not. Commander Spock might well say, "It's not logical to destroy your life-support system," but only a few of us are going to take heed.

So perhaps it's time to step back and ask what might have moved our ancestors. What would it take to rally the tribe in the Paleo? What kind of appeal would inspire people to journey to the next valley, cross a big river, or do battle with a pride of lions for a juicy carcass?

Obviously, data wouldn't move anyone in such conditions; charts and graphs just aren't going to do the job. Instead, people would have looked to one another for courage, conviction, passion, and intensity. Who's stepping up? Is someone sticking their neck out? Is someone taking a personal risk to advance the cause? This is what gets our attention and inspires us to action.

Ultimately, people are moved by seeing others taking risks for what they believe. We're moved by Colin Kaepernick, Emma González, Ken Ward, Paul Watson, Tim DeChristopher, and others who stand up for a better world, people who take risks for principle and for a functional future. When I see you wading out into the crocodile-infested waters to lead us across the river, I'll be moved to follow. Words may be helpful, but they are not sufficient. If you really want to move people, put your body where your mouth is.

FUN APPEAL

But it doesn't need to be all blood and guts either. To be sure, there's plenty to be serious about, but don't focus your messaging on deprivation and the grim details of dreary, low-impact living. Don't talk about the need to live in the bush, subsist on a diet of kale, or live a stark Amish lifestyle. Your pitch will fall on deaf ears.

Instead, make the case for enjoyment and meaning. In fact, it's fun and rewarding to live a low-impact lifestyle and share your experience with others. It's fun to learn about the plants and animals of your local bioregion. It's fun to protest in the streets and join with others in the fight for a functional future.

Don't focus on the labor involved or the fact that it usually takes a significant amount of hard-core labor to move the needle on social policies. Instead, tell this story: There *will* be dancing at this revolution—and drumming and art and good food. Come and join us. This is going to be the greatest party on the planet!

CHAPTER 59

BREADTH BEFORE DEPTH

Try to learn everything about something and something about everything.
—Thomas Huxley

It's the dilemma faced by every gambler, every fisher, every online dater, and every person who's encountering an ambiguous predicament. Shall I put my energy and bets down on a single spot, or should I spread myself out over the terrain and hope that I strike it rich?

We can think of this dilemma in terms of the letter "T." The vertical axis suggests digging a hole in one spot, finding a specialization, and going as far as we can with it. When it works, the payoff can be substantial, but it's always a gamble. If you dig your hole in the right place, you'll hit the jackpot, but if you dig in the wrong spot, you'll waste years of your life.

In contrast, the horizontal bar of the T implies "shopping around," digging a series of shallow holes here and there. The risk here is that you'll spread yourself out so thin that you won't be effective or functional at any one challenge. Your understanding might be "a mile wide and an inch deep." You might be a jack-of-all-trades, but sometimes you really need to be a master of one.

We might also think of this as a "cocktail party dilemma." As we all know, it's risky to show up with a single deep specialization. You'll end up wandering the room, unable to engage anyone in conversation unless you get lucky and stumble into someone who happens to share your particular field of expertise. But if your knowledge base is broad, you'll be able to connect with almost anyone. The conversation might be superficial, but at least you can get some rapport going.

Success in human life often seems to come down to exercising the right choice in specializing and generalizing, and everyone seems to have their own personal style. Some of us like to choose a single issue and dig deep; others like to travel widely and take a deeper dive every now and then. But there can be no right answer or perfect strategy. When you're working with an ambiguous, unpredictable reality and incomplete information, you've got to make your best guess and go with it. All of which brings us to our planetary predicament and our looming encounter with a monstrously ambiguous near-term future. Shall we go deep or broad?

Sadly, we receive almost no guidance on this score. Schools teach isolated subjects, and rarely, if ever, are students encouraged to develop a meta-strategy for navigating the dilemma of the T. Typically, school is just a bunch of knowledge, some of it broad, some of it deep. Consequently, students generally have no idea which direction to go. Is this class about the horizontal or the vertical? Will I be rewarded for specializing or going far afield in my search? Students are whipsawed from one direction to the other, never sure how deep to dig or how far to look.

Later, at the university, students are explicitly pushed to specialize on the vertical axis. Students are permitted to "shop around" in their freshman and sophomore years, but then they're expected to sober up and focus. In other words, start going down a rabbit hole. Keep digging long enough, and someone will give you an advanced degree and a good job or maybe a professorship.

As a culture, we believe that professionalization is the ideal path to success, and we encourage our young people to dig deep. It's worked in the recent past, and we assume that it's going to work in the future. The economic rewards—at this point, at least—are going to those who specialize and learn "everything about something."

But the world is lurching toward a completely new and unpredictable reality, and in this world, specialists are going to be exposed and vulnerable. When the world shifts, as it surely will, your specialization might be left out in the cold, useless and irrelevant.

Even worse, specialists have a notorious tendency to lose track of big pictures. When you're deep down in the rabbit hole, it's easy to forget the panoramic views that are so essential to keeping us and the planet whole. Or to use another metaphor, you might know everything about a particular bicycle spoke, but if you lose sight of the whole wheel, what good is it?

There's also a set of psycho-spiritual considerations here. That is, some of us choose a strategy based not on curiosity and conscious intent, but on avoidance and the desire for safety. For example, those who go all-in on the vertical hole-digging might simply be trying to escape the wide-open reality of the larger world. Rigid, narrow specialization involves a lot of work, but it also protects us from having to deal with the messy, ambiguous nature of the wider world. It's a security strategy; the world may be in chaos, but at least I know what's happening in my particular rabbit hole.

Alternately, those who go all-in on horizontal wandering might well be trying to escape the focused labor that goes into actually doing something. And so the question becomes obvious: Why are you digging or wandering? What's driving your quest? Are you seeking meaning and knowledge, or are you trying to protect yourself from ambiguity?

In any case, the beauty of "breadth before depth" is that it gives us the lay of the land and the panoramic views that are essential for getting our bearings. If we simply start digging where we're standing, we might waste years, even centuries, of effort before we realize that we've been digging in the wrong place. That's why it's essential that we take students up on the mountain as often as possible: the beginning of the academic year, the beginning of the semester, and the beginning of each new area of investigation. Show them the map and point: "This is the landscape. This is where you could go."

And practically speaking, our new, chaotic world is about to challenge us with an entirely new range of systemic breakdowns and dysfunctions. We'll no longer be able to count on specialists to fix our cars, our houses, and our meals. Individuals are simply going to have to learn how to perform a wider range of tasks, everything from growing food to cooking to fixing houses to performing basic medical care. The jack-of-all-trades will be a vital person to have in your community.

This implies that the horizontal bar of the T will be our best bet for education and living. Keep it broad and wide; learn something about everything. A little specialization is a good thing, but don't dig the hole too deep. Come up for air every now and then and look around.

CHAPTER 60

ONE MORE GRAIN

> The man who moves a mountain begins
> by carrying away small stones.
> —Confucius
> *The Analects*

If you've ever tried to change something in the world, you know how easy it is to fall into a state of despair. When we compare our personal power with the inertia of the status quo, our efforts often feel insignificant, even irrelevant and meaningless. We try and try, but nothing seems to change. It's easy to lose heart.

Perhaps a metaphor will help. Prior to the 1960s, most people thought of scientific progress as the simple accumulation of knowledge, a process in which new evidence builds on established structure, brick by brick, fact by fact. It all seemed pretty linear and maybe even boring, but in 1962, the philosopher Thomas Kuhn told us a different, highly disruptive story. In his classic work *The Structure of Scientific Revolutions*, he argued for an episodic model in which plateaus of stasis are interrupted by periods of revolutionary discovery and reimagining.

The process begins with the appearance of minor, inconvenient anomalies that seem to contradict the dominant paradigm. At the outset, the countervailing evidence goes largely ignored and is even ridiculed. No one pays much attention, but over time, the weight accumulates, leading eventually to a sudden and dramatic shift in thinking and attention: the famous paradigm shift.

For Kuhn, this is precisely what played out in the Copernican revolution, beginning in 1543. When Copernicus first proposed a heliocentric solar system, the evidence was actually rather weak and unconvincing. It was only later, when Galileo filled in gaps in the model, that it took on the power to overthrow the existing paradigm.

In essence, Kuhn argued that the process of scientific and cultural change operates like an enormous balance scale. A scientist or activist adds a contradictory idea to one side, but nothing seems to happen. The process continues for some time, and during this period, the scientist/activist may well conclude that his efforts are having no effect. Thus the despair.

But the grains of sand add up and shifts do come, sometimes in an instant. In 1991, the former Soviet Union collapsed almost overnight under the weight of its own incompetence. In 2015, same-sex marriage reached a sudden tipping point of popular acceptance. Mass acceptance of the reality of climate change might be following a similar trajectory. And in 2020, popular support for Black Lives Matter also reached a new level of cultural significance.

In fact, this process is consistent with the findings of political scientist Erica Chenoweth and her "3.5% rule of social change." Working with Maria Stephan, a researcher at the International Center on Nonviolent Conflict, Chenoweth performed an extensive review of civil resistance and social movements from 1900 to 2006. In short, they discovered that it only takes a small shift in people's attitudes to make a substantial difference. They also discovered that nonviolent campaigns are twice as likely to succeed as violent campaigns. These findings have been instrumental in inspiring the work of Extinction Rebellion and other activist groups.

All of this should give us some hope and encourage us to stay in the fight. The grain of sand you drop upon the scale may look and feel invisible, but it is not nothing. You may not see the effect, even in your lifetime. But the scale will move as people add their grains of effort and courage. Sooner or later, the paradigm will shift, and the shift may be bigger, faster, and more significant than we think.

In the end, it's all about the doing. Times are hard and the odds are long. Conditions feel overwhelming, and our future is in mortal danger. But the odds have always been long for the activist. Risk is inevitable, and the chance of failure is substantial. Your efforts may well feel inconsequential, but there are others out there fighting too. The tipping point may be closer than you think.

CHAPTER 61

THE UNKNOWN DECATHLON

The measure of intelligence is the ability to change.
—Albert Einstein

Suppose you're an athlete. You've got a sport that you love, and you spend long hours and years trying to improve your performance in that realm. You focus on exactly what needs to happen in each phase of the game, and all your sets and reps are crafted specifically to the final goal of turning in the best possible performance and winning a championship.

It all makes sense in its own way, but there's a paradox here. Hyper-specific training can produce amazing results, but it's not really designed to deal with novelty—or the larger world, for that matter. If anything goes wrong, the whole enterprise can fall apart. That's why Wisconsin-based athletic coach Steve Myrland takes a more expansive view. Concerned that the modern athlete is becoming too specialized, he encourages his athletes to think and train bigger. In workshops and presentations, he poses the question, "Are you *adapted* or *adaptable*?" And for many, this becomes a Zen koan that reorients both their training and the trajectory of their lives.

Myrland's approach is obviously valuable for athletes, but it also contains an essential perspective for all of us modern humans. Like today's athlete, many of us—most of us, really—are in serious danger of becoming too narrow in our skill sets. The modern world channels us into particular lifestyles and careers, and before long, most of us are doing essentially the same things each day: habitual patterns of food, transportation, living arrangements, screen time, communications—all of it standardized and driven by routine. After a few decades of living the standard American lifestyle, most of us are deeply adapted, not adaptable.

But this is an incredibly dangerous position to be in, especially in a world that's on the brink of radical change, a hockey-stick world of increasing acceleration. In this kind of world, the adapted will struggle and perish, whereas the adaptable will go on to create something new and viable.

This also tells us something crucial about stress. In a static world, those who are highly adapted can function at a high level, but when the world shifts, narrow specializations become increasingly out of sync, vulnerable, and brittle. This is what so many of us are feeling today, consciously or otherwise. We specialize and adapt, but lurking in the background is the possibility—even the probability—that our expertise may soon become irrelevant. And then what? We've spent our entire lives becoming adapted to a particular set of circumstances, skills, and values, all of which may soon be left out in the cold. It's no wonder we're so on edge.

PRACTICE

Ideally, our schools and universities would play an intentional, highly focused role in developing human adaptability, but as it stands, this vital skill is mostly ignored in favor of prepackaged, standardized curriculums. Students are expected to learn, metabolize, and regurgitate mountains of information, but there's no real effort to foster their physical, cognitive, or spiritual flexibility.

So how do we become less adapted and more adaptable? This might seem like a bit of a puzzle, but in fact, we already know how to do this: the SAID (Specific Adaptations to Imposed Demands) principle tells us so. We become more adaptable by practicing precisely this very thing. We become more adaptable by putting ourselves in new situations that force us to be adaptable. There's no mystery to this at all.

But this calls for a unique kind of training, one that will be counterintuitive for most of us. Instead of trying to perfect particular skills or capabilities, we'd practice moving fluidly from one domain to another. Build some capability, then switch. Gain some mastery, then go back to being a beginner in some new art. As soon as you're feeling competent, switch again. You'll never become great at any one thing, but you will develop something even more vital: the psycho-spiritual ability to move into new situations, confident that your body and mind will eventually figure out what to do.

FANTASY SPORTS AND STUDIES

To get a feeling for how this might work, imagine a new kind of sporting competition or even a new Olympics. Instead of producing standardized athletic events for participants, we'd deliberately put them in ambiguous situations. Each country would send a few athletes, and on arrival, they'd be assigned a handful of events, chosen at random. Think of it as an "unknown decathlon." For example, an individual might be called upon to swim a hundred meters; compete in a gymnastic event, a long jump, and a bicycle race; and play a musical instrument.

It would be impossible to train for each of these challenges in any kind of depth beforehand, so the whole thing becomes a test of adaptability. It would be exciting to watch and would also serve as a powerful metaphor for the average fan. After all, most of us can't relate to the professional athlete who has the time and resources to dig a specialty to the maximum, but all of us know the struggles of adaptability. Wouldn't it be fun and inspiring to watch athletes move from one novel challenge to the next?

Schools and universities could function the same way. Instead of driving people toward isolated, narrowing specializations, we could rotate academic challenges. In this kind of adaptability training, pursuing a single "major" for years on end would be frowned upon. Instead, students would be encouraged to focus in one domain for a semester or a year, then switch, then switch again, reinventing themselves along the way. To be sure, students would lose some degree of sophistication in their understanding, but they'd gain immensely in their psycho-spiritual ability to adapt to novel circumstances.

The beauty of this orientation is that it's maximally relevant for the world that we actually inhabit. If the COVID-19 pandemic has taught us anything, it's that we can't really predict what conditions will be like a year from now, much less ten years from now. Some specialization is obviously useful, but for most of us, the time has come to practice fluidity. Whatever your sport, lifestyle, or profession, the question of our day is simple: "Are you adapted or adaptable?"

CHAPTER 62

THE POWER OF SUBTRACTION

> The truth is revealed by removing things which stand in its light, an art, not unlike sculpture, in which the artist creates, not by building, but by hacking away.
> —Alan Watts

There are thousands of teachers in our world, but if we take a closer look, it soon becomes apparent that there are really two basic styles of engagement.

The dominant form is additive. In this style, the teacher sees his or her job as delivering information and knowledge, and more is always better. Cover ground, deliver the material, and set the student up for the next level, where another additive teacher will deliver yet more content, information, and knowledge. Success is a matter of quantity; the great student knows a lot of stuff and can prove it on a standardized test. Far and away, this is the most common form of teaching in most school settings.

In contrast, the subtractive teacher begins with the understanding that the modern world is far too noisy and confusing as it is and that health and sanity depend on quieting things down. Get back to the body, back to the Paleo, back to a realm of coherence and quiet equanimity. Simplify, clarify. These are often spiritual teachers, but they can be found in many domains.

LESS IS MORE

The problem with modern education is that the additive model just doesn't know when to quit. In essence, it's a kind of addiction. More is never enough. More content, more curriculum, more assessment. Study hard to learn more facts so that you can get into a good college, where the additive model goes exponential, culminating in the PhD, also known as the "Piled higher and Deeper" degree.

In some cases, this approach succeeds in producing happy, healthy people, but just as often, it overloads people with mountains of confusing, irrelevant, and worthless content. It also distracts people away from their bodies and the primal knowledge that comes through their physical experience.

This is what makes the subtractive model so vital. As noise becomes ubiquitous, stressful, and even life-threatening, it becomes increasingly important for people to hear and feel the clear messages that come from their habitat, their people, their bodies, and yes, from the heart. Knowing a mountain of facts is impressive and occasionally even useful, but when the process obscures our very humanity and life experience, we might well ask, "What's the point?"

In fact, many students resist the additive paradigm instinctively and are right to do so. Their bodies are built for the Paleo, sculpted for life in a wild, outdoor setting. They crave clarity, and yet teachers insist on piling on the knowledge, higher and deeper every day. These students don't have a "learning disorder." Rather, the school has a "teaching disorder."

And maybe the real "core curriculum" is already there. The body is already wired to learn habitat, with no cognitive training whatsoever. Experience is the teacher: Hunt and learn. Listen, touch, feel. Watch the animals and learn. The human body is a sponge for the natural world. Every time we add another layer of cognitive content, we obscure the primal instincts that are so vital to human function and happiness.

In the extreme, the additive model is actually destructive, and as Ivan Illich would have put it, "iatrogenic." That is, piling on content can ultimately destroy the curiosity and motivation that drive learning in the first place. This is why the subtractive teacher is so vital. Strip away the clutter, let go of the nonessentials, and get back to primal understandings. Your students' bodies are fully capable of learning as it is. In this sense, the fundamental teaching is, "You already know this."

To be sure, there's a risk that your students might miss out on some piece of information that might prove useful in the coming years, but you'll also find yourself in touch with things that truly matter. In the end, quality is more important than quantity.

CHAPTER 63

EXPERIENTIAL DESIGN

> The highest and most beautiful things in life are not to be heard about, nor read about, nor seen but, if one will, are to be lived.
> —Søren Kierkegaard

At first glance, education seems like a pretty complicated enterprise.

There's all that content to teach, and according to the experts, it's all got to come in the correct order, in the right form, and at the right pace. Make sure you've got the right textbooks, websites, and audiovisual aids all lined up, and you might have a shot at success.

But all of this misses the point. From the body's perspective, cognitive content is all pretty much the same. Sometimes it's exciting and sometimes it's mind-numbing, but it's still a matter of sitting still, listening or reading, trying to capture and metabolize a set of abstractions that will, so they say, serve you well in the future.

But the body isn't really wired for any of this. The animal body learns via experience and engagement, typically with habitat and other human beings. In other words, *experience is the language of the body*. If you want to talk to the body in a meaningful way, you're going to have to create the right kind of experience.

Experience, after all, has been the dominant form of learning for virtually all animals for virtually all of history. All mammals, including primates and early hominids, have learned exclusively by and through their experience. The natural world has been our university, and life has been our education.

This has been the experience of all animals, ever since the Cambrian explosion some five hundred million years ago. Every animal that has ever lived has learned about the world through contact, engagement, and experience. Think about it: five hundred million years of experiential education—a definite proof of concept.

But today, we attempt to leapfrog over this most essential educational truth. Living under the long shadow of Descartes, conventional education begins with the premise that the mind is separate from and superior to the body, and in fact, the body isn't really invited to the party at all. School is little more than a symbol-fest, an orgy of abstraction, a decades-long stint in a chair, strapped to a keyboard. This is the lived experience.

But no matter the details of the cognitive content, the body will always be inevitable. If you're a teacher, it doesn't matter what your subject is. Chemistry, physics, geology, language—you're always working with human bodies and their embodied nervous systems. In this respect, every teacher is ultimately a physical educator.

Going back to the Paleo, so much becomes obvious. People learned their habitat not by listening to lectures on flora and fauna in camp, but through actual encounters with the world. Grandparents surely joined in and tried to direct the attention of young people in particular ways, but the real action was in the daily adventure, inside and outside of camp: see, feel, touch, listen, get surprised—use the whole body to engage. Take risks to sharpen your attention and your memory. Human bodies are really, really good at this. Experience is the ultimate teacher.

We are the first animal in the history of the world to attempt to do it some other way. And in this sense, modern educational practices are profoundly, radically abnormal.

EXPERIENTIAL DESIGNERS AT WORK

All teachers, coaches, and trainers are—or should be—experiential designers. Our primary job description is not to "deliver content" or "administer the curriculum" but to create the right conditions for learning to take place.

Sadly, many of today's teachers simply take the experiential template that's been handed to them and replicate it with some personal touches. School is school. It has its own familiar look and feel, its own environment, culture, and tasks that must be performed. Tradition tells us what to do with our students: line them up outside the door, ring the bell, get them seated, then direct their attention to the chalkboard or the computer screen. This is the experience.

It's easy to fall back on this established pattern, but this simply perpetuates the status quo and leaves students with the same experience they've always had. You can tweak the content all you like, but unless you change the body's experience, nothing much will change.

Other teachers will take matters into their own hands and craft the experience from scratch. To do this, it's essential to start with a beginner's mind and an empty cup. Think about the totality of the student's encounter, from beginning to end, seen through the experience of the body.

What does it feel like to start the day or the practice session? What is the physical quality of each step in the process? What does the body experience when engaging with the people, the setting, and the content? What does the student's body see, touch, smell, and taste? What is the body's emotional reaction to these encounters? And most of all, how is your student or client going to feel at the end of a session, a semester, or a year?

Don't take these things for granted. Map them out in detail and revise them if they don't add up to the kind of engaging, immersive experience you're after. Then, once you've got a sense of the experience you're looking for, layer in whatever content you like.

CHAPTER 64

DOJO RULES

> Talent without discipline is like an octopus on roller skates. There's plenty of movement, but you never know if it's going to be forward, backwards, or sideways.
> —H. Jackson Brown Jr.
> *Life's Little Instruction Book*

As we've seen, experience is the language of the body. The content of our teaching is obviously important, and we are right to care about the details, but the body understands on a deeper level. With this in mind, it's essential to create a culture of excellence that supports a highly focused experience.

Fortunately, you won't have to create this culture from scratch. Around the world, almost every martial arts program includes some version of "dojo rules," time-honored guidelines for success in training. The typical set includes the following:

- Show respect for people, process, and place.
- Keep the training hall clean and orderly.
- Participate completely. Do not arrive late or leave early.
- Everyone works with everyone else.
- Come to training with an empty cup, ready to learn.
- WAIT: Why Am I Talking?

These rules work because they set expectations and put limits on behavior. They make it clear: This is not a nightclub. This is not a restaurant. This is not a shopping center. It's a place to focus, concentrate, and deliver your best possible performance every day. This is a special place, home to a sacred experience that's worth protecting.

The beauty of the dojo rules is that they set the body up for an experience that's focused, intentional, and meaningful. The body understands: Bow to the mat, bow to your partner, pay attention. The teacher's words may or may not be inspiring, but it's the experience that does most of the teaching.

WOODEN'S RULES

This emphasis on discipline is common to all high-performance environments. Legendary basketball coach John Wooden began each season with a review of "Wooden's Rules." Not suggestions, not requests—rules. Among them were the following:

- Be dressed, on the floor, and ready for practice on time every day.
- Work hard to improve yourself without having to be forced. Be serious. Have fun without clowning. You develop only by doing your best.

- No cliques, no complaining, no criticizing, no jealousy, no egotism, no envy, no alibis. Earn the respect of all.
- When a coach blows the whistle, give him your undivided attention and respond immediately.
- Take excellent care of your equipment and keep your locker neat and orderly.
- Do things the way you have been told. Correct habits are formed only through continuous repetition of the perfect model.

In describing Wooden's philosophy and success, NBA All-Star Bill Walton said, "A culture of yes is built on a foundation of no." In other words, we get the best out of people by prescribing and enforcing clear boundaries. Wooden's teams won precisely because of their disciplined practice. By investing energy into focused practice sessions, Wooden created habits of excellence that would remain true, even under the stress of high-intensity playoff games. His players performed well in competition because they were accustomed to putting in their best efforts every day.

This is a proven formula for success. We see variations on dojo rules in all high-performance environments around the world: aircraft cockpits and control towers, intensive care and surgical wards, firehouses, courthouses, and elite restaurant kitchens all are operated by clear, consistent rules for the facility itself and the behavior of the people who work there.

As teachers, trainers, and coaches, our objective is to create similar high-focus environments and programs that move students and clients toward disciplined engagement. But sadly, our efforts are often undercut by today's culture of convenience. Marketing professionals advise us to make our programs "as easy as possible." Pamper the customer, they tell us;

make it easy to sign up, easy to participate, easy to drop in, and easy to drop out.

The result is that people now feel free to come and go as they please, talk to anyone, and of course, play with their phones whenever they choose. The end result is chaos. The educational experience is now devalued, scattered, and often, nearly meaningless. Coach Wooden and every traditional sensei would be appalled by the wholesale dilution of our practices. Just imagine trying to drop in or drop out of training at the Shaolin Temple or any other school of high performance. Things would not go well for you.

GRAVITY AND LEVITY

Naturally, fun-loving critics push back against this emphasis on discipline. They value play and the freedom to explore. Go too far with the rules, and you'll wind up with a boring program that kills the playful spirit.

But it doesn't have to be this way. In fact, this is precisely the point. By bringing a sense of safety and predictability to the process, students can actually have *more* fun. When people know what's expected, they can cut loose. This creates a "safe emergency" that challenges people but doesn't put them over the edge.

The challenge is that for humans, the field of play is immense. We play with everything under the sun: rocks, sticks, words, bodies, ideas, materials, tools, colors, shapes, sounds. The possibilities are mind-boggling. The end result is that we just don't know where to go with our energy or when to stop. This is why the blank page and the wide-open spaces of keyboards, fretboards, canvases, and dance floors can be so intimidating. We're overwhelmed with possibilities.

This is where the teacher, trainer, or coach steps in with smart guidelines and clear expectations. We say, "Play within this range." Legendary Hollywood screenwriter Robert McKee calls this "the principle of creative limitation." In his landmark book *Story: Substance, Structure, Style, and the Principles of Screenwriting*, he put it this way:

> The principle of Creative Limitation calls for freedom within a circle of obstacles. Talent is like a muscle: without something to push against, it atrophies. So we deliberately put rocks in our path, barriers that inspire. We discipline ourselves as to what to do, while we're boundless as to how to do it.

Even in the world of comedy, we see a similar theme. Jon Stewart, former host of the *Daily Show*, put it this way: "Creativity comes from limits, not freedom." In other words, the purpose of rules isn't to inhibit the creative process but to channel and liberate our energies.

CHAPTER 65

NO STICK, NO CARROT

> Reward and punishment is the lowest form of education.
> —Chuang Tzu

Why do a thing? Why work hard to learn a new art or craft? Why go outside your comfort zone? Why take a risk in trying to create a functional future?

The conventional "wisdom" holds that people need motivation to do unpleasant things like exercise and learning, so we're quick to offer up carrots to modify their behavior. And if that doesn't work, well, there's always sticks.

Sometimes this approach works, for a while anyway. But over time, the consequences become extremely negative, and we wind up with a population of reward-seeking people, people who are automated to get the treat, the biscuit, the gold star, and the bonus. As Alfie Kohn put it in *Punished by Rewards*, "Do rewards motivate people? Absolutely. They motivate people to get rewards." In the long run, this is highly destructive to human creativity and our ability to create a functional future.

DOMESTICATION BY REWARDS

Conditioned by the structures of modern culture, we've grown so accustomed to working for rewards that we scarcely ever stop to question what they might be doing to our minds, our bodies, and our futures. Starting well before kindergarten, we're manipulated by sweets and treats, and from there, it's but a short step to the abstracted rewards of gold stars, As, paychecks, and stock options. As Kohn put it, the entire enterprise—in both schools and the workplace—has been reduced to a single overarching narrative: "Do this and you'll get that."

But have we ever stopped to ask why we're doing this? If pressed, we might suppose some benign, even prosocial intent: "Education, work, exercise, and prosocial behaviors are inherently unpleasant. The rewards are there to pull people in the right direction, to lead them to do the right thing for themselves and the world." But is any of this really the case?

Taking a historical perspective, it all looks quite different. Prior to the age of agriculture, people lived by a gift economy, and there was little need to manipulate others into any particular behavior. People hunted and gathered because they were hungry and their bodies liked the action. No one ever had to be bribed to go out on the hunt or to gather food; the rewards were inherent in the activity itself. Likewise, prosocial behavior was—for the most part—perfectly natural and obvious. No carrots required.

But agriculture changed everything. Tilling the fields was hard work, and any sensible hunter-gatherer would avoid it if at all possible. Threats and punishments might have gotten some people to drive the plow, but agriculturalists soon discovered that carrots worked better. In turn, rewards became instrumental in the process of human domestication. If people could be trained to pursue carrots, they could be subdued and manipulated.

This is all creepy enough, but the real question is this: How did we ever come to the conclusion that education, work, exercise, and prosocial behavior are inherently unpleasant? In fact, there is nothing inherently distasteful in any of these things. Maybe it's just the way we've been framing it. In fact, there are a good many people who actually love education and physical movement, and some even love their jobs. It sounds like we've been working with a flawed assumption.

The solution to this manipulation is to be wary of rewards, just as any wild animal would be. Someone is trying to modify your behavior; someone is trying to get you to do something that maybe you'd rather not do, and there's a pretty good chance that they may not have your best interests at heart. You might have to play a rewards-based game to get along in the modern world, but know this: rewards are not your friends. In fact, if we go all-in on chasing rewards, we'll eventually lose contact with the pleasures that are inherent in the thing itself. We might get the carrot, but in the end, that's all we'll get.

As teachers, trainers, and coaches, it's essential to get clear on what we're trying to do and why we're doing it. Carrots have been part of our system for so long now that we can scarcely even imagine any other way of organizing the process. As it stands, most of the carrots we offer are "extrinsic." That is, they lie outside the domain, art, or discipline in question. We give gold stars for doing homework, we pay people to exercise, we give them perks for doing their jobs well. But research shows that these extrinsic rewards are only partly effective at best, and more likely, they distract students, clients, and workers from the intrinsic pleasures and satisfactions they might gain from the activity itself.

The superior way is to forget carrots and reframe the process to promote "autotelic" activity. Point to the pleasure of the activity itself. In this, the carrot is contained within the actual doing. This means promoting the pleasure and satisfaction that come with engagement. Do your homework not because you'll get a gold star, but because the subject is interesting and mastery feels good. Go to the gym not because someone will give you a "like" for your FitBit score, but because it feels really good to move with power and grace. Extend yourself in art, language, and reading not because you'll get a good job one day, but because it feels good to know what's going on in the world.

This might well sound preposterous and unrealistic, but if it does, maybe that's because you don't really believe in human creativity or self-motivated learning. Maybe you've never seen or heard of anyone doing something simply for its own sake. But people have done this countless times in history. We can be sure that no one ever used carrots or sticks on the Paleolithic cave artists to get them to produce the outrageous artwork of Lascaux, Chauvet, or Altamira. In fact, autotelic behavior is profoundly normal for our species.

Naturally, this changes the entire game of teaching. No longer is it an administrative task, a laborious grind of tracking carrots, sticks, and outcomes. Instead, this is all about belief, engagement, and contagion. If you really, really believe in the power of your art and your discipline, it will show through.

If not, you might want to find another path.

CHAPTER 66

ADVENTURE-DEFICIT DISORDER

> You know you're truly alive when you're living among lions.
>
> —Isak Dinesen
> *Out of Africa*

The world calls, incessantly, powerfully. The child's body grows, becomes strong, and in turn, a sense of wonder emerges. What am I capable of? What will happen when I meet the wild habitat outside of camp, the unfamiliar terrain, and most especially, the animals? Will I fight the good fight and prevail? Will I get lost, or will I find my way? Will I be smart and strong? I need to test myself, to throw my body up against the world and see what I'm made of. I need to know this, and I will not rest until I find out.

Every young man or woman has these desires, this drive and passion to experience the world in the flesh. And in the

Paleo, it was a perfect fit. Hunting was the ultimate test, the ideal way to find out who you were and what you were capable of. The bush was a proving ground: How will I perform when faced with a wild animal? What kind of decisions will I make? Will I be sensitive enough to follow the tracks in the dirt? Will I be able to smell the wind and get the drop on my prey? Am I up to the challenge?

These questions have animated thousands of generations of young men and women, humans in the prime of life, eager to know the world and their abilities. This longing is a human universal and is unquestionably a product of healthy human biology. When the body is operating at its peak, it craves engagement. This is no fleeting muse or superficial desire; this is a deep biological need, a need as vital as breathing itself. It is our birthright.

But sadly, modern culture tries to pretend otherwise. Our priority is domestication, control, regularity, and above all, order. Physical adventure and engagement just don't fit the paradigm. It's too wild, too unpredictable, and worst of all, not given to assessment on a standardized test. If the children would like to read adventure stories, that would be acceptable (and testable), but as for actually doing something authentically engaging, well, that's something you'll have to do on your own time.

To be sure, some students find the adventure they seek through sports, and yes, athletic competition can be a proving ground and an opportunity for discovery—if it's presented that way. But of course, that's not what we do. As professionalization spreads ever downward from the pros to the college ranks and high schools, the value system comes along for the ride, and winning becomes the prime directive. If a student finds adventure and discovery along the way, so much the better, but it's the championship and the glory that really count.

Even worse, competitive sports are ruthless in eliminating less-talented athletes. This means that the opportunity for adventure is only granted to kids with talent, aptitude, or more likely, affluent parents who have provided them with additional training. This makes it a win-win for the fortunate but a lose-lose for everyone else. It's hard to have an adventure when you're riding the bench.

To be sure, some students are lucky enough and affluent enough to have genuine adventures outside of school. And still others are rebellious enough and wild enough to demand adventure, even if it means throwing everything else to the wind. It's a risky move, but it speaks to the body's innate and nonnegotiable drive for experience. In this sense, adventure is an actual psycho-physical need, not altogether different from our need for food, water, and air. It shouldn't surprise us in the least that students will rebel in order to get it.

So what happens to adventure deferred? Exactly what we're seeing today: a public health crisis of students under stress, with all the familiar dysfunctions—attention problems, neurological disorders, depression, apathy, anxiety, physical lethargy, and social conflict. We wring our hands and write prescriptions as fast as we can, but all to no avail. We speculate about neurotransmitter deficiencies and all manner of genetic complications. Maybe, someday, if we fund enough research, a large corporation will come up with the right cocktail to keep all our students "on task."

But as so often happens in this modern world, we fail to look upstream. We fail to remember our history, and we fail to address root causes. And in this case, the root is obvious—by denying the human need for authentic physical engagement and adventure, we damage both the body and the spirit. In short, this is educational malpractice.

BE AN ADVENTURE ADVOCATE

Of course, we can't really expect modern schools to take young people on hunts in the wilderness, chasing down dangerous animals with rocks and sticks; schools have enough to do as it is. But there are vital lessons to be learned here. Instead of pretending that the drive to adventure doesn't exist or, worse yet, that it's some kind of flaw in the young organism, we should embrace it as a normal, essential part of young adulthood.

In this, we find a helpful new perspective. Suddenly our student's behavior makes a lot more sense. Yearning for adventure, they push back against our authority, and they're right to do so. Unable to engage the world directly, they seek out risky experiences. Locked into a world that can only promise a "good job" with even more time at a desk, they rebel. And when that fails, their bodies begin to withdraw, and their spirits turn dark.

None of this should come as a surprise to us as teachers, trainers, coaches, and therapists. So instead of trying to "cure" their "affliction," maybe we should celebrate it, harness it, and honor it. Our students are simply doing what young human animals do. They want to be educated as a whole animal. Let's give them the chance to do just that. So instead of medicating or punishing the adventurous spirit, be an advocate for its expression and vitality. Practice giving this kind of counsel to your students, clients, and patients:

> *Adventure is important. It's essential that you engage with the world and find out what you're capable of. This is vital to your health, happiness, and future success. Find an adventure path and take it. Your life depends on it.*

You may lose your job if you talk this way, but then again, you might be setting yourself up for a powerful adventure of your own.

CHAPTER 67

ARE YOU COACHABLE?

> Routines and habits are the Known, protecting us
> from the Unknown. Habits are also called home.
> Habits tame the raw wilderness of existence
> into the civilized comforts of everyday life.
> Unfortunately, as we all know, habits gradually
> domesticate all the wildness and energy out of life.
> So much energy gets bound up in routines and
> habituated patterns, keeping them alive, that your
> life goes dead instead. Thus, if you want to discover
> again the wild side of life, you have to leave "home";
> you have to break or dissolve your habits in order
> to release the energy locked up inside them.
> —Ed Buryn
> *Vagabonding in America*

Back in the late twentieth century, the neuroscience community announced a breathtaking new discovery. "We've cracked the code of learning," they declared. A fascinating series of insights into the human nervous system was all the rage, promising to revolutionize the educational process. It was all pretty technical, and it took a few decades to sort it all out, but the findings were clear and even inspiring. For the first time, we began to realize that the brain, far from being a static organ, was constantly remodeling itself throughout life, according to how it's used. In other words, the nervous system is *plastic*.

This was an incredibly powerful finding because it overturned the existing dogma of *neurofatalism*, the belief that the adult brain is fundamentally static. For decades, teachers simply assumed that children had fixed aptitudes and that the best you could do is test them and assign them to various educational pigeonholes. In this, neurofatalism was an incredibly depressing doctrine. If you were lucky, you were born with aptitude and talent, but if not, well, better luck next time. The best students could do was to play the hand they were dealt.

But the discoveries of neuroplasticity changed all that and revealed a wide-open playing field for education, training, and personal development. If teachers and trainers could get the sets and reps right, people could learn virtually anything. This doctrine has since been described as *neuro-optimism* and has been widely embraced by the performance, meditation, and coaching communities.

Neuroplasticity has three elements: First is long-term potentiation, the process in which synaptic membranes of downstream neurons become sensitized with repeated stimulation. In short, the more you fire the circuit, the more receptive it becomes, making subsequent firings that much more likely. Second is myelination, the process by which living cells act as insulation around the axons or "wires" in neural circuits. Incredibly, these cells wrap tighter around neurons that are fired frequently, increasing the speed and efficiency of those circuits. Third is cortical remapping. When we engage in new activity, the sensory-motor cortex of the brain recruits neighboring cells into the relevant circuitry.

Taken together, these neurological changes add up to some very real and powerful transformations in our ability to learn and perform. But what's really important to understand is that all of these changes are "use dependent" and incredibly specific. That is, the remodeling of synapses, nerve fibers, and cortical areas is extremely precise and is driven by the activity of the student, patient, or athlete. This, of course, is the neural analog to the famous principle of "Use it or lose it."

SHADOW SIDE

Neuroplasticity is astonishing in its subtlety and sophistication. Anytime we engage in activity of any kind, the nervous system is continuously remodeling itself to meet the demand. The implication is profound and inspiring: if we get the sets and reps right, humans can pretty much learn anything under the sun.

It sounds promising, but it's not all good news. Repeated use of the system makes learning possible, but it also creates ruts in our nervous system, our minds, our behaviors, and even our spirits. The system resembles a watershed in that early learning is like the drop of water that falls on a ridgeline. As it flows, it carves a shallow groove, which in turn tends to capture the flow of the next drop, and so on. After a while, you've got a rut, then a culvert, a stream, a river, and eventually a valley or a canyon. The river is the learning, but it's also a sensory-motor habit.

There's no getting around this simple fact: habit is an inevitable by-product of learning. You might even say that habits and learning are simply two names for the same thing. Get the habits right at the outset and you'll wind up with a champion, but get the habits wrong and everyone will struggle. And if poor habits go too deep, the movement or behavior in question becomes effectively "locked in" and difficult or impossible to change.

This adds up to a new job description for teachers, trainers, coaches, and even health professionals. In essence, the core objective is to get the sets and reps right. Or to put it another way, the entire enterprise consists of habit creation and habit revision. Set up the best possible habits at the outset, then readjust as necessary along the way.

CULTURAL PLASTICITY

In most discussions of neuroplasticity, the focus is on individual learning, but it's also safe to assume that entire cultures are also plastic. Early stories and experiences are drops of water on the cultural landscape, creating shallow grooves for the subsequent passage of more drops. And as the grooves become deeper, they capture more and more of the water that falls from the sky, turning the grooves into rivers, then valleys and canyons. This is why it's so hard for activists to change anything. When people and institutions are deep inside the cultural canyon, their natural tendency is to keep doing what they've always done.

This also explains why it's so difficult to be truly creative. As ruts deepen in society and culture, more and more of our thoughts, feelings, and psycho-spiritual energies are channeled into existing valleys and canyons. The result is that many of our so-called creations are really just clones of existing work. Movies, books, visual art, and music mostly follow what's already there, one cliché after another.

When people say that something is "systemic," "structural," or "embedded," that's just another way of saying that it's deep inside a cultural valley or canyon. Systemic racism, for example, has a long history that started on a historical ridgeline hundreds, even thousands, of years ago, with the earliest forms of slavery and imperialism. Once the groove was established, it only grew deeper over the centuries, and today it's become, as we might say, entrenched. The only way out is to climb back up to the ridge and start over with equality and mutual respect. It's a lot of work to carve a new groove, but the effort is vital.

REWIRING

The metaphor is solid, and the challenge is obvious. No matter whether we're working with individual human bodies or culture at large, the goal is to build functional habits at the outset, then revise or rewire those that are no longer working. And while breaking bad personal habits strikes many of us as notoriously difficult or even impossible, good coaches know how to do this.

First, do whatever you can to get the process pointed in the right direction at the outset. Whether you're working with a young athlete or a young culture, early reps are by far the most powerful. Discipline at the beginning leads to success down the line. The first day of the season or the first day of class is always golden.

Then, once the training is underway, keep revising. Keep adjusting the rut, the groove, the watercourse. If the movement isn't perfect, go back up to the ridgeline and focus your attention on getting the next drop—the next repetition—in precisely the right place. Monitor the flow, keep the focus, and repeat.

In athletic training, this process is well understood and highly effective, but it takes a lot of work and focus. This is why coaching is so essential. The solo athlete can be seduced by her existing skills and may not be inclined to do the heavy lifting of habit revision. But as an outsider, the coach can bring the necessary vision and discipline to bear, repeatedly bringing the athlete back up to the ridgeline to do it again and again. Without a coach, the athlete has a powerful tendency to fall back on old habits of attention and movement.

COACHABILITY

The problem with habits—both personal and cultural—is that the deeper they get, the harder they are to change. And for ideas and behaviors that are really entrenched, it takes a sincere, sustained, persistent effort to get back up to the ridgeline. Good intentions aren't going to do it. "Thoughts and prayers" aren't going to do it. "Exploratory committees" aren't going to do it. Change requires hard work, repetition, and leadership. Or if that fails, a crisis.

So maybe what we need are cultural coaches—individuals or organizations that can stand outside the ruts in our society and tell us where we're going wrong, people who can take us back up to the ridgeline to start over and do it right. These are our artists, writers, teachers, and activists, people who are willing to take some risks and carve some new pathways for our social and psychic energy.

In traditional societies, tribal elders once served this role, but today, we don't listen to our elders, not much anyway. We're so busy being busy and living the established order that we can scarcely even imagine that there's life outside our established ruts and valleys. But if we're going to survive, we've got to listen to someone, which is to say, we've got to be coachable. We've got to be humble enough to listen to what our teachers, trainers, and therapists are telling us.

In fact, there are plenty of people in our midst who are willing and able to coach us into the future, people who can guide us back up to the ridgeline and give us the discipline to carve a better groove. But as a people, we've got to listen. And even more to the point, we have to be willing to climb up out of our ruts, stand on the ridge, and carve some new behaviors.

But as it is, most of us are too distracted and stressed to listen. We're preoccupied with personal dramas and our standing in life. In other words, we aren't particularly coachable. We're like the stubborn athlete who insists that he's already the greatest to ever play the game. And when you're the greatest, your coach is just a sideshow. But every experienced coach knows what happens to athletes who claim to be the greatest: they usually fall by the wayside, eclipsed by humble athletes who are willing to do the work.

CHAPTER 68

FREEDOM, DISCIPLINE, REPEAT...

> The organism will not absorb the fruits of the task unless its powers of apprehension are kept fresh by romance.
> —Alfred North Whitehead (1861–1947)

If you spend much time in educational circles, you're sure to hear people discussing—or more likely, arguing over—the various merits of freedom and discipline. Advocates for play and freedom point to the innate curiosity of the human being and the natural desire to know the world. All teachers really need to do is leave students alone or put them in interesting settings, and things will take care of themselves. Disciplinarians counter that the only way to learn anything is to put in the reps, over and over again, until you get it right. And naturally, each side seeks to prove its superiority and take over the process.

This antagonism has been going on for hundreds, even thousands, of years.

Enter the philosopher Alfred North Whitehead. Writing in the early twentieth century, Whitehead was a keen observer of education and was well versed in the freedom–discipline debate. But instead of taking sides, he moved to higher ground and advocated for both points of view. As he put it:

> Freedom and discipline are not antagonists, but should be so adjusted in the child's life that they correspond to a natural sway, to and fro, of the developing personality.

The solution, as with so many other dualities in life, is oscillation. Playful education works, but so does focused, dedicated striving. To make the experience complete, simply move from one phase to the next, back and forth. In this, Whitehead's advice sounds natural and organic:

> The only avenue towards wisdom is by freedom in the presence of knowledge. But the only avenue towards knowledge is by discipline in the acquirement of ordered fact. Freedom and discipline are the two essentials of education.

For Whitehead, there were two distinct phases of the process. In the *romance* phase, students are encouraged to fall in love with the art, the discipline, and the experience. This is a time for discovery, curiosity, big ideas, divergent questions, adventure, and novelty. This is the time for passion.

In the *precision* phase, students are instructed to perform their tasks with discipline and rigor. Whether it's doing a problem in mathematics, shooting a basketball, or performing a surgical procedure, make sure people do it just so. As

Whitehead put it: "This stage is dominated by the inescapable fact that there are right ways and wrong ways, and definite truths to be known." Work this phase until fatigue sets in, then rest or return to the romance phase, and so on.

This pattern of oscillation just feels right. No longer do we need to argue about the merits of one philosophy or the other. Instead, we simply set up the broad outlines of the experience and begin. The beauty of this method is that it's consistent with everything we know about the neuroscience of learning, as well as the experience of our Paleolithic ancestors. Engage–relax–engage. Hunt, relax in camp, go hunting again. We've been doing this for hundreds of thousands of years.

FLATLINE EDUCATION

But of course, this is not how it's done in conventional schooling, where most programs try to split the difference between freedom and discipline by being somewhat playful and somewhat disciplined. The end result is a muddy, vague process that fails to move people into deep engagement with the material and the process. The problem is that there's not enough contrast, and students are left confused about their level of engagement. It's a mixed message.

Even worse, many modern schools bypass the romance phase entirely. It's just not part of the narrative of "Get into college so you can get a good job." Rarely does a school year or semester begin with an academic adventure story about a protagonist who, fired by intense curiosity, dives into engagement with science, art, mathematics, or the humanities. Rarely do we hear about the personal risk, sacrifice, or mastery that comes with the passionate pursuit of an art or discipline. There's time for all that, and besides, romance and passion are fundamentally untestable, so why bother?

And even in the domain of athletics and personal training, we tend to leapfrog over romance. Eager to get into the "real training," we forget to tell the vital stories of athletic excellence or personal transformation that are so crucial for sustaining the effort over months and years.

All of which leaves students and clients out in the cold, unmotivated and unfocused. Without romance, there's no fuel for the endeavor, no power to carry students through a serious program of sets and reps. Some students manage to pick up romantic juice on the outside, but if not, education will prove to be little more than an endless slog, a meaningless grind in search of a target.

BE AMBIDEXTROUS

To make the process work, we've got to be bilingual and flexible. In a sense, every teacher must be two teachers—able to move fluidly from one domain to the other. The romantic teacher tells the story of adventure and the life satisfaction that ultimately comes with mastery. She speaks with emotion about pride in craftsmanship, the joy of engagement, and the pleasure of a job well done. The precision teacher is all about focus, rigor, and execution. She expects students to give their best in every moment, polishing their work to the highest possible standard. It will take some effort to develop both personalities, but when you do, the results will be powerful.

CHAPTER 69

THE HEAL CURRICULUM

> The saddest aspect of life right now is that science gathers knowledge faster than society gathers wisdom.
> —Isaac Asimov

Something called STEM is all the rage in educational circles these days. It stands for "Science, Technology, Engineering, and Math." On the face of it, the whole thing sounds perfectly reasonable and even valuable. Advocates present STEM as a solution to everything that ails our schools and our society at large, and it's advertised as a win-win for students. Not only will their hard work "save the planet," but it will also help them secure good, high-paying jobs and financial success.

But the implicit assumption of the STEM curriculum is deeply flawed. Proponents assume that the challenges of the future will be primarily technical in nature and that STEM will be the solution. In the years to come, human life will consist of a series of problems to be solved, data to be gathered, calculations to be performed, and buttons to be pushed. We'll have to track things, build things, and fix things, and STEM skills will help us do just that.

But is this an accurate description of our predicament?

To be sure, modern humans can benefit from some level of technical knowledge and expertise. It's good to know how to fix things, and we can be thankful for having this kind of understanding in our midst. But the challenge of our present and our future is *not* primarily technical. It's spiritual, emotional, physical, and above all, relational. It's our relationship with life that's broken, and no amount of calculation and analysis can change that.

When we see the future as nothing more than a series of technical challenges, we restrict our vision. As the saying goes, "When all you've got is a hammer, the whole world looks like a nail." When all you've got is a toolbox of Newtonian–Cartesian perspectives, the whole world looks like nothing more than a dysfunctional mechanism in need of repair. STEM might well be necessary in the creation of a functional future, but it isn't even close to being sufficient. In fact, if all we do is STEM, our troubles are only going to multiply. In this respect, STEM is little more than an avoidance tactic; it merely kicks the can down the road to the next inevitable reckoning.

MAN FROM MARS

The common thread of science, technology, engineering, and math is distance, rationality, and objectivity. These are hard, even "macho" disciplines that are built on a foundation of non-participating consciousness. Stand back from the object or process in question, and above all, don't touch it or engage in it in any way. Keep your hands on your keyboard, and whatever you do, don't get emotionally involved. Distance is essential.

To put it another way, STEM is a story of an atomistic world and knowable, linear, mechanical cause and effect. STEM is useful in a practical sense, but it's not pointed in the right direction. In fact, it's not really pointed in *any* direction. It gives us no guidance on relationship, values, or meaning. It's just a tool that can be used for any purpose, good or ill. In fact, many of the products of a STEM education are already harnessed for planet-hostile behavior: fracking, pipelines, off-shore drilling platforms, factory farming, mountaintop removal, and dams all rely on STEM to do what they do. Just because a student learns STEM doesn't mean she'll act with sapience.

STEM is sold as a solution, but it's really a symptom of our alienated, disintegrated relationship with the world. STEM does nothing to address the separation anxiety or angst that we feel. What we really need at this moment in history is *less* distance and objectivity. We need to *feel* habitat, feel one another, feel our bodies, the pulse of the planet, and the grandeur of the living Earth. STEM completely fails this requirement. Rationality has its place in our cultural toolbox, but as always, the dose makes the poison. Too much distance becomes a liability, if not a disease. A healthy life is built on participation, not distance.

THE HEAL CURRICULUM

So if STEM is a path to alienation, what's the alternative? Perhaps a HEAL curriculum would give us a better result:

>Health, humanities, and history
>Ecology and experiential education
>Art, anthropology, and activism
>Life lessons and philosophy

These HEAL studies don't offer the promise of power or control over the natural world, and they don't offer much in the way of profit for anyone involved. But they do offer something far more valuable: a sense of integration with the world. They build continuity and give us a sense of values, aesthetics, and morality. They may not lead students into high-paying jobs, but they will give us something far more important: the possibility of participation with life on Earth.

The beauty of the HEAL disciplines is that they help us feel safe. They put us back into participation with the world and close the rift that's been exacerbated by STEM. They dissolve the fear and stress that are coursing through our population, driving us to reactivity and polarization. In short, HEAL heals.

In this paradigm, we teach health not as a pile of facts about nutrition, exercise, and lifestyle diseases, but as a broad-based panorama of integration with the world. We teach the humanities not as a set of academic subjects to be tested and scored, but as vital human stories, essential for the creation of a functional future. We teach history as a way to understand where we came from and who we are.

We teach ecology not as a dry set of facts about animal behavior and habitat, but as a way to really understand interdependence and our place in the world. We teach by experience because experience is the language of the body and the most powerful way to make a difference in students' lives.

We teach art not as a way to make pretty pictures, but as a way to see and relate to the world. We teach anthropology to understand the power of cultural creativity. We teach activism because we want to be relevant and effective.

We teach life and philosophy because we're curious about what it means to be alive on a pale-blue dot in a remote galaxy, somewhere in the universe.

Naturally, some will push back against this entire line of thinking and claim that without STEM, the entire world will fall back into irrationality, superstition, and madness. But this is simply another case of Eurocentric imperialism and assumed supremacy. As we've seen, rationality is a modern and arguably abnormal invention. Prior to the age of agriculture, no human culture lived by data collection, syllogism, or research findings. People used both sides of their brains, as well as their entire bodies, to learn and navigate the world. No one gathered data. No one consulted research. And yet, many people managed to live in ways that were healthy and largely free from the stress, lifestyle diseases, and suffering we see today. The Paleo way was a proven concept. In contrast, STEM is not.

This is not to say that we should abandon STEM entirely or try to find our way in a complex world simply by impulse, but it is to say that we need a sense of perspective and balance. To put STEM on a pedestal is to make a grievous error. And to advance STEM while leaving the humanities in the dust would be a catastrophic choice that would spell the end of the human enterprise. To put it another way, this would be a relational disaster on an epic scale.

Taken together, the HEAL curriculum goes directly to the heart of the matter, our relationship with the world and the universe. It won't give us technical power, but it would give us something far more important: a chance to reflect on our values, our relationships, and our sense of meaning. STEM can have a place in our classrooms, but it's HEAL that will keep us alive, functional, and maybe even happy. As Justice Oliver Wendell Holmes once put it: "Science teaches us a great deal about things that are not really very important; philosophy a very little about those that are supremely so."

CHAPTER 70

PLANET OF AMBIGUITY

> Security is mostly a superstition. It does not exist in nature, nor do the children of men as a whole experience it. Avoiding danger is no safer in the long run than outright exposure. Life is either a daring adventure, or nothing.
> —Helen Keller

> Creativity requires the courage to let go of certainties.
> —Erich Fromm

It's some hard medicine to swallow: If we're really honest with ourselves, we're forced to admit that we really don't know what life is all about. We don't know why we're here or even if our lives have any significance. We don't know how our behaviors influence society or if our actions will make any real difference. And to make it worse, there's the nasty reality that each of our lives is coming to an end, sooner or later. Death is on the calendar, and even worse, we don't know what any of it really means.

Of course, this kind of cosmic and existential ambiguity is nothing new. It's been a regular, daily feature of human life, beginning deep in the Paleo. For the vast, overwhelming majority of human history, ambiguity, doubt, and uncertainty have been our reality. No one ever wondered if there might be some other way, and until quite recently, no one ever had the ability or even the desire to do anything about it.

It wasn't until the scientific revolution that the promise of certainty and control first emerged. For the first time in history, humans imagined that maybe they could nail down the cosmos, solve the riddle of life, and live in a world of security and predictability. Thus began a frenzy of activity, research, and investigation, all of it seemingly designed from scratch to take control of life once and for all.

Science, religion, and modern medicine all participate in this quest to solve the "problem" of ambiguity, to seize the cosmos and give us the certainty we seek. We see a similar spirit in modern efforts to "save the world" with environmental science. Around the planet, well-meaning researchers are now tracking every animal, plant, and substance they can. We might well imagine where all this is headed and can envision a day in which every molecule in the biosphere has its own radio-tracking collar so that we can monitor its whereabouts, trajectory, and state in real time. We imagine a master control room with giant computer monitors, a vivid display of every life-form on Earth.

But where will it end? Are we really going to treat the entire biosphere as a managed zoo, a game park, a laboratory experiment, a giant biological process in a petri dish? Even if—especially if—such a scheme was successful, the end result would be essentially dead or, in other words, de-natured. This would be the ultimate self-defeat.

Across every level, from the personal to the planetary, the quest for security in a fundamentally dynamic world is doomed to fail. As Alan Watts put it:

> There is a contradiction in our desire to be secure in a universe whose very nature is fluidity and movement . . . If I want to be secure, that is, protected from the flux of life, I am wanting to be separate from life. Yet, it is this very sense of separateness that makes me feel insecure. In other words, the more security I can get, the more I shall want . . .

We crave security, but we're never going to get it. And if we do get it, it's only going to be temporary at best. And at worst, it will kill the life that we claim to cherish. Our lives and the biosphere are always in flux, living and dying. There is no security. We try to lock things down with rituals, beliefs, and technologies, but the most we can do is hold the insecurity at bay for a while. But then the ambiguity comes roaring back, often with catastrophic consequences. The harder we try, the harder we will fall.

The uncertainty and ambiguity persist at every level. According to paleontologists, the average life span of mammalian species is one to two million years. The species life span of invertebrates is longer, at about eleven million years, but the exact numbers don't matter. What's really important is the understanding that even species are temporary, always in transition to some new form. Nothing in biology is eternal, not our bodies, not ecosystems, not species. The Buddha was right: impermanence is the law of life.

THE ART OF IGNORANCE

The implicit message in all of this is simple. Human knowledge, as impressive as it may be, is only a glimpse of a magnificent and fundamentally incomprehensible whole. Ambiguity is and will always be the sea we swim in. It's the normal, default condition, and it's not going to go away, not with faster computers, not with better technologies, not with superior policies and practices.

The life lesson is simple, but it challenges us to the core: Embrace this ignorance as the human condition. Stop trying to solve ambiguity. Stop trying to nail down the cosmos. Stop trying to make everything fit into human-generated boxes. We are one temporary, semi-sapient species with a very limited view of the universe. We cannot and should not attempt to play biological or cosmological king of the hill. Mastery isn't just an illusion; it's a counterproductive trap.

Become a connoisseur of ignorance. There's no shame in admitting any of this. We are fundamentally ignorant about the nature of the cosmos, human life, human behavior, and even the workings of our own minds and spirits. Further acts of discovery may be exciting, but they will mostly serve to reveal the awe-inspiring breadth and depth of the world around us. This is the paradox of education. The smarter we get, the smaller we get. Embrace the mystery.

CHAPTER 71

KEEP YOUR EYE ON THE WORK

It is forbidden to despair.
—Nachman of Bratslav, Hasidic rabbi (1772–1810)

There's a new word going around in conversations about our future. We usually hear it when someone looks at the trajectory of our planetary predicament and concludes with a tone of resignation and despair, "WASF"—We Are So Fucked.

Given all the bad news these days, it's an easy conclusion to draw. The daily drumbeat of ominous reports is now incessant, each one telling a story of disappearing habitat, the loss of biodiversity, more warming, and more feedback loops on the verge of a cataclysm. But WASF really puts a damper on our conversation and brings us right to the end of our psycho-spiritual rope. Why do anything at all? Why fight back against the forces that are wrecking the world? Why even try to build better relations with the planet and each other?

Of course, all of this depends on your point of view. If your reference point is conventional, civilized, industrial-capitalist reality, then of course WASF is obvious. We're overshooting the carrying capacity of the planet, and vital ecosystems are breaking down before our eyes. The warning signs are everywhere, and the facts cannot be disputed. A society that's devoted to economic growth and profit over all other considerations will have to face a reckoning sooner or later. In this sense, modern life as we know it is well and truly fucked.

But other reference points are possible. We could, for example, put our attention on the biosphere herself and attach our identity to the living world. Suddenly, new insights emerge. When we study the vast scope of biological history, we're struck by the fact that the biosphere is enormously, outrageously resilient. She's suffered monstrous, near-fatal wounds from asteroid strikes, oxygen holocausts, rising and falling sea levels, and tectonic shifts, but she always rebounds with new diversity and new health. In this sense, we aren't fucked at all. The planet may not be habitable by humans in the near future, but Life on Earth is going to be just fine. So relax. Life will find a way.

Or we could put our attention on the human capacity for cultural creativity. For thousands of years, people all across the planet have devised new rituals, stories, tools, and relationships to meet the needs of the moment. The study of anthropology reveals that humans are really good at this. To be sure, there's going to be chaos and suffering in our future, but people are fantastically inventive. We might be reduced to living in small communities in impoverished habitat, scattered across the planet, but we will create. That's what humans do.

Likewise, we could focus our attention on the worldview that's typical of Paleo, native, and indigenous people: this is a circular world, marked by integration, interdependence, and the belief that all life is kin. When we adopt this view, everything changes. We don't feel so alone, so vulnerable, so at risk.

Our individual lives may be shattered, our local futures uncertain, even our species extinct, but the circle remains.

NO HOPE, NO DESPAIR

In any case, WASF tells us that the time has come to stop deluding ourselves with the notion that, with just a little more effort, everything will be OK. In fact, everything is not going to be OK. It's time to wake up to ecological reality and accept the situation for what it is. Accept the destructive culture that we have created. Accept the ignorance, arrogance, and violence that have led us to this point. Give up the cheerleading and the magical thinking and get real.

The problem with WASF is that it's deadening and boring. And of course, it ultimately becomes a self-fulfilling prophecy. Most of us want to be optimistic about the future, but WASF throws a wet blanket over all our dreams and leaves us stranded and depressed. We are wired for hope, it would seem, and we'll do almost anything to keep that spirit alive, but WASF knocks it dead.

Hope is honorable and maybe even noble in its way, but it can also make us blind to the realities of our age and the magnitude of the challenges we face. By itself, hope becomes "hopium," a narcotic that keeps us out of touch with the changes we need. Hope, after all, is so much easier than actually doing something.

But despair is not an option either, personally or collectively. On a bad day, of course, it's easy to fall into the quagmire, but it's bad practice to set up shop there. Over time, despair leads to cynicism and depression and, ultimately, the end of meaning. This is no way to run a life or a culture and no way to create a future.

So if hope and despair are off the table, what are we left with? We are left with the work.

We are left with the challenge humans have always faced: how to persevere and create, even in the face of radical doubt and uncertainty. The world is vast beyond our comprehension, and the outlook for survival is unknown. We might even say that despair is a product of our hubris and our faith in our dark predictions. In a way, it's a kind of narcissism.

Modesty and sapience tell us that our predictions—no matter how well grounded in research—may well be misguided. We simply don't know how things will play out, so it's foolish to jump to psycho-spiritual conclusions. In a vast and mysterious universe, anything can happen, so it's best to stay with the art, stay with the work, and stay with what gives us a sense of meaning.

Be strong and remember the words of Edward Abbey. As he saw it, courage is the master virtue because "without courage all other virtues are useless." Stand tall in the face of ambiguity and uncertainty and stick to your work, however you see it.

And then, when we finally come to see the doom for what it is, we gain a sense of freedom. Yes, the prognosis is dark, and yes, there will be losses and suffering, but we can still live with clarity. Conditions are far from ideal, but we can still make choices. We can live with balance, integrity, compassion, and maybe even sapience. And in this knowledge, there's a sense of liberation. No longer constrained by hope and the frantic, desperate desire for conventional stability, we might even find ourselves happy.

As eco-theologian Michael Dowd reframes it, WASF might even stand for "We Are So Fortunate."

CHAPTER 72

TRIBAL ELDERSHIP

> The eyes of the future are looking back at us and they are praying for us to see beyond our own time.
> —Terry Tempest Williams

Sapience does not arise from a vacuum. It's a product of our history, our culture, our struggles, and the leadership of our elders. In traditional cultures, this much is taken as obvious, but in the modern world, there's something seriously amiss with our narrative about aging and seniority.

Everyone knows the narrative by now: aging is one long, depressing decline into degeneration, illness, and loneliness. Certain events are said to be inevitable: decreased physical and cognitive function, massive medical bills, neurological meltdown, and perhaps worst of all, social and cultural irrelevance. In short, getting older is a slow-motion train wreck to be avoided by any means necessary.

The outlook is grim, so we medicalize the process and conjure up all manner of treatments to slow, stop, or reverse the process. Gripped by anxiety, we promote the virtues of "healthy aging." Experts claim that we can stop the clock, reverse the damage, delay the onset, and dampen the symptoms. In the process, time becomes our enemy.

But the personal, social, and cultural consequences of this narrative are catastrophic. Not only does it make us increasingly miserable and fearful as time goes by, but it also drives the widespread practice of ageism. We begin to see our seniors as nothing more than a drag on society and the economy; old people are a burden and an inconvenience. Human value, in other words, decreases over time.

Not only does this narrative devalue great swaths of human life, but it also puts us under an insane level of stress. If you believe your best years are your thirties and forties, followed by a progressive decline into illness and irrelevance, the clock is going to be ticking loud and hard. You've got to hurry up and make something happen because once your body starts slowing down, it's game over. Even worse, you've got to make yourself a big pile of money right now because once you hit your golden years, the medical-industrial complex is going to step in and take most of it away.

Sadly, the modern health-and-wellness industry is a powerful enabler of this narrative. For every age-related insult to the human body, someone claims to have a solution. Diets and substances galore, exercise programs for every ailment, exotic treatments of every description—the list is endless. Magazine covers and websites glorify youth and sell us the promise of eternal life. According to the marketing pitch, aging is not inevitable—it's simply the failure to buy the right products and services.

But in the context of human history, today's narrative is profoundly abnormal. In the Paleo, tribal survival was highly dependent on the experience, knowledge, and wisdom of the elders. The old ones had participated in many hunts and observed the waxing and waning of animal life over the course of decades; they'd seen the tribe suffer and flourish through good times and bad. In this context, their words and judgment carried enormous weight. As keepers of vital knowledge, they were the most valuable and respected members of the community. In the Paleolithic world, human value actually *increased* over time. This is why Native Americans still say, "When an elder dies, a library burns."

SERVANT LEADERSHIP

Tragically, ours is the first culture in human history to devalue its elders, the first culture in history to reject the very people who might help us create a path forward. To make progress, it's essential to turn this narrative around, but where shall we begin?

An obvious first step would be to give up our obsession with youth and start taking responsibility for our role as elders-in-training. This means learning the ways of the world and sharing our knowledge with those within our reach. It is not acceptable to simply long for an easy retirement on the golf course. We must step up.

In the Old Way, the elders were fully aware of their role and their responsibility. Experience in wild outdoor environments made it clear: the primary duty of elders was to act on behalf of the tribe, to share their knowledge, to give away their insights so that the tribe could live another day, perhaps another year. There would have been no thought of retirement, no notion of self-pampering or hoarding. For the Paleolithic senior citizen, the primal directive was simple: give away your knowledge so that the tribe can live.

Seen in this light, our modern practice of hoarding and monetizing knowledge seems particularly perverse. Instead of giving our knowledge away to help the next generation survive, we do whatever we can to guard it, monetize it, and profit from it. In a Paleo society, such a practice would be considered profoundly antisocial and even immoral. To hoard knowledge when the tribe might benefit from it is very close to being criminal.

In short, the tribal elder is the ultimate servant leader. As she looks out at the immensity of the world outside of camp, she feels the exposure and the vulnerability. She knows how hard it is just to stay alive. She worries about the state of her people and what it will take to keep them whole. Has she done all she can to help them navigate the world? Do the young hunters know all they need to know about the ways of the animals, the weather, and the threats from neighboring tribes? What else must she teach before she makes the great journey?

As a servant leader, the tribal elder understands her health in a unique way, one that will come as a surprise to modern ears. In today's culture, we're constantly bombarded with messages, products, and services designed to keep us forever young. Heeding this call, we begin to do everything possible to maximize our individual welfare. We focus on ourselves, our training, our practices, our bodies. We try to hoard our health and keep it intact as long as possible.

But this strikes the tribal elder as preposterous. The purpose of health is not to hoard it but to give it away. Give it away to the tribe and your loved ones so that they can carry on. Give it away so that your people might thrive. Of course your body will start to decay. Of course you will die. But by giving her health to the world, the elder fulfills her role and her purpose. What else is health for, if not to spend it on the people and causes that need it? Hoarding one's health is the ultimate foolishness.

THE ELDER'S WAY

Being a tribal elder is no easy path, of course. The problem is that you're not going to be rewarded for your efforts, not in a conventional sense, and almost certainly not in your lifetime. The events you set in motion today might take a long time to play out, and successful outcomes won't materialize for years, decades, or maybe even centuries. In this sense, you're working for people who aren't even alive yet.

But that's just how it goes when you're working for the seventh generation. You're working hard to sustain the tribe and the future of our blue-green world, but you're not going to earn a big salary, and even more likely, you're going to be paying out of pocket for transportation, meals, lodging, and everything else that needs to happen. If you're firmly attached to a big, immediate payoff, you're going to be disappointed.

Conservation and social activism mean sacrificing big chunks of your life for people you will probably never meet, people who will never be able to thank you. In other words, the activist's art is highly speculative. In rational, economic terms, it is absurd. What kind of fool would invest in an outcome they will never see or experience?

But activism is not rational economics. It's something deeper and more powerful. And in this domain, sacrificing for a distant, tribal good isn't folly—it's an act of sapience. Giving one's life for downstream improvement not only feeds the greater good, but it also makes us happier and healthier as individuals in this lifetime. The way to be healthier, in other words, is to give your health away.

If you're looking for a quick payoff, you're in the wrong line of work. Instead, take your sense of satisfaction directly from the activity itself and from the meaning that it holds. In other words, connect with the intrinsic pleasures that come with activism: working with people, organizing, creating curriculum, and crafting narratives. It's a tough gig, but that's just the way it is when you're working for the future. Big, audacious goals require a long view. As American theologian Reinhold Niebuhr put it, "Nothing that is worth doing can be achieved in our lifetime."

BE A GOOD ANCESTOR

To put your work in perspective, imagine this scenario: Out there in the future, some one hundred years from now, there's a young boy and a young girl, eking out a marginal living in a coastal region, anywhere in the world. These are the people you're working for—your employers, if you will.

These kids are refugees from some unnamed regional conflict, driven from their homes by flooding, food shortages, and dark, faceless men with weapons. Separated from their parents and friends, they're insecurely attached to the people around them, and their bodies and spirits are suffering. Their world is hot, chaotic, and unstable. Events are inexplicable, arbitrary, often frightening.

They manage to make a rough living on the roadside, selling snacks and water to the thousands of workers who're building sea walls along the coast, but ecosystems are down in several regions, and food is scarce. Agriculture is collapsing, and fresh water is a luxury. Social services, education, and medical care are spotty and mostly reserved for those in affluent, gated communities. These children are smart and resilient, but the trauma is beginning to settle into their tissue. Sleep is a rare luxury, and every day is a fight for survival and dignity.

These kids are too busy getting by to think much about their ancestors and the events and values that led the world to this point, but imagine this: If you could just make their lives better in some small way, that would be something. If you can help stop a pipeline project, divest a big organization from fossil fuels, turn agriculture back toward the Earth, save some habitat from destruction, move some people away from violence and toward compassion—these children would thank you. Their lives will remain difficult and challenging, but your efforts will mean something.

Ultimately, the effort is worth it. The beauty of getting older is that it gives us perspective. We give up some of our strength, endurance, and vitality, but we also begin to see the world with far deeper clarity. In fact, growing older is not unlike the process by which our vision adapts to darkness. Spend a few hours out at night, and the sky begins to reveal itself and the awe begins to settle in.

Nonetheless, being a tribal elder is no easy matter. Conditions are often wicked, and tough decisions and judgment calls must be made, usually with incomplete information. Along the way, you'll sometimes falter and mislead your people. You'll misjudge your habitat, the weather, and the capabilities of your hunters. You'll be strong when you should have been flexible. You'll be yielding when you should have been assertive. You'll communicate poorly and mix your messages. You'll get scared, confused, and doubt your capabilities.

All of this is quite inevitable, but remember this: practice is perfect. No matter how difficult the situation, you can lead with a spirit that's sincere, curious, and compassionate. You can maintain your focus on health, sapience, and a blue-green future. The seventh generation will forgive your screwups, your missteps, and your awkwardness, and they'll remember the dignity, effort, and sincerity you brought to the process.

ABOUT THE AUTHOR

Frank Forencich is an internationally recognized leader in health and performance education. He earned his BA at Stanford University in human biology and neuroscience and has over thirty years of teaching experience in martial art and health education.

    Frank holds black belt rankings in karate and aikido and has traveled to Africa on several occasions to study human origins and the ancestral environment. He's presented at numerous venues, including the Ancestral Health Symposium, Google, the Dr. Robert D. Conn Heart Conference, and the Institute of Design at Stanford University. A former columnist for *Paleo Magazine*, Frank is the author of numerous books about health and the human predicament and is a member of the Council of Elders at the MindBodyEcology Collective.

www.ingramcontent.com/pod-product-compliance
Lightning Source LLC
Chambersburg PA
CBHW032024290426
44110CB00012B/653